IN SERVICE TO
THE HORSE

IN SERVICE TO THE HORSE

Chronicles of a Labor of Love

SUSAN NUSSER

LITTLE, BROWN AND COMPANY
New York   Boston

COPYRIGHT © 2004 BY SUSAN NUSSER

Little, Brown and Company
Time Warner Book Group
1271 Avenue of the Americas, New York, NY 10020
Visit our Web site at www.twbookmark.com

First Edition

The author is grateful for permission to reprint the following
previously copyrighted material:
"A Dream of Horses," from *Lupercal* by Ted Hughes.
Reprinted by permission of Faber and Faber Ltd.

Library of Congress Cataloging-in-Publication Data

Nusser, Susan.
    In service to the horse : chronicles of a labor of love / Susan
Nusser. — 1st ed.
        p.   cm.
    ISBN 0-316-80631-5
    1. Horse grooms — United States. 2. Event horses — United States.
    3. Eventing (Horsemanship) — United States. 4. Burton, Samantha.
    I. Title.

SF284.42.U6N87 2004
798.2'4'092 — dc22

                                                    2003020582

            10 9 8 7 6 5 4 3 2 1

                        Q-MB

            Design by Renato Stanisic

        Printed in the United States of America

For Michael

A Dream of Horses

We were born grooms, in stable-straw we sleep still,
All our wealth horse-dung and the combings of horses,
And all we can talk about is what horses ail.

Out of the night that gulfed beyond the palace-gate
There shook hooves and hooves and hooves of horses:
Our horses battered their stalls; they jerked white.

And we ran out, mice in our pockets and straw in our hair,
Into darkness that was avalanching to horses
And a quake of hooves. Our lantern's little orange flare

Made a round mask of our each sleep-dazed face,
Bodiless, or else bodies by horses
That whinnied and bit and cannoned the world from its place.

The tall palace was so white the moon was so round,
Everything else this plunging of horses
To the rim of our eyes that strove for the shapes of the sound.

We crouched at our lantern, our bodies drank the din,
And we longed for a death trampled by such horses
As every grain of the earth had hooves and mane.

We must have fallen like drunkards into a dream
Of listening, lulled by the thunder of the horses.
We awoke stiff; broad day had come.

Out through the gate the unprinted desert stretched
To stone and scorpion; our stable-horses
Lay in their straw, in a hag-sweat, listless and wretched.

Now let us, tied, be quartered by these poor horses,
If but doomsday's flames be great horses,
The forever itself a circling of the hooves of horses.

—TED HUGHES

CONTENTS

IN SERVICE TO THE HORSE

METICULOUS NOTICING

At seven a.m., the barns of Stonehall Farm, in The Plains, Virginia, are shrouded in a cold, discouraging November mist. Samantha Burton and her fellow grooms arrive and scatter among the stalls. They feed their horses hay and grain, and change their stable rugs for the rugs they wear outside. After the horses eat, they cheerfully follow their grooms out to their individual paddocks in front of the barn. Sam is the head groom for David O'Connor, Olympic gold medalist in the Three-Day Event. Stonehall is where he and his wife, fellow medalist Karen O'Connor, train their horses.

If Samantha had been born a horse, she would have been a plain bay. She is medium height, with brown eyes and brown hair that she wears in a sensible ponytail. Her broad forehead is surprisingly smooth

3

for someone who focuses so intensely on her work. At twenty-five, she is strong limbed and athletic, the human counterpart to the hardworking Irish Thoroughbreds she grooms. She is quick to smile and quick to laugh. Economical in her speech, she frequently brings conversations to an abrupt end by nodding and saying, "Exactly."

She has been with the O'Connors for almost four years and even though she is the senior member of the team, responsible for the rest of the O'Connors' staff, she still works side by side with them until chores are done. "The second I stop being a team player," she explains, "the second I don't muck out with everybody in the morning, that's when I lose respect for myself and that's when everybody else is going to be like, 'Screw her. I don't want to work for her anymore.'"

Sam's life with horses began when she was four years old, when she tagged along with her older sister, who was taking riding lessons. "I wanted to do everything she wanted to do," Sam admits. Next to the horses, her sister's star faded, and it was for them that Samantha kept returning to the barn. By the time she was eight, she knew what she wanted to do with her life. "I was in the kitchen," her mother, Chris, remembers. "And she said, 'Mama, I want to ride horses for a living.' I was thinking, 'Yeah, I want to be a prima ballerina.'" Chris laughs. "I should have known she would do it." Divorced and maintaining separate households, the Burtons didn't have any extra money. "We struggled to keep a horse under her," Chris says. From an early age, Sam was "very good at making happen what she wanted to happen," and her unwavering devotion and persistent lobbying compelled her father to buy her a pony, the first of several horses she would own. With little money to spend, Sam ended up with horses who were, in her words, "a bit loony, and had a bit of history." In partnership with her father, Sam bought horses, retrained them, and then sold them for a profit. "He'd buy something cheap and I'd turn it over," she says. After high school, she went to Virginia Tech, in her hometown of Blacksburg, and got a degree in animal science. Still pursuing her dream of being a professional rider, she took a position as a working student with an advanced competitor but found that she couldn't support herself. "I had free board and free lessons and I had no money. I couldn't live." She got a phone call from her old riding coach, who told her that the O'Connors were looking for a groom. Taking the job meant that she could no longer afford to keep her mare, but, her mother says, "Sam knew exactly what her opportunity was."

David O'Connor, at thirty-eight, resembles Sam, dark eyes, brown hair, medium height. One shoulder droops lower than the other, the result of an old riding injury. He also has a similar history. His family didn't have money either, though they were a horsey family. His mother, Sally O'Connor, wrote one of the textbooks of his sport, *Practical Eventing*. When he was fourteen, she took him and his older brother on a quixotic horseback trip across country during their summer vacation. It was a preposterous endeavor, and even the boys' father didn't believe they would get out of Maryland. They rode all day, and when it was time to stop, they approached a farm and asked if they could put their horses in the pasture and sleep in the barn for the night. Almost always, the farmers said yes, and invited the family in for a hot supper. It took them three months to get to California. But the days on the road and the nights spent with strangers gave David a tremendous respect for how people make a living.

Like the rest of the O'Connors' five grooms, Sam lives on a neighboring farm, High Acre, where the O'Connors rent cottages for their staff. A quarter mile separates the two farms, and the grooms drive over every morning in separate cars. Mornings are Sam's favorite time of the day. It is quiet, and the methodical execution of her chores leaves her free to think ahead to the rest of her day. Mornings, she says, are when the horses "love you best. You're bringing them all the things they like": hay, grain, fresh water, a turn in their paddock, a clean stall, and the company of their best friend — their groom.

After the horses are fed and turned out, the grooms pour themselves some coffee from the pot in the tack room and, balancing the cups on trunks and stall walls, they start mucking out the stalls. David and Karen have about forty horses, from unbroken babies to retirees. In pursuit of efficient management and marital harmony, their barn is divided between them. They rarely ride each other's horses and they each have their own head groom. Their independence from each other is so complete, Sam says, that she's often surprised by what they don't know about each other's business.

Nursing a cold, Sam holds her coffee mug close to her face and then takes it with her to the small white barn behind the main barn, where she joins Karen's head groom, Nicole. Although neither tall nor long legged, Sam covers ground quickly, having spent her entire walking life keeping up with horses whose average stride length is eighteen feet.

Nicole is in the last few weeks of her four-year tenure with the O'Connors. Vicky Jessup has been hired to replace her, but the management responsibilities that Nicole and Sam have been sharing will become entirely Sam's when Nicole leaves. Sam and Nicole chat over the stall walls as they chuck heavy pitchforkfuls of soiled straw, some of it still steaming, into the back of a tractor parked in the aisle.

Nicole is just getting over the cold that Sam is starting, and they compare symptoms.

November is the off-season for Karen and David. They are both out of town teaching clinics, the proceeds of which help fund their competitive endeavors. It is up to Sam and Nicole to start bringing the horses back from the monthlong holiday they get after the fall roster of competitions. David calls in only every few days to check on his horses. By the time the O'Connors return, their horses will be ready to begin the serious training that starts when the O'Connor team moves to their winter training facility in Florida in January.

After she and Nicole finish mucking stalls, Sam takes her coffee, gone cold, and stands under an eave, out of the rain, at the end of the barn's aisle and points to a chestnut mare named Bally Mar who is grazing in her paddock. Nicknamed Amber, the mare arrived in David and Karen's absence, and Sam isn't sure what to do with her. Amber's former rider, Jim Stamets of Hamilton, Massachusetts, died suddenly of a heart condition after having qualified the mare for this year's Rolex, the premier Three-Day Event in North America. Amber's owners, honoring Stamets's commitment to her, want her to have her shot at Rolex and passed the ride on to the O'Connors. They also sent her groom, Max Corcoran. Sam doesn't know what to do with her either. Max would like to be part of the O'Connor team, but until Sam gets some direction from David and Karen, she can't assign any other horses to her care. Trying to be helpful, Max pitches in with chores and offers bits of information about her horse. Amber, she says, is "really quirky." She needs to be sedated for even routine procedures like clipping and having the long hairs of her mane pulled out. Before "pretty much about everything," Max jokes, the mare needs a mild sedative. "Are you sure?" Sam asks. "We have a lot of mean horses here. There's always *something* you can do."

Sam watches the mare amble in her paddock, the drizzle sluicing off her waterproof turnout rug. She shrugs and heads back into the barn to finish up her morning chores. In the feed room, she lines up rows of identical blue pails. (The O'Connors' barn colors are blue with gray, so everything in their barn — buckets, stall guards, horse blankets, bandages, wraps, the two horse vans, lead ropes, wheelbarrows, pitchforks, brushes, grooming totes, everything except the horses — is blue and gray.) The horses' names have been written on pieces of tape on the sides of the buckets. From the feed bin, Sam scoops chaff and grain. Combined, they look like a delicious, if somewhat grassy, breakfast cereal. On top of that she adds the supplements that seem to outweigh the horses' actual food. Yeast-colored rice bran for adding weight is mixed in, along with orange and white powders containing minerals and electrolytes, pomegranate-red liquid iron, and vitamins in the form of green pellets. For the horses who need anti-inflammatories, up to ten white pills the size of peanuts are plopped on top. All of this, including the pills, the horses will gobble up greedily. Getting them to eat, Sam jokes, is not a problem. The pails are stacked up and covered with a blanket. The horses' dinners are ready, leaving one less chore for the afternoon.

Setting up dinners in the morning, like completing every chore possible before they start riding, is part of the O'Connors' system, what the grooms call "the program." Chores follow the exact same order every morning. With military precision, the horses are fed and turned out, stalls mucked, water buckets scrubbed and refilled, trunks and stall surfaces dusted, doorways swept, and finally a Zamboni-like vacuum is run over the rubber mats in the aisle. Always having an eye on the end of the day, never putting off until later a chore that could be completed immediately, is how the O'Connor team manages the volume of work that a top competitive barn creates for its employees. That efficiency, David believes, lowers the stress on his horses. If the grooms are rushed, the horses pick up on that. Likewise, if the barn hums along efficiently, the horses get that too, the sense of purpose and order. When the horses are on the road, traveling to competitions and staying in unfamiliar places, that consistency keeps them as relaxed and happy in their strange surroundings as they are at home.

As if on cue, the grooms whirl around and head out of the barn. They're going to the tack room, a separate building the size of a small warehouse, to change and get their gear. Like a stage in the seconds after the final scene, the barn buzzes with residual energy. In their stalls, the horses who weren't turned out blow big sighs through their nostrils and slop their lips in their water buckets. Moments later, as if they are returning for an encore, the grooms reappear in breeches and boots, or with chaps zipped on over their jeans. Bridles hang over their shoulders and saddles over their arms. They dump their gear on racks and march out toward the paddocks, which are nearly invisible in the heavy mist. Only Sam comments on the miserable weather. "Great," she says, waving the mist into swirls with her arms. "We can't even see them."

Preparing the horses for training, or "legging up," means long walks in the woods and light drills in the indoor arena. In another month, when David and Karen are done traveling, the horses will be ready for interval training and jumping. Sam is responsible for all of David's horses and she splits their day-to-day care between herself and the recently hired Vanessa Roman. Vanessa was recommended to the O'Connors by her equine studies instructor at the University of Massachusetts. Sam worries that Vanessa might be too small to ride David's horses, to "really get her leg on them." She has given her David's two senior horses, both Olympic medalists, to groom. Custom Made is only ever called Tailor around the barn, and Giltedge's nickname is Tex. These two horses, Sam says, are "absolute teachers in different ways." Tailor, the more powerful of the two, knows all the tricks and won't perform what he is asked unless he is asked correctly. Tex, the pure-hearted, figures out what the rider wants even when the request is muddled. While Tex and Tailor teach Vanessa how to ride upper-level horses, Sam is getting to know David's younger ones. His newest arrival is Persistent Rain, called Percy for short. Like most of David's horses, he is a bay. He is such a powerful jumper that the rider David bought him from had to give him up because Percy's jump was hurting his back.

Sam leads Percy in from his paddock and drops the end of his lead shank to the ground. Horses who are "with the program" at the O'Connors' know that this means they are supposed to stand still. Percy thinks it's an invitation to investigate his surroundings. He pokes his nose into the empty stalls and turns to greet another horse coming down the aisle. Max, who is also new to the program, offers to hold Percy for Sam, but she declines. "He needs to learn to stand by himself," she says. She faces Percy forward and pulls off his blankets, repositions him again after she puts the blankets away, and turns him again when she starts to groom him. He is still fidgeting, and Sam hauls him around to face her. "Percy," she commands, "you have to pay attention to me." Percy looks down his long nose at her while Sam keeps her hands on his halter. When he lowers his head, she rubs his face and goes back to work. Percy stands still. Under his black forelock, his eyes follow Sam, as if he wants to be sure she sees how well he is behaving.

*   *   *

Horses are prey animals. Their survival depends on their ability to spot and run away from predators, and their eyesight is their most reliable sense. According to equine behaviorist George Waring, horses have 215 degrees of peripheral vision. Having such a broad range of vision means that their depth of field vision isn't very good. Broad range of vision is better for spotting predators but not so good for the kinds of things riders ask their horses to do. By the time they reach the takeoff point for a jump, horses can no longer see it; they jump their memory of the fence that they saw a few strides before. In a two- or three-jump combination, only the first jump is visible to them as they approach. It's not until they land that they know there is another jump only a stride or two away. They also have a blind spot that starts between their eyes and extends over their head and down their spine. When Percy lowers his head for Sam, he is offering not just his cooperation but his trust. To keep it, Sam can never do anything that hurts or scares him.

To some extent, women share the horse's visual acuity. Two psychologists at York University in Toronto conducted a study in which their subjects, with no explanation, were asked to wait in a room and then, after having moved to another room, to write down what they had seen. The women in the study could recall 70 percent more of the objects and their placement in the room than the men could. Malcolm Gladwell, describing the study in a 1997 *New Yorker* article, wrote, "This was not a test of memory so much as it was a test of awareness — the kind and quality of unconscious attention that people pay to the particulars of their environment." Unconsciously maintaining a visual inventory of their environment is exactly how horses stay alert to predators. Sam's ability to notice and remember the placement of objects in Percy's environment means that she is just as aware as he is of any changes that he might perceive as a threat. If he plants his hooves and balks in the doorway, Sam's visual acuity will notify her that someone has moved a tack trunk, or replaced a bucket, or left a blanket hanging where it doesn't belong. She can simultaneously identify the source of his resistance and reassure him by moving confidently past it and expecting him to do the same, just as the lead horse in his herd would. In the wild, horses live in open territory. They eschew closed places that inhibit their ability to run away. The security that domestic horses have in a barn or a closed stall comes from the other horses in their company and the leadership of their human handlers.

As Sam works with Percy, she will ask for and expect increasing degrees of his trust. From standing still when his lead shank is dropped, to lowering his head to the point where he can no longer see what she is doing, to following her into the cargo hold of a plane, Percy's trust in her will allow him to inhibit his own instincts. He'll learn to quell his instinct to flee, turning instead to his groom, waiting for her leadership. If she makes a mistake, by angling him too sharply into his stall, for example, causing him to painfully bump his hip on the doorway, she will have to start all over again. David's training of Percy for competition will build on that trust. Methodically, David will present Percy with ever more difficult challenges that Percy will be able to meet. By never asking Percy to do something he can't, David will teach Percy that he can do anything David asks of him, like jumping into water or through a covered bridge.

Sam uses her entire body to groom Percy. One hand follows behind the currycomb and brush. Her palms slide over his coat, quick fingers probing for scabs and abrasions. She bumps against him and rolls around his sides. She stoops underneath him and crouches directly behind his hocks, where a backward swat with a hoof would land in the middle of her face. She runs her fingers through his tail, gently separating tangles, and smoothes her hands over the muscles of his hindquarters, chest, and shoulders. Most important, she feels his legs. "In this sport," she says, "they do gallops, they jump, they do everything else, and if you miss even the slightest change in their leg, you could be missing a tendon that's starting [to tear]." Percy's history is in his legs. Sam says they're the best she's ever seen, an indication that Percy has been lightly used. She expects that to change, though, once he starts competing and the impact of all the galloping and jumping he will do starts to show up in his legs.

The three other grooms with her in the barn are doing the same thing. Vicky Jessup is working over one of Karen's horses. Max is grooming Amber in her stall. Vanessa Roman, the least experienced groom, copies Sam's movements as she tentatively feels Tex's legs, trying to teach her hands to feel what Sam's hands feel.

Competition horses live rarefied and isolated lives. They live around other horses without ever being among them. Too valuable to risk getting injured in the paddock, they're turned out alone, within sight of their stablemates but unable to create relationships with them by nuzzling and mutual grooming, the language horses use with their families. But their need for social interaction dominates their lives. Breeder and veterinarian Michael Shafer has observed that horses have such an overwhelming need to be part of a community that they will overlook differences in species if there are no other horses around for them to interact with. Practitioners of natural horsemanship, a popular form of training, base their entire system on the horse's need to interact with *something*. In a round pen that has nothing in it but a human being, even a wild horse will turn and face the person. If that human drives him away again and again, denying him the chance to make contact, the horse will eventually lower his head and lick his lips, the gesture that horses use among themselves to indicate submission. They are less interested in being in charge than in getting along with their peers.

Valuing harmony over individual dominance is a behavior that education specialist Carol Gilligan found when she researched adolescent girls for her book *In a Different Voice*. Gilligan was refuting the theoretical methods that had documented an earlier and more resolute moral development in boys than in girls. The research methods that had been used to come up with that finding, she argued, favored individuals who resolved tensions through conflict and resolution. Boys, her study revealed, identified themselves as part of a merit-based hierarchy. The identities of the girls, Gilligan found, took their strength from the quality of their web of relationships.

Even though horses rely on leadership, and even though their herds have a hierarchy, that hierarchy is a situational one. The horse who leads the herd to safety isn't necessarily the same horse who leads them to food. The mare who is the first pick of the stallion in the breeding season might willingly allow one of her girlfriends to drink first. There is also no correlation between physical prowess or intelligence and herd order. The horse who leads is the horse who most wants to lead. As long as that horse doesn't lead the herd into trouble, the rest are content to follow.

The O'Connor training program is built on keen observation and relationship building. David relies on his grooms to know his horses even better than he does. The meticulous noticing of the changes in the horses, from their moods to their physical well-being, is the biggest part of their job. The grooms are to the horses what the combined services of physical therapist, manager, counselor, assistant, and chaperone would be to an NBA star. As their coach, David knows best how his horses respond to the challenges of the game of Three-Day Eventing, but it's the grooms who know the horses' quiet, emotional side best.

Percy and his stablemates are saddled and bridled, or "tacked up," and ready to be ridden. Max, Vicky, and Vanessa mount up just outside the barn. The grooms lean down and make sure the saddle girth is tight and adjust their stirrups. "I always get the saddle with your stirrups," the long-legged Vicky jokes to Vanessa. They zip their jackets up to their chins and pick up the reins with their fingertips. Three abreast and chatting with one another, their ponytails swinging in the same rhythm as the horses' tails, they crunch down the yellow gravel drive.

On this particular morning, Sam is going to work Percy in the indoor arena. Up a steep hill behind the barn she mucked out earlier and past a small clearing, the Stonehall indoor sits against the tree line. Its upper third is encased in glass block that lets in a watery gray light. Nicole is already there, schooling one of Karen's horses. After checking her girth, Sam pushes Percy forward into a walk. When she starts trotting, Percy rounds up his back under her, carrying her weight evenly. His nose is almost perpendicular to the ground as he balances lightly on the bit that connects him to Sam's hands. She rides him in schooling figures: circles, serpentines, and figure eights. As Sam pushes him into his bit with her legs, Percy steps farther under himself with his hind legs, strengthening the muscles of his back and haunches. The difference between a horse who is using these muscles and one who isn't looks like the difference between a ballerina stepping to center stage and someone schlepping down the street to catch a bus. At the two-beat trot, Percy lands squarely on diagonal pairs of hooves. The only indications of Sam's cues to him are the flick of his ears and the changes in his gait. After half an hour of hard work, Sam quits. She and Nicole ride out together for a hack — a long walk on the trails where the horses can relax.

The Plains, Virginia (home of, among other things, Robert Duvall), sits in the northwestern corner of the state. In the heart of Virginia hunt country, it is an hour and a lifetime away from Washington, D.C. Where Sam grew up, in Blacksburg, horses live behind barbed wire in unkempt fields. "You come up here," she says, waving her hand to indicate not just Stonehall but all of this corner of Virginia, "and it's, like, heat lamps and four-board fencing." At night, the light from the capital glows on the horizon, but during the day, only mile upon mile of green pastures and black board fencing are visible stretching out to the foothills of the Shenandoah Mountains. There are a dozen active foxhunts in the area, and the shops and pubs in the village centers are all equestrian themed. Nearby Middleburg is the editorial home of *The Chronicle of the Horse,* a weekly magazine that has for sixty-five years been dedicated to "Sport with Horse and Hound."

Stonehall's electric-eye gates open at the approach of visitors, who have a short drive down a smoothly blacktopped road before they arrive at the main barn, surrounded by yellow gravel. Stonehall's sixteen roomy stalls, fronted by oak paneling, are evenly divided between eight of the O'Connors' horses and eight belonging to Jacqueline Mars, the owner of Stonehall and the neighboring property, High Meadow. They maintain separate staffs, separate offices, and separate tack rooms; the O'Connors' tack room is in a separate building and Ms. Mars's, with its hunt prints and portraits of beloved hounds, is in the main barn.

Done riding, Sam and the other grooms deposit their gear in the tack room, and Sam heads out to check on the other two barns in the O'Connors' purview. The combined acreage of Stonehall, High Meadow, and High Acre is about a thousand acres. The little cottage that Sam lives in with her boyfriend, Kenny Johnson, is at High Acre, where the O'Connors' students keep their horses and where the horses who are sent to them for training live. Sam greets the working student who has been assigned to that barn and then peeks into the stalls. She stops at the end of the row. "Obviously," she says, pointing to two well-fed Thoroughbreds, "these two just arrived." The horses look comfortable in their shaggy coats. Their whiskers are long, their ears are fuzzy, their fetlocks have grown over the tops of their hooves, and their manes and tails are uneven. They look like normal horses, the kind whose owners ride them on weekends. They don't look like competition horses. "We'll take care of them before Florida," Sam says grimly, as if she's distressed to have such common-looking horses in close proximity to her own.

On the other side of Stonehall is High Meadow, the second barn owned by Ms. Mars. A mile-long gravel driveway switches back and forth up a steep hill and then crests at open pasture and what on a clear day would be a million-dollar view of the Shenandoah Mountains. High Meadow is where the young horses live, those who are a year or so away from their first competition. The O'Connors' students are getting the horses started for them, and as Sam drives by, she eyes the lithe, straight-backed riders who trot and canter their horses on a grassy plateau.

One of Sam's horses, The Native, is up here too. Nicknamed ET for "extra trouble," the horse was described by John Strassburger, editor of *The Chronicle of the Horse*, as David's "problem child." ET started out in life as a racehorse. After retiring from the track, he came to the O'Connors as a sale prospect, and it was hoped that his speed and jumping ability would attract a buyer. Unable to sell him because his past life on the track had exacerbated his already combative and aggressive personality, David arranged for Ms. Mars, his patron, to buy the horse for him. Sam characterizes ET's history as abusive, though David stops just short of that. He believes that it was the atmosphere of the track, where horses are asked to give "one hundred and ten percent every time they go out," that made ET such a defensive animal. Sam calls ET her "little black horse," both for his appearance and his moods. A favorite of Sam's and David's, ET is the least popular horse with their vet, who is afraid of him. ET, Sam explains, "feeds off the atmosphere. He gets wound up, and the more wound up he gets the more he starts lashing out."

Sam doesn't like having ET so far away from the rest of her horses in the main barn, but the move to the remote High Meadow has put him in a quieter environment, one that seems to be soothing his nerves. As she stands in front of his stall, ET pokes his delicate black face with its bright star and wiggle of white between his nostrils over the door. This past fall, ET won the Fair Hill CCI Three-Day Event. "We all looked at each other," Sam remembers, "and said, 'Oh, my God! ET's grown up!'" He watches her as she talks about him, his ears pricked in her direction. When she turns to him, he pins those ears, pulls his head back into his stall, and turns his butt to the door, as if he's trying to deny that he's been eavesdropping.

"The horses I take care of," Sam says. "I know from the

tips of their toes to the tops of their ears. David could ask me any question and I could answer it. No problem." She wasn't as confident when she first arrived at Stonehall. Even though she'd spent her life riding and training horses, she'd never worked with horses at this level. As a young rider, Sam was obsessed with Karen's career, when she was still Karen Lende. Back then, Sam says, "I'd never heard of David O'Connor." Since Sam arrived at Stonehall, David has won Badminton, the world's premier Three-Day Event, and individual gold and team bronze at the Sydney Olympics. Winning competitions is a bonus to Sam, the just reward for meticulous good care and enlightened training methods. She knew nothing about the O'Connors' methods and practices before she arrived at Stonehall, but since then, she has become a convert. As new grooms come to the barn, Sam says, David expects them to rise to the standards of the program or they will wash out.

Sam's specialty is working with young horses, ones who don't come with the baggage of someone else's mistakes, and she prefers new grooms who are talented but inexperienced as well. She is less concerned about Vanessa's lack of experience than she is about the fact that she has to "chase her a bit" to get her to keep up with the pace of the work. Vicky has ample experience, both as a groom and as a competitor, and since she started, she's been working more independently than Sam likes. The two women have already clashed, and Sam worries that Vicky isn't going to get in line with the O'Connor program. Sam is not shy about recommending that a groom be fired. Recently, she was frustrated by David's insistence that she give more time to a groom who, eventually, as Sam had predicted, didn't work out. She is fiercely loyal to Ms. Mars, the O'Connors' sponsor, but in the past, she's had no problem letting go of grooms recruited from Ms. Mars's side of the barn who weren't working hard enough to be part of the O'Connor team. "They wanted to take coffee breaks," Sam explains.

Once the competitive season starts, Sam's six-day work-week turns into seven days. After Christmas and Thanks-giving, there are no more holidays until next fall, when she gets her two-week vacation. She works when she's sick and when she is injured. If her horses are sick or injured, she will stay up all night at their sides rather than entrust their care to someone else. For Sam, whose earliest memories are of "watching, just watching my tiny little Shetland pony," that's the whole point of her job. "That's why I came here. To learn more, to increase my love of the horses." Sam is no more able to articulate why she loves her horses than most people are able to articulate why they love their children. It is as if her purpose here on earth is to love horses, a purpose that is so obvious it's inexplicable.

Her time with the horses is spent actively learning about them: "You get quite good at reading their body lan-guage." Her eye and her keen observation draw out her horses' personalities, just as her hands extract their history and condition from their bodies. Earlier in the year, David's horse Tigger Too, a bright chestnut whose red coat shows through his white blaze in spots that look like freckles, had a little bit of swelling, a degree or two of heat, that showed up in one of his legs after he was ridden. Sam caught it, and the horse was sent off to the vet to have his leg scanned. An old tendon injury was just beginning to flare up. "If you don't get your hands on their legs, on their feet, everything, every single day," Sam warns, "you could end a horse's ca-reer." They backed off his training, and Tigger was later able to complete Fair Hill. If they had pushed on, Tigger would be convalescing right now instead of being legged up and prepared for Rolex in the spring.

Back in Blacksburg, Sam wouldn't have noticed a slight change in a horse's leg because that wasn't the kind of care she was accustomed to providing. She learned her skills under the sharp eye of David's former head groom, Colleen, who trained her, as well as under David's. "David kind of lets you make mistakes," she explains. "So that you'll never do them again. It's not even that he comes and yells at you; you're just so embarrassed and ashamed that you've screwed up that you'll never do it again."

Of all the equestrian disciplines, Three-Day Eventing is the most rigorous and comprehensive test of the skill, athleticism, and bravery of horse and rider. Its first appearance as an international sport was in 1912, at the Stockholm Olympics, where competition was open only to members of the military, for whom the disciplines of Three-Day Eventing had been developed to train brave, fit, and obedient cavalry mounts. In Germany, the sport is still known as the *militaire.* In 1952, the sport was opened to civilians at Badminton, England. The CCI *(concours complet internationale),* which is ranked from one to four stars depending on the degree of difficulty, is the highest competitive level. It was labeled Three-Day Eventing by the British because the three phases — dressage, speed and endurance, and show jumping — took three days to complete, though most contemporary CCI competitions have been extended to four days because the number of entrants requires two days for the dressage tests.

The first phase, dressage, is performed on the flat (as opposed to over fences), and riders execute a predetermined test of a horse's three basic gaits: walk, trot, and canter. Those three gaits are themselves broken into their relative paces, working trot and the longer-strided extended trot, for example. Horses execute basic lateral movements, such as the half-pass and the shoulder-in, which demonstrate their suppleness from side to side. Dressage is the only phase of competition for which the horses are subjectively judged, receiving scores for each of the required movements that reflect the quality of those gaits. The quality is determined by how supple the horses are, their impulsion — the extent to which they propel themselves forward by engaging their hind ends rather than dragging themselves along with their forelimbs — and their obedience to their riders' commands. It is usually the least favorite phase for most event riders, akin to the compulsory exercises that figure skaters must perform before they advance to their freestyle performances. "Sam would kind of putz through the dressage with a frown on her face," her mother, Chris, remembers. Her "Evel Knievel grin" appeared on cross-country.

Phase two, speed and endurance, is the phase for which the sport is known. At the highest level of the sport, the four-star CCI, of which there are only four in the world, the horses trot, canter, and gallop through four separate endurance phases — eleven miles over rolling terrain at speeds up to thirty-five miles an hour. The final phase of speed and endurance, called cross-country, is the most arduous. Horses gallop at top speeds for four miles and jump about thirty-five obstacles arranged in combinations that create close to fifty jumping efforts. It is dangerous and thrilling because the fences are solid and won't fall down if a horse crashes into them. They're built into the terrain, requiring horses to jump uphill and downhill, into and out of water, into dark woods and out to bright, sunlit fields. Rather than the straightforward standards and poles of the show jumping ring, cross-country fences are made out of things like whiskey barrels, stacks of timber, tables, benches, hay bales, little cottages, doghouses, covered bridges, and wagons —

all the things a cavalry horse might encounter as he charges across country on his way to battle. They also jump canoes and pickup trucks with flowers in the bed. Anything that fits within the height and width requirements set by the *Fédération Equestre Internationale* (FEI) and is judged safe by that organization's technical delegates can be used as a cross-country fence. The maximum height of the obstacles is just under four feet, but their width and spread are so varied that the FEI has established seven different measurements of their dimensions.

If the riders make it through cross-country without accruing too many penalties — because they fell off, or their horse refused to jump, or they galloped too slowly, or, worst of all, their horse fell — *and* their horses pass the compulsory vet inspection the morning after cross-country, they proceed to show jumping, the final phase. Show jumping takes place in an enclosed and mostly level arena in which the footing has been carefully groomed. The fences, constructed of upright standards and poles or boards that are suspended in cups attached to the standards, *do* fall down. They're spaced at precise and challenging angles so the horses, tired from the previous day's efforts, have to be accurate in their turns and their striding between fences. They also have to be conscientious about not tapping the rails with their feet, which will knock them down. The winner of the competition is the horse and rider team who receives the highest score for dressage and racks up the fewest faults over the ensuing two days. The CCI four-star is the equine equivalent of an Ironman Triathlon.

Before she came to the O'Connors, Sam had only done horse trials, the beginner version of the CCI four-star. Horse trials, ranked from novice to advanced, have only one speed and endurance phase — cross-country. Slower, smaller, and shorter horse trials serve a function that is similar to that of the Little League and the NCAA. At the lower levels, they're a safe, fun place for an amateur to compete their horses; at the upper levels, nascent professionals (both horses and riders) can build experience before they face the rigors of a CCI. Even at that level, Sam knew that eventing was what she wanted to do with the rest of her life. "I thought it was cool. That I had a horse that trusted me enough and that I trusted enough to go out there at high speeds and leap over these huge fences." That trust, deepened by having to be competitive at all three phases, Sam believes, creates the intense relationship between event horses and their riders.

By late afternoon, it's already dark. Because it is the off-season, Sam can count on getting out of work by five or six p.m. She's hoping a good night's sleep will take care of her cold, but that seems optimistic. Her face is flushed, and her eyes are glassy with fever. Her voice is so hoarse that words disappear from her sentences, forcing her to say everything twice. She still has chores ahead of her, and even though they aren't leaving for Florida for another month, she needs to start packing. Between the O'Connors' horses and those of their students, almost fifty horses are going to Florida. A move that would be a once-in-a-lifetime event for a normal horseman has become routine for Sam. Still, she has already used up her yearly equipment budget, and anything that she forgets will have to be shipped down or she'll have to do without.

Vanessa is in the barn, getting Tex ready for bed. At this early stage in Vanessa's apprenticeship, one that is designed to last about eighteen months before she'll be trusted to work on her own, Sam has to double-check everything Vanessa does. Tex stands in the aisle while Vanessa chats with one of

Ms. Mars's grooms. Sam bustles in the door and zeroes in on Tex's left front leg. She runs her hand down his thin cannon bone, closing first the vee of her hand and then her fingers around the tendon that runs the length of it. Vanessa stops talking and steps forward, watching. Under Tex's left knee, Sam pauses a minute and then switches to his right leg. She goes back and forth while Vanessa chews her thumbnail.

"Feel anything?" Vanessa asks.

"A little heat," Sam says, staring at the floor in concentration. "Keep an eye on it."

Vanessa squats under Tex, who drops his nose to the top of her head. She copies Sam's procedure while Sam watches, though it's clear that Vanessa doesn't feel any difference between the two legs. Sam leaves her underneath Tex and steps outside the barn. Beyond its perimeter, a row of mammoth pine trees creates a dark and foreboding wall between the barn and Ms. Mars's house. Originally, Sam explains, Vanessa was supposed to take Nicole's place as Karen's head groom, but she was passed over when the more experienced Vicky was hired. Inexperience, Sam says, "drives Karen crazy." David told Sam that he liked Vanessa's way with his horses and he has placed her under Sam's supervision. Sam is a little worried about Vanessa's diligence in her chores and whether she's tall enough to get her leg on David's big horses, but the one thing she's not worried about is Vanessa's inexperience. "When I first came," she says, "I couldn't feel a tendon either."

Ahead of Sam are five months of increasing intensity. In Florida the horses will start competing at small horse trials that will prepare them for the CCI starred competitions in the spring but that will also increase their risk of injury. She'll live in motels for weeks at a time as the team travels from competition to competition. A homebody, Sam likes training horses more than competing them and would rather stay in Virginia, but *her* horses are the ones doing all the traveling. And, like her boss, Sam believes that competition is what pushes riders and their grooms to be better horsemen. Her next bit of downtime won't be until after Rolex at the end of April. Then she'll gear up for the World Equestrian Games that are being held in September in Jerez de la Frontera, Spain. Tex and Tailor are David's best chance of making the United States team, but they won't know if the two veterans, who at sixteen and seventeen are on the verge of retirement, can hold up to another grueling year of training and competition until they get started. "What David keeps saying," Sam says, "is that those two are going to determine what they do next year." David will be relying on her to monitor the minute daily changes not only of his veterans but of almost a dozen actively competing horses, each at a different stage in his career.

Sam looks tired when she turns to go back into the barn, as if it is not just the last couple hours of chores weighing on her but all the hours ahead and all the hours from her three and a half years at Stonehall that are behind her. It's dark, and it has been raining since she arrived, a depressing end to a bleak November day. In the barn, the horses are buckled into their stable rugs, done for the day. The ones who've had baths are napping under their heat lamps, whose red light glows in the barn's windows. Shaking the shimmering raindrops from her ponytail, Sam aims for a side door, escaping the cold for the warmth and comfort of her barn.

Chapter Two

THE DESCENDANTS OF THE STEPPES

Between 35,000 and 125,000 years ago, our Neanderthal ancestors discovered in the horse a ready
supply of food. Scavenging their already preyed upon
remains, Neanderthal hunters dragged the horses' skulls,
which would have been impossible for other animals
to crack open, back to their encampments, where they
scooped out the nutritious brain matter. By 30,000 to
35,000 years ago, early man had developed greater hunting skills — chasing and spearing animals rather than
scavenging their remains. In Solutré, France, archaeo-
zoologist Sandra Olsen investigated a boneyard of
equine remains that represented 20,000 years of slaughter in a single location. Olsen believes that a cul-de-sac
at the site enabled hunters to divert migrating horses
into a natural corral and slaughter them. Between
32,000 and 100,000 horses were killed at that site. At

its densest, there were bones of more than eleven horses per cubic meter.

Yet at the same time that we were eating horses, we were revering them. In cave paintings like the famous ones at Lascaux, France, the hunting of horses was routinely depicted in what Olsen believes was some form of prehunting ritual. Horses were painted on cave walls, and one of the oldest three-dimensional art objects is a thirty-thousand-year-old horse figurine. Called the Vogelherd horse for the cave in Germany where it was discovered and carved from a mammoth tusk, the sculpture depicts a lovely, rounded horse with a proudly arched neck. Paleolithic people used horse teeth as decorations and carved human figurines out of them. Their tools were decorated with images of horses. Out of the bones of horses, they carved horse heads, sometimes stringing them together for necklaces. Horses were not the most often eaten animal; their bones appear less frequently at Paleolithic sites than those of deer, yet horses appear more often than any other animal in their artwork.

The history of our consumption of horses is as old as the history of ourselves. But the moment when we became *riders* of horses has been much more difficult to pinpoint.

Archaeologists are looking for that evidence in the vast grassland steppes of central Eurasia. In a three-thousand-mile area between the Carpathian Mountains in Hungary and the Alta Mountains of Mongolia, researchers are doggedly seeking proof of what they know must have occurred there: an early Indo-European settler looked at the horses he was slaughtering for food and made the decision to slide onto the broad, comfortable back of one of them.

What researchers have been unable to find is the evidence that tells them exactly when that happened. David Anthony, who pioneered a method for determining bit wear on a horse's teeth, thought he had found it when, in

1989, he analyzed worn teeth that had been unearthed by a Russian archaeologist in the 1960s at a site in Ukraine known as Dereivka. The teeth were from a single stallion that had been buried along with two dogs, which indicated this particular stallion had been sent to the next world with a great degree of ritual. The evidence was so appealing, so suited to our ideas of the value of horses, that despite the skepticism of other scientists, Anthony's findings beat a very short path into the textbooks and popular-science journals. Carbon dating of the remains that occurred after initial publications revealed that the horse was not part of the prehistoric Sredni Stog culture that lived in the area but actually dated much later. The Dereivka stallion, apparently, belonged to the Scythian nomads and warriors who dominated the plains in the seventh century BCE. Undeterred, Anthony has moved on to another central Asian site at Samara.

Sandra Olsen, who was skeptical about Anthony's bit wear evidence, has found the same evidence of wear on 28,000-year-old horses who had no contact with humans. And, as the contemporary evidence of riders in the school of natural horsemanship demonstrates, it is entirely possible to ride a horse with no bit. But she agrees with Anthony that since horses appear to have been domesticated, they may also have been ridden in central Asia as long ago as 4200 BCE.

Olsen's interest is less in determining when horses were ridden than when they were first domesticated. Still, she and Anthony are both playing a game of probabilities. Without what they call a "smoking gun" that points to the precise moment in time when horses were first ridden, archaeologists are building their case for domesticated horses empirically, from the changes in the environment they've discovered once horses appeared on the scene.

At the site in Kazakhstan of the Botai culture that

Olsen is studying, the bones of horses were buried all around the settlement, and it is unlikely, if not impossible, that Botai hunters killed thousand-pound wild horses and then dragged them back to their settlements to skin them. Her colleague Charles French has also uncovered what he believes to be manure pits in Olsen's excavations, indicating that as soon as we kept horses, we had to muck out after them. There are foreign objects at Botai as well, quartzite, for instance, even though there doesn't appear to be a nearby quarry. The settlements are also huge, 50 to 160 houses, indicating that these people could stay in one place, as they had a ready supply of their own horses to eat at hand. Anthony also pointed out that horse bones have appeared in graves with humans as early as 4000 BCE, a burial distinction that was not bestowed on wild animals.

Failing to find firm evidence in central Asia alone for the domestication of horses, David Anthony turned to comparisons with Native Americans. He identified nineteen different behavioral patterns among the people of the steppes that were identical to the patterns that, in earlier research, he had found among North American Plains Indians after the Spanish introduced horses to them in the sixteenth century. Starting around 3500 BCE, Anthony found an increase in flint weapons, indicating a rise of warfare. An increase in weapons in farming communities indicated that their residents were trying to protect themselves from something. "Steppe-type" graves were discovered as far away as Hungary and Transylvania, a breadth of travel that would have been far easier on horseback than on foot. The presence of foreign objects in the settlements, like the quartzite at Botai, provided evidence that once they traveled, they returned home with souvenirs.

The earliest equestrian elite among the American Indians, the Comanche, the Apache, and the Sioux, mounted on horses, were able to seize ever larger portions of territory, pushing unhorsed tribes to the fringes and ultimately to extinction. They waged wars and stole from their neighbors; one horse-stealing raid, according to Anthony, traveled seven hundred miles and back again. They traded goods, brought home treasures, and developed a class structure that reflected what Anthony found in central Asia. Once horses appeared in the archaeological record there, certain inhabitants were not being buried in traditional communal graves but in individual ones. Buried with them were copper ornaments, shell beads, and flint tools, as well as "exotic prestige objects." The individual graves, Anthony writes, represent the beginning of a horse-owning "incipient elite."

In the six thousand years between the steppe settlements and contemporary society, horses were the key to prosperity and social hierarchy. They fed us, transported us and our goods, brought us victory in war, and tilled our soil until their position was usurped by the machines of the industrial age. Outside of developing nations that still rely on horsepower, horses, even more than trophy wives, watches, boats, or cars, are a universal symbol of wealth, power, and prestige. Arrivistes to the class of wealth and power can use horses as a kind of money-laundering service, washing away the newness of their riches by investing in a tradition that enables them, at least while they are with their horses, to have a position in the coterie of families that Gore Vidal once characterized as America's "stealth rulers."

One of the best places to view the contemporary cult of the horse is at the Cosequin Winter Equestrian Festival. Held every year from January to March in Wellington, Florida, and then Tampa for two weeks in April, the festival attracts riders from North America, Europe, and South

America. Many of them will make Wellington their winter home. Others arrive for a week or two and then leave. On average, there are four thousand horses per week in the four permanent barns and thirty-seven tents on the Wellington show grounds.

Wellington features three different kinds of classes for riders and their horses: the subjectively judged hunter and equitation divisions, and the jumper classes. In the hunter classes, the horses are judged by a set of criteria that evaluate their suitability as field hunters, who follow packs of hounds through the countryside, though the idea that any of these horses, worth about $50,000 each, would gallop through woods and fields after baying hounds is laughable. In the equitation divisions, *riders* are judged on the correctness of their seat and their style. In the jumper divisions, horses complete a timed course of fences, and the fastest one who gets the least penalties is the winner, similar to the show jumping phase of the Three-Day Event. Eventers sometimes compete in jumper classes to hone their skills.

The elite among the elite at Wellington are those riders who compete in the Grand Prix jumping classes. The highest level of the jumper divisions, Grand Prix competitions require horses to jump fences between four and a half and five and a half feet high. Courses have about fifteen to twenty jumping efforts, arranged in single fences and combinations. They're placed at oblique angles and on "bending lines." Traveling at speeds up to twenty-five miles an hour, horses jump, land, sprint, change directions, and explode over another jump. The cups that hold the fence rails in place are a mere eighteen millimeters deep. As much as Three-Day Eventing is about bravery and stamina, Grand Prix jumping is about precision and power.

At five-thirty in the morning, when most of the

grooms report to work, it is still dark in Wellington. The headlights of battered compact cars and dually pickup trucks slide across the faces of the security guards who wave them through the entrance gate. They park on the grass in the rows closest to the permanent barns. Car doors open and close in the dark, releasing clutches of grooms and clouds of marijuana smoke that linger, along with the smell of horses, manure, car exhaust, and dry grass, on the moist south Florida air.

The lights inside the barns glow through the doorways, creating patchwork squares on the ground outside. In the parking lot, on top of the tallest pole on the show grounds, a single spotlight casts a nimbus of light into the tops of the palm trees. In a nearby ring, the grooms who have already arrived are working their horses from the ground. Attached to their grooms by long ropes, called lunge lines, they canter around them in circles, bucking and burning off energy. In the hunter and equitation divisions, the "beauty contests," horses who shuffle along laconically with dropped heads and lowered knee action are the ones most likely to be rewarded with a ribbon. Lunging an excitable horse makes him more manageable. But lunging is also used to exhaust horses, producing, as one trainer says, "robotic, opinionless obedience." Some of the horses have been in the ring since three a.m., and others, as one former professional reveals, have been kept awake and lunged at intervals all night long. As the horses settle into a canter, the steady rhythm of their hooves is as soothing as the gentle creak of a rocking chair. In the dark, the grooms can't even see them. The one bright spotlight blinds them every time they face it. They monitor their horses' positions by the tension on the lunge lines and the sound of their hooves thudding around them.

Most of the show grounds are still shuttered and dark.

The eight competition rings have been cleared of their jumps, and a white tanker truck lumbers in concentric circles, squirting jets of water onto the arena footing. The coffee kiosk by the secretary's office is open, and a few riders and barn staff whizz up in golf carts for lattes and blueberry muffins. The Porta-Potty service truck beeps insistently as it backs up to the toilets and sucks out their contents.

In a schooling ring lit by the truck's flashing yellow light, a painfully thin woman on a muscular chestnut trots the entire length of the ring. She is cushioned in her saddle, her feet resting lightly in her stirrups. She sits erect as her horse punches off the ground in fluid, powerful strides. Arching his neck, he tunes his twelve-hundred-pound body in to his rider. With arms as thin as pencils, she holds the reins that connect her to the horse's bit. His ears flicking, he responds to the messages that she is giving through his bit, his back, and his sides.

The woman on the chestnut is making use of what Anne Kursinski calls the best time of day to ride. Forty-two years old, four-time Olympian, Anne arrives at the barn an hour later, at 6:30, before the circus of golf carts, riders, kids, dogs, and trade fair shoppers descends on the grounds, when, she says, "It's just you and your best horse." The early hour, like daily workouts at the gym, is just one of the disciplines that has kept her competitive on the Grand Prix circuit for more than twenty years. Although it's been a few years since she dominated the sport, the memory of her accomplishments compelled one trainer to comment, "At the top of her game, *no one* could beat her."

Anne's head groom, the one who rallies the rest of her staff of four at five-thirty in the morning, an hour before Anne's first ride, is Brooke Lowe. Twenty-two, tall, fit, round-faced, with a long brown ponytail that she pulls up over the strap of her visor, Brooke speaks with the shortened, twangy vowels of her native Illinois. She grew up in the Crystal Lake area outside of Chicago. A college classmate recruited her into Anne's barn the previous May, right after Brooke graduated from William Woods University in Fulton, Missouri. Her start in life as a horsewoman was late compared to most of her peers. She and her mother spotted horseback riding in their local park district's catalog of summer classes when Brooke was eleven. "I already played soccer and I'd tried gymnastics. I'd tried ballet. We saw horseback riding, so we gave it a shot." Like Samantha Burton, Brooke fell in love with riding and then had to nourish that love on the paltry sustenance of once-weekly lessons. She sustained her interest throughout high school, and in college she majored in equine business administration. "If you're going to be doing something that's going to take up a lot of your time, like normal jobs do," she explains, "you might as well be doing something you enjoy."

In the dark early hours of morning chores, Brooke's job looks a lot like Sam's: mucking stalls, setting up feeds, scrubbing buckets, and turning horses out in their paddocks. When the chores are almost done, Brooke leaves the remainder to the other grooms and walks over to the secretary's office, where the day's class lists are posted. Her job is to find the lists for the classes that Anne and her students are competing in and see where they are in the order. She then writes that order down on a marker board in the barn. She is responsible for making sure the horses get to the ring on time. "Some classes take hours and hours and hours. Some classes you fly through, so it's always kind of guessing when you have to get your horses ready."

Once she writes down the order on the marker board, Brooke pulls a magnetic blanket out of a tack trunk. Anne's jumper Escapade is competing later in the day, and the magnetic blanket helps ease the tension in his muscles.

Brooke lays it over his back and plugs it into its power pack. While Escapade's free radicals are being polarized, Paula Pozzi, one of the other grooms, cross-ties Anne's "best horse," Eros, in the aisle. Eros is sixteen and has one major injury behind him. He's been assigned to Paula because Anne and her partner, Carol Hoffman, who's nicknamed Hoffy, think that Brooke's management responsibilities might distract her from the attention that Anne's senior horse needs. "I don't want him," Brooke says. "He doesn't even like me, because every time I'm with him I'm with the vet or giving him shots or worming him."

The vigor of Paula's brush strokes rocks her small, wiry body and makes her glasses slide down her nose. Still brushing, she pushes them into place with the back of her free hand. Eros pins his ears, and when Paula is close to his front end, he opens his mouth wide enough to bite her head off and gnashes his teeth. One hind hoof is cocked as if he means to kick. Brooke thinks Eros's behavior is a game that's meant to intimidate his grooms. "He thinks he's better than everyone else," she says, adding, "He's got a right to think that."

Paula finishes with Eros just as Anne arrives. Snapping her cell phone shut, Anne bends her knee so Paula can give her a leg up. Anne adjusts her helmet strap and holds her feet out of the stirrups while Paula gives her boots a quick polish and wipes the grit off their soles. Anne thanks her, picks up Eros's reins, and disappears into the darkness just beyond the perimeter of the barn.

At eight a.m., the loudspeaker pops to life, announcing the first class of the day, at eight-thirty, in the hunter ring. In the food court next to the stabling area, a bristling grill cook flips fried eggs onto sandwiches for a queue of impatient customers. Next to him, a French family, in lilting accents, takes orders for crepes. Like an invading army, riders uniformly clad in beige breeches and black boots swarm out of the barns and tents, their cell phones to their ears as if they are all receiving instructions from some central location. The ring of perfectly shod hooves reverberates off the walls of the barns as the horses are led out for their baths or to be ridden. From the tents at the farthest edge of the show grounds, over a mile away from the main ring, horses plod down the lanes of the stabling area. Their grooms are in the saddle, letting their sneakered feet dangle at their horses' sides rather than adjust their stirrups, as they deliver them to their riders.

By nine a.m., the shuttered kiosks that line the walkways throughout the grounds are opening, their merchants unfurling awnings and dragging display racks to their fronts. The first traffic jam of the day has clogged the gate between the stabling area and the show grounds as horses and riders, pedestrians, grooms, dogs, bicycles, and golf carts wait their turn to file through. The Cosequin Winter Equestrian Festival is open for business.

Outside the show grounds, which have almost no signage, the 45,000 residents of Wellington are dropping their kids off at school and heading to work, this a Wednesday like every other. Most of them are unaware that four thousand horses and their attendant grooms, riders, owners, and trainers are in their midst. The residents of Wellington don't know about the festival because the organizers don't promote it locally. The money they need to run the festival comes not from spectators but from the competitors and their corporate sponsors. Even on Grand Prix Sundays, the majority of the spectators on the grounds are other riders and the owners of the horses. The professional horsemen who winter in Wellington live anonymously and keep company with one another. When they go out at night, they frequent only a few of Wellington's restaurants and clubs.

They do their shopping at the festival's trade fair. An administrator at the local chamber of commerce says she sometimes sees them in the Publix supermarket, but "when they want a haircut, they fly home."

The scene at Wellington will be repeated at shows throughout the United States and Canada in the coming months. The changes in location provide different backdrops to the airborne jumpers in the Grand Prix ring, but the rules, the competition, the competitors, the riding style, and even the fashion in riding clothes remain the same at almost every A-rated horse show. Devon in Pennsylvania in May, Spruce Meadows in Calgary in July, the Hampton Classic on Long Island in August, the summer shows organized by HITS (Horse Shows in the Sun) in the Catskills, are all inhabited by this self-supporting segment of the überwealthy.

Only a small portion of the participants at Wellington make their living as professional horsemen. The remainder, even those who compete full time, fund their sport out of their own pockets. Forty percent of Wellington's participants make over $150,000 a year. Though that average includes the wages of the grooms and barn workers, and so is considerably lower than what the owners and riders actually earn. Their average home value is over $400,000, and 81 percent of them own their homes outright. They own, on average, five horses each, and an informal estimate of the price of a horse at Wellington is $50,000.

Anne Kursinski calls the wealthiest participants at Wellington, those with independent incomes for whom there is no bottom line, no price too high for a horse they want to buy or a groom they want to hire, "the millionaires."

Trying to distinguish any group of people at Wellington by calling them millionaires, though, is like trying to distinguish a group of scientists at a convention by describing them as the ones wearing glasses. Like most of her professional peers, Anne actually supports herself with her riding and teaching. She is at Wellington with sixteen horses, the majority of whom she jointly owns with other investors or is riding or training for their owners. She has some students with her as well, who have their own horses. The $4,500 cost per stall for the season to stay in one of the four permanent barns is shared by the co-owners of the horses. Paddock space is an extra fee that, like the cost of the stalls, she shares with the owners. She rented empty stalls for feed and tack rooms. This very expensive stabling came with crooked doors that have to be wrenched open and slammed shut and uneven flooring that dips so deeply in the middle of the aisle that the wheelbarrows tip over. Although water is free, the drain at the entrance to her section of the barn clogs every morning. Nevertheless, Anne and Hoffy are lucky to be in the permanent barns. Horsemen without her tenure keep their horses in tents. Marvelously decorated tents, but ones that can blow down in Florida's high winds.

Despite its somewhat down-at-the-heels accommodations, Wellington is one of only a few horse shows of its caliber in the United States. Anne competes almost exclusively as a jumper rider, and at Wellington, there is a Grand Prix every weekend with purses ranging from $25,000 to $300,000.

Anne is taking Escapade, one of her younger horses, in a low-level jumper class, smaller, shorter, and slower than the Grand Prix. Her horses are so thoroughly groomed every day that other than pulling out the extra-white saddle pads, Brooke doesn't have any special preparations. When her horses compete in the Grand Prix, Anne hires a professional to braid their manes. Braiders are part of the roving band of specialists who ply their skills from barn to barn.

There are massage therapists, chiropractors, farriers, and even equine psychics on call as well.

Brooke curries and runs a soft brush over Escapade's reddish-brown coat and lays a spanking-white saddle pad on his back. She buckles leather boots onto his legs. Into his ears she stuffs earplugs to muffle the sounds of the show grounds that might get on his nerves. Hoffy makes the earplugs by rolling up cotton in the cut-up toes of nylons. Under his bridle, Brooke ties on a crocheted hat that keeps the earplugs from falling out and whose fringe keeps the flies away from his face.

The Market Street gear is a mix of specialty products and old-fashioned homemade goods. Along with his silly hat, Escapade wears a hand-stitched saddle. The horses' legs are treated with lasers but are wrapped in plain old flannels, cut from a bolt in the tack room and pinned on with bandage pins. Their dietary supplements, many provided by Anne's corporate sponsors, are the cutting edge of equine pharmaceutical development, but every one of the horses' meals gets stirred with a carrot that is then dropped in. The horses' legs are bathed in Ivory dish soap, and a specialty horse shampoo is used to wash their bodies.

Sparing no expense for the horses' care at the same time that she resists the marketing frippery of Wellington helps Anne keep the influence of the millionaires at bay. She is reluctant to replace a product that works, like the flannel leg wraps and bandage pins, which most barns have long since replaced with leg wraps that have Velcro closures. But like all professional riders, Anne needs to cultivate corporate sponsorships to keep up with the expenses of running a professional Grand Prix barn. In the permanent barns and the tents, the banks of stalls assigned to professionals are distinguished from those of the amateur riders by the corporate banners. Companies who want to be in the eye of America's equestrian elite fly their colors everywhere they can.

When Escapade leaves the barn, he is wearing his hand-stitched saddle, provided to Anne by one of her sponsors, Hermès. Over the doorways of the barns he passes are banners advertising everything from equine pharmaceuticals to horse snacks. More banners, from huge corporations like Fleet Bank, FedEx, and Century 21 ripple on the rails of the schooling rings as he goes by. The Grand Prix classes he may compete in during his ten weeks in Florida are attached to the names of their sponsors: Bayer, Jaguar / Land Rover, Zada Enterprises, Tommy Bahama, Samsung, and Budweiser. When he enters the international ring, he will pass through two giant replicas of the containers that Cosequin, Bayer's equine joint supplement, is packaged in. The jumps in the ring have company names written across their panels and when Budweiser sponsors a class, there are two jump standards in the shape of Shamu the whale, whose image, like that of their Clydesdales, is one of their corporate logos.

Having arrived at the schooling ring, Brooke waits with Escapade under a shelter that protects him from the sun. Horses with the names of equine retailers stitched to their saddle pads canter by. If you were to replace the riding boots with work boots, the breeches with jeans, the hunt caps with baseball caps, and the horses with cars, Wellington might look like a NASCAR rally.

Anne and Hoffy meet Brooke at the schooling ring. While Anne warms up, Brooke and Hoffy claim one of the three warm-up jumps that bisect the center of the ring. It is dangerously crowded. Grooms and helpers wait at the jump standards, mere inches away from the leaping horses. Other riders, grooms, and barn people mill around the edge of the ring as horses brush by them at the canter. Anne starts her warm-up with a small fence and then, almost inaudibly, calls out a change to Brooke and Hoffy, who scramble to raise the jump cups and replace the pole before Anne approaches it from the other side. The view from the hill between the warm-up and competition rings is a magical spectacle of flying horses. Sometimes all three practice jumps are being cleared at the same time and in different directions: sixteen hooves passing over the heads of a dozen grooms who stand immobile, like the girl in the knife-throwing act, trusting their safety to the skill of the riders.

When Anne enters the competition ring, Brooke and Hoffy take their places next to each other on an observation deck reserved for riders and owners. They lean over the railing holding their breath as Escapade races toward each jump, lands, turns, and races for the next. Anne isn't sure yet that Escapade is a Grand Prix horse. She knows he can jump high enough and that he's fast enough, but she's not sure he can handle the pressure. Eros, her veteran, she says, "could care less." Escapade is clearing the jumps, but he seems worried about them, not listening to Anne as carefully as he should. Toward the end of the course, a rail drops with a heavy thud. Both Brooke and Hoffy let out their breath. With only one rail down, he might still make it to the jump-off, the second round for the top ten horses in the class, but it's not likely. At the last fence, he drops another rail. "Ah, well," Hoffy says, and then turns to Brooke. "*You* did a good job," she says, and thanks her. Outside the ring, Anne is surrounded by her consultants: Hoffy; her assistant trainer; and the coach of the United States Show Jumping Team, George Morris, who has been a mentor to Anne for most of her career. Brooke takes Escapade's reins. A dark film of sweat spreads over his flanks and has pooled in the pockets over his eyes. When she can, Brooke likes to hear what Anne says about the ride. "I like to know what was going on in the ring from her perspective. It makes my job a little easier." Learning that Escapade was too fresh or a little sluggish lets Brooke know that she needs to change his lunging routine. If he wasn't listening to Anne, Brooke reviews her day to see if he wasn't listening to her. Maybe she was too abrupt or short tempered leading him around, which, she thinks, can make a horse sullen and unwilling to go forward.

Back in the barn, Brooke bathes Escapade and puts him away. She still has Anne's students to deal with. Although their ride times are posted, Anne's students can't seem to get to the barn on time without calling Brooke throughout the day from wherever they are on the show grounds. One of the students, a wired and overwrought New Yorker, has flown down for the long weekend. Her horse, a bay, has had some kind of allergic reaction and has hives all over his body. The student rushes to Brooke. "Oh, my God! What are those? They look horrible!" Brooke reassures her that they'll clear up, and when the student goes to change, she curries the horse. His coat is coming out in big hunks, leaving bald patches. Brooke looks at the hair in the currycomb and shrugs. "Hopefully she won't notice," she says.

Brooke studies Anne's students the same way she studies Anne's horses, figuring out how best to prepare them for their classes. The bay's rider, for instance, needs to be rushed, but she can't know she's being rushed or she gets frantic. "It kind of goes along with the job," Brooke says. "It's natural for me to do it. I like working with them and they enjoy it too." The bay's rider is ecstatic about Brooke. At her old barn, he had gotten into the habit of refusing to stand still when he was mounted. His rider had to be launched into the saddle as he jigged away. When he was assigned to her, Brooke made it her responsibility to get him to stay put. Now, as his rider lowers herself into the saddle, she points out how still he is standing. "Brooke did that," she says excitedly. "Brooke is the best."

As fond as she is of Anne's students, Brooke finds it painful to watch them ride. She's made do her whole life: once-weekly riding lessons, horses at college that she had to share with other students, and infrequent lessons at Anne's. As a rider, Anne thinks Brooke is safe but not skilled enough to ride Anne's jumpers over fences, and she also expects her grooms to be professional grooms, not people who've signed on with Market Street expecting to get free lessons. Brooke wants to train horses someday and she worries that her riding is suffering because she spends so little time in the saddle. During the ten weeks of Wellington, she won't get to ride at all.

The bay with the hives ends up with time faults in his class because his rider missed a shortcut between fences. Brooke knew it as soon as she saw it, and though she doesn't necessarily think she would have done a better job, it hurts to know that as long as she's a groom, she'll never get the chance to try.

Anne is particular about who rides her horses because her philosophy centers on "getting inside the horse and really trying to understand the being on a different level," and errors by other riders come through as static on her lines of communication to them. She questions her own decisions about her horses all the time. After each ride she will listen to the input of those few people she trusts: her assistant trainer, other Grand Prix riders, her former coach, and Hoffy; making sure that she has to question only her own riding keeps her task from being overwhelming.

On top of that, Anne isn't the sole owner of her horses. When she first entered the international ranks, she pioneered the use of investment groups to buy horses for her.

Many of her horses, some of which are worth hundreds of thousands of dollars, are owned by a handful of people, including herself. The owners get to participate in the sport and share the prize money. More important for Anne, having multiple owners protects her from the caprice an individual owner sometimes exercises on the riders of his or her horses. In the back pages of equestrian magazines, readers are occasionally treated to scandalous stories of internationally famous riders sneaking into the barns of their competitors and stealing back horses whose owners, they believed, had injudiciously taken the horses away from them. The abrupt departure of a horse can also lead to lawsuits. Anne is protected from the capricious transfer of horses from one rider to another because her horses are owned by multiple investors, including herself. This means that each investor is free to create a unique relationship with Anne, and she is still able to provide continuity in each horse's training. But Anne also has to answer to not one but several people about each of her horses' performances. The horses are top priority at her barn. She has lost students in the past because she argued with their powerful parents about competing horses she believed were lame. After the horses come her own riding and the needs of the owners, then the students and the corporate sponsors. The grooms and their aspirations end up at the bottom of the list.

The results at the end of the first week of Wellington are mixed for Market Street. Anne's younger horses did well, as did those of some of her students. Because he was fractious and unfocussed early in the week, Escapade was pulled out of Sunday's Grand Prix competition, which was a disappointment. Still, Brooke says, "they're all sound, knock on wood." The grooming team hasn't yet gelled. They're still bickering over who is doing the most chores, but as Brooke says with a shrug, "no one is killing each other."

Sunday night is the night out for the Wellington crowd. Monday is a day off for the horses, and though Brooke has to work, she has a light day. Her friends who work in other barns ring her cell phone all afternoon making plans. Brooke is going to a friend's for a steak dinner and swim in the pool and then afterward, everyone is meeting up at a bland local watering hole called Cobblestones, where the drinks are cheap. Then they're off to the Player's Club for dancing until three a.m. None of the other Market Street grooms make plans with Brooke. Paula Pozzi is married and lives in nearby Loxahatchee. She is going home to her husband. Gustavo has just been hired because Jesus Valdivia, nicknamed Chuy, never came back from Mexico, where he went to renew his visa before the Florida season. The other groom who came down from New Jersey, Jesse, the only groom who shares the Market Street condo with Brooke, isn't making plans with Brooke either, but that's fine with Brooke because she doesn't like him. He never does his dishes and is always threatening to quit. "When I first started," she says, "it was me and Heath and Erin and Rene, and the four of *us* got along really well and *Chuy* was the oddball." Now, as the only member of the staff who doesn't speak Spanish, Brooke is the oddball.

In the New Jersey barn, away from the horse shows, Brooke felt "shut down" by the routine and seeing the same people every day. At horse shows, she says excitedly, "you get to see all these other people and you can interact with them. You get to see new places." At Wellington, Brooke has other friends to hang out with, so her oddball status isn't as hard on her as it is at home. Besides, she says, she's doing all the "oddball stuff," like mixing feeds, giving medications, and administering the therapeutic treatments. Still, she hopes the next groom Anne and Hoffy hire (they're shorthanded by one and everyone believes that after payday Jesse is going to make good on his threat to quit) will be someone like her. "Another girl, in her twenties, someone I can go dancing with."

The grooms wait together companionably enough for the last horse to come back from his class. "We all start at the same time," Brooke explains. So it's not fair for one groom to have to stay late just because his or her horse is in the last class. Paula is humming around with a feather duster, swishing dust off the trunks and the stall bars. Brooke and Gustavo sit on a tack trunk, drumming their heels against its side. Anne appears, followed by Jesse and the last horse. Anne writes down Monday's schedule on the marker board and then peeks into her horses' stalls, where they're gobbling up their grain, chewing sloppily and snuffling in their buckets like piglets. Dusk is seeping into the barn. The last horse is put away and the cross ties are clipped across the aisle, closing off the barn for the night. Market Street's day is over.

The loudspeaker is silent. The barns are almost empty. In the lounge areas next to the stalls, some lingering riders and barn managers share pitchers of margaritas. The potted plants glisten with their recent watering and an orchid stretches suggestively out of its hanging basket. In the stalls, the four thousand horses who passed the week at Wellington are snug for the night. The ribbons the horses won or lost this week have added to or detracted from their value. The flawless among the flawless, their individual beauty is no longer visible to many of the horsemen at Wellington, jaded as they are by the abundance of riches. In their stalls, the horses sleep peacefully, unaware that they have prices on their heads. A hired service will check on them hourly throughout the night, logging their activities on sheets posted in the aisle: "3 AM, down, sleeping. 4 AM, up, resting. 5 AM, up, waiting for breakfast," the sheets will say in the morning.

In addition to not knowing exactly when the original horseman of the central Asian steppes climbed onto a horse's back, archaeologists also don't know why. What made him think he could control a thousand-pound biting and kicking animal? Sandra Olsen suspects it was a young man. "Why do you think they draft eighteen-year-olds?" she says. "Because they'll do anything." And how was the first horse chosen? Was there one that was more beautiful than the others? One that was more friendly, more inviting? Was it a foal who had been hand raised after being orphaned by his mother? Or maybe it was just the first horse they could catch. Had a contemporary horseman from Lexington, Kentucky, the Thoroughbred breeding capital of the world, made that decision, the single overwhelming criterion would have been speed.

In November of 2001, two months after the fall of the World Trade Center, with the American economy on shaky footing and the collective nerves of the horse breeding industry jangled and out of sorts, Betty Moran, a breeder from Pennsylvania, paid $4 million for a middle-aged broodmare at the annual bloodstock sale at the Keeneland sales pavilion in Lexington. The mare, Twenty-Eight Carat, was the daughter of Alydar, the dam of stakes winner AP Valentine, and pregnant by, or in foal to, Kentucky Derby winner Fusaichi Pegasus. Her *curriculum vitae* was so exceptional that the industry was shy about pointing to her sale as a sign that it was in good shape. Mares like Twenty-Eight Carat, according to Geoffrey Russell, Keeneland's director of sales, are special.

"They're jewels. They're things people crave. Even in the depth of a depression, they will still bring a lot of money because they are collector's items."

Twenty-Eight Carat was consigned to the Keeneland sale by Lane's End farm in nearby Versailles. Perennial top consignor at the sale, Lane's End is owned by William Farish Sr., friend of the Bush family, U.S. ambassador to Great Britain, and breeder and purveyor of Barbara Bush's famous spaniel, Millie. In its twenty-six-stall stallion complex are some of the finest and most valuable breeding stallions in the world.

At the beginning of the 2002 breeding season, Lane's End has twenty-two stallions standing at stud. For a fee in the $50,000 to $75,000 range, broodmare owners can purchase the services of Dixieland Band, Gulch, Summer Squall, or Lemon Drop Kid. For $200,000, they can have Lemon Drop Kid's sire, Kingmambo. The top stud at Lane's End is A.P. Indy. At $300,000, A.P.'s fee is second only to that of Overbrook Farm's Storm Cat, whose fee is $500,000. A.P. is booked to almost a hundred mares for a breeding season that starts in February and ends in July.

A.P. Indy's groom is Kenneth Burrus. Well over six feet tall, barrel-chested, and with a bit of a hay belly, Kenneth is nicknamed Big K. When his horses are behaving, he moves with the ponderous, deliberate steps of a draft horse, and when they're not, he reacts with a sprinter's speed. Kenneth is in his late fifties. He has a ring of carefully barbered white hair that peeks out like a fringe from under his Lane's End baseball cap and small, fierce blue eyes that almost disappear under crow's feet when he smiles, which is rare. For the ten years that A.P. has been at Lane's End, Kenneth has been the first person he sees every morning and the last one to put his hands on him before he's turned out for the night.

Kenneth has been a groom for thirty-six years, his entire professional life. Lane's End is only the second place he's worked. It wasn't his love of horses that brought him to the barn. "I was fixin' to get married, and I needed something more regular than the farming end of it." The son of a tenant farmer, Kenneth is one of eighty thousand people in the state of Kentucky who draw their livelihood from the Thoroughbred breeding industry. Thoroughbred racehorses are Kentucky's biggest agricultural crop, bigger even than that other vice, tobacco. In another part of the country, Kenneth would have turned to the local factory when he settled down. In Kentucky, the most lucrative factories around are the stud farms. As far as he can remember, until he started working with horses, he never had an interest in them. "I was just a farm boy," he says. "I'd never seen a horse."

"Presumably because they are so valuable, Kentucky horses are in general the most protected, pampered and undisciplined animals in existence," writes Jim Squires, a Kentucky breeder and author of *Horse of a Different Color*. "As a result, many of them — stallions in particular — are prone to bite, strike, kick and eat the very 'hardboots' who care for them." Part of Kenneth's job is to teach a new stallion what's expected of him at Lane's End. "You just try to get to know him," Kenneth says. "The good parts and the bad parts." Lane's End doesn't expect too much of its stallions. Once they retire from racing, they will never be ridden again. After their five-month stint in the breeding shed, they'll spend their days napping in their stalls and their nights romping in their paddocks. "We want to coexist with him," Bill Sellers, the stallion foreman at Lane's End, explains, "handle him when we need to and leave him alone the rest of the time." When they arrive from the track they're fit and aggressive. A.P., Kenneth recalls, "was a little feisty." But soon enough, they settle into a routine with Kenneth.

After he retrieves his horses from the paddock at around six a.m., Kenneth grooms them. Each horse has his own grooming kit, which Kenneth parks on top of a ledge outside his stall. Other than their leather halters with engraved brass plates bearing their names, the horses have no other equipment. The halters are frequently replaced, the old ones auctioned off for local charities. There is hay in the feed room that is replenished regularly from a supply stored away from the barn. Their grain is custom blended by equine nutritionists at the University of Kentucky. There are a few tools, and Kenneth has a battered radio, tuned to a country-western station, sitting on a wall. Other than that, there is nothing in the Lane's End aisle besides varnished paneling, the gleaming brass bars that separate the stallions' stalls, and the shafts of sunlight that shoot down from the cupola atop the vaulted roof.

Kenneth catches A.P.'s halter and clips him to a heavy chain mounted to the wall of his stall. Shin-deep in straw, Kenneth brushes A.P.'s left, or near, side and then crosses behind him to brush the right, or off, side. He polishes A.P. with a clean towel while A.P. bobs his head and pins his ears. When Kenneth brushes his face, A.P. closes his eyes and leans into the brush. Then, as if embarrassed by that show of tenderness, he pins his ears again. When Kenneth stoops to pick out his feet, A.P. lifts them up for him, as if in deference to Kenneth's age and their long history together.

In addition to A.P., Kenneth grooms Dixieland Band and the 1999 winner of the Kentucky Derby and the Preakness Stakes, Charismatic. Dixieland Band has his own routine too. When Kenneth opens his door, Dixie charges at him, teeth bared. "That's his mission in life," Kenneth says: "'See if I can get this big boy. I done put stitches in him once. I think I can do it again.'" Dixie, despite his ingratitude, is brushed exactly the same way A.P. is, and the routine is the same for Charismatic, who stands quietly and somewhat dully, as well. "You could video him a hundred days in a row," Bill Sellers says of Kenneth, "and you'd see the same thing every day."

All that routine is good for the horses but a little boring for Kenneth. When he was first promoted from the yearling barn to working with the stallions, he was excited; it was something different. But "after you been doing it twenty years," he says, "you get tired of it." He doesn't follow the races or have a horse of his own. He is mildly interested to see how his stallions' yearlings do at the sale, but what he most looks forward to every year is his vacation.

Kenneth is less impressed by a horse's race record or stud fee than by his personality. He heaps his highest form of praise on A.P. when he calls him a "great horse." The stout, seal-brown son of Seattle Slew, A.P. inherited from his sire a rim of white around his eyes. From under his dark forelock, A.P. seems to look at the world askance. Belmont Stakes winner, Horse of the Year, A.P. earned his spot at the top of Kentucky's stallion roster by passing his speed, and that of his sire, on to his foals. His mother, or dam, was Weekend Surprise, one of Lane's End's foundation mares. She was such a successful broodmare for Lane's End that she had the rare honor of being buried in its graveyard, along with her dam, Lassie Dear, and the other storied bloodstock of Lane's End. (Actually, it is only her head, heart, hooves, and ovaries that are buried here. The rest of her was carted off to the rendering plant. There is clearly a limit to sentiment spent on horses.) Visitors to the farm can't visit the graves, because they are still unmarked. The planning of the cemetery, Bill Sellers jokes, has been held up in typical Lane's End style. They have been dawdling over expensive proposals for a monument that is in keeping with the simple, astonishing beauty of the farm. He wants them to hurry up, because there are only two people, Bill and a woman in the office, who actually know where the horses are buried.

A.P. is a bit of a homeboy at Lane's End. He was sold off the farm as a yearling for $2.9 million, the best-selling yearling in his crop. When he retired, he boomeranged back to take his place in the front barn. Since then, he's won the heart of every groom at Lane's End. He is fond of his food, and the staff is sensitive to jokes about his broodmarish appearance. When they talk about him, they characterize him not as a blooded Thoroughbred who has largely led a patrician life of leisure, which is the truth, but as a horse who is like them, a workingman. "If he were a guy," Bill Sellers says, "he'd be a construction worker, black lunch box, 'Where's my dinner?'"

In his thirty-six years of being a groom, the only other horse Kenneth has been as fond of was Alysheba. Alysheba won the first two legs of the Triple Crown in 1987 and was Kenneth's first Derby horse. Kenneth liked him because he was something different. In his paddock, he raced the fence line and reared up and pawed the air, "showing off and stuff," and he once yanked an earring out of a woman's ear. Both Alysheba and A.P., Bill Sellers says, seemed like they knew what you were saying when you talked to them. Unlike A.P., however, Alysheba was not a potent sire. His first crop of foals set records at the yearling sales but didn't produce at the track. His stud fee fell off, and he was sold to a breeder in Saudi Arabia. "I would like to have seen Alysheba do well," Kenneth says. "I guess you always try to look forward instead of back, but every now and then you think about a horse like Alysheba. Why he didn't make it."

★   ★   ★

SUSAN NUSSER

Pedigree is the first consideration in establishing a stallion's fee. Charismatic, even though he won two out of three races of the Triple Crown, has a stud fee of only $35,000. Lemon Drop Kid, whom he bested in the Kentucky Derby, has a stud fee of $75,000 because he is of the more fashionable Kingmambo bloodline. Kevin Conley, in his book *Stud,* points out that our obsession with equine bloodlines predates our obsession with our own. James Weatherby's *General Stud Book* was published thirty-six years before *Burke's Peerage.* Speed, speed, speed is what breeders have always looked for in Thoroughbred bloodlines. Spectacular Bid, the son of Bold Ruler and the 1980 Triple Crown winner, was unable to pass on his speed. A half-brother to Secretariat, Spectacular Bid possessed heart and courage and desire but not potency. A dud at stud, the Bold Ruler line fallen out of fashion, he was expelled from the blue bloods in Kentucky and retired to a stud farm in New York, where his services sold for a few thousand dollars.

Unlike A.P.'s or Dixieland Band's, Charismatic's future at Lane's End is uncertain. A slight, unprepossessing chestnut, Charismatic has been underestimated for his entire short life. Just months before he won the Derby, his trainer, D. Wayne Lukas (whom the grooms called D'Wayne), risked losing the horse by entering him in a claiming race. Claiming races are races where for the price of the purse, anyone can buy any horse in the race. Before the horses leave the starting gate, a potential buyer must pony up the fee. According to Elizabeth Mitchell, who wrote about Charismatic in her book *Three Strides Before the Wire,* the claiming race was Lukas's attempt to find a race he knew his horse could win so Charismatic could taste what it felt like to be a winner. He won that claiming race and, luckily, went unclaimed, but by the Derby he had so little experience as a winner that he went off at 31-1 odds. Most in-

54

dustry insiders would have assigned the same odds to his jockey, Chris Antley. He had won the Derby once before, on Strike the Gold, but confessed that he had been on so many drugs at the time he didn't remember it. Plagued by weight gain, addiction, and depression, the trinity of afflictions that comes with a jockey's journeyman card, Antley had penitently dieted and exercised and abstained his way back. His ride on Charismatic, he said, was his chance to ride a Derby he could remember. After winning the Derby and the Preakness Stakes, the first two legs of the Triple Crown, Charismatic went off as the favorite in the Belmont Stakes, the final leg, in front of 85,000 fans. Just over the finish line, as the crowd gasped, Antley leaped off his horse's back and wrestled Charismatic's left front leg off the ground, calming the horse and supporting his weight with his own small body. Charismatic had broken his leg and lost the Belmont. The leg healed. Sellers reports being proud of the "small part we played in that horse's recovery." Under Kenneth's tender care, the horse was hand-walked for months until he was sound. Sadly, Antley was found dead in his California home less than a year after his Derby win. Officially and absurdly, investigators declared that, loaded with drugs, Antley had staggered and crashed around his house with enough force to deliver a blunt trauma to his own head. His friends, his family, and many in the racing community believe that he was murdered by the son of a wealthy man with whom he had been doing drugs. Charismatic's own hard-luck story, Kenneth believes, makes people want to like him more. But, he says, "we've seen a lot of [stallions] come and go since we've been fooling with them. Most of them don't make great sires," he warns. "More of them don't than do."

In the last weeks of the off-season, before the breeding shed opens the week of Valentine's Day, Kenneth and the other grooms are waiting — for the end of the day and, down the road, the beginning of the season. At two o'clock, Kenneth turns his horses out in their paddocks for the night. Poor A.P. has to wear a grazing muzzle to keep him from eating too much grass. The night watchman is supposed to bring him in around midnight. Kenneth suspects that A.P. will not only elude the night watchman but will also get the muzzle off, both of which he does most nights. The grooms watch Ricki Lake in the office, arguing about whether or not she's better than Jerry Springer. Kenneth stands by the front fence, looking toward his house, several hundred yards down the drive on Lane's End property.

Kenneth owns a farm in Harrodsburg, but when his wife stopped working, they moved to Versailles and left the farm in the care of their son. He goes home for lunch, and he drives his truck to work every day so he can leave it in the parking lot when he wants to sneak home before quitting time. He likes to talk about his family, as if talking about them will somehow make up for all the weekends he missed with them in a lifetime of six-day workweeks. "A lot of time your kids and your wife had to go off to reunions and family gatherings and stuff, and 'Where's Kenneth?' He's working. He can't go."

About ten years ago, Kenneth broke his neck in a car accident. "Only new truck I ever had went straight up into the air." Before the accident, he had been thinking about taking a job in a factory, where he'd have weekends off. Or switching to carpentry, which he likes because "you could stand back and see what you've done." But while he convalesced, immobile in a neck brace, he missed his work: "You don't realize until you set home." His doctor told him he didn't think it was a good idea to return to the stallions, but Kenneth said, "I gotta get back."

In his house down the lane, Kenneth's wife is babysitting their two-year-old granddaughter. She loves horses. Kenneth knows she does because she talks about them all the time. After all his talk about having chosen his life as a stud groom because it was a regular paycheck and not because he loves horses, he's still thinking about getting his little granddaughter a pony and keeping it at his farm in Harrodsburg. "It wouldn't cost me much," he says, as if it's already planned out. "I got a little barn and fence and stalls." Then he changes his mind. "Right now," he says, "as long as I got quarters for those horses outside Wal-Mart, we're all right."

In another job, in another part of the country, Kenneth might have had those weekends off with his family, but he would never have been in the position he is at Lane's End. When his boss, William Farish, wants to know how his most valuable horse is feeling, he asks Kenneth. But despite his professional success, his intimate knowledge of the most valuable animals in the world, like Brooke Lowe, he still doesn't have what he most wants — to be the master of his own fate. Despite the prestige of the horses they handle and the people they work for, grooms' days are dictated by the immense needs of the very horses who have bestowed on them their professional respect. If not for the horses, Kenneth and Brooke would never have found themselves in the company of the elite, the power class. But the horses who have brought them there have also shackled them to a servant's role, tending to the possessions of the very wealthy. In an odd reversal, though, when those powerful people come seeking information about their horses, the people they turn to are Brooke and Kenneth.

Chapter Three

PERSONALITY

Samantha Burton is accustomed to being good with horses, but being good at managing people is new to her. Under her supervision, the other grooms have become chatty since they arrived in Florida. It is as if leaving behind the blanched fields and naked branches of Virginia for the green grass, giant oaks, and blue skies of Florida has warmed their hearts, and they are now overflowing with affection for one another and their horses.

The O'Connors lease their winter training barn from Lambholm South, a Thoroughbred training facility just outside of Ocala, in Reddick, Florida. In their little corner of the farm they have two barns: an older traditional one and a new shed-row-style barn built for them in 2002. In the new barn, the stalls face outward and the aisle runs around its perimeter. There are no exterior walls. On one side, the horses look at someone's backyard. On the other side, they look out over a pasture where cattle graze. Sam hopped off the rig when they arrived and immediately snagged the stalls with the best view for David's horses. For Tex and Tailor, Reddick, Florida, is a place of cows.

The new barn, Sam says, makes her feel like it's the first winter the O'Connor team isn't camping out. Last year, the O'Connors were in the old barn and the students were in tents. Their new bright and airy tack room is just being finished when they arrive. As David screws in the bridle and saddle racks, he calls Vanessa, the shortest groom, to his side. "See if you can reach this," he says. There is a feed room, a real bathroom, and a washer and dryer that save on twice-weekly trips to the Laundromat. The grooms are still roughing it, though. Down the road, next to a storage shed, is a row of campers that they call home. The students live there as well, and add to the grooms' responsibilities by doing things like coming home late after a night of partying and driving over the central water pipe, forcing the water to all the campers to be shut off.

In the main barn at Reddick, the O'Connors have twenty horses, plus another five or so in with the students' horses. There are more than forty horses under their supervision. David has some of his young horses with him, those that will be tackling their first competitions this year. Along with Karen's other horses are her two retirees, Biko and Prince Panache. On the first weekend in February she is taking seven horses to the Rocking Horse Stables horse trials in nearby Altoona — the first competition of the season. David is skipping the competition because he'll be teaching in North Carolina the same weekend. On Thursday afternoon, with a groan of reluctance, the grooms agree to start at three-thirty the next morning so they can get all of Karen's horses braided before they leave at five a.m. Five horses will go over in Blue Thunder, the O'Connors' horse van, and the remaining two will travel in the students' trailers.

At three-thirty in the morning on Friday, the dim yellow lights of the O'Connor barn throb through a dark and heavy fog. The moss-laden branches of the giant oaks reach out toward it, as if they are trying to cloak it even further. Beyond the lights of the barn, the paddocks are invisible, and a report of a dead panther on the highway causes Sam to look into the mist, rethinking her decision to turn Biko and Prince Panache out overnight.

Four of Karen's horses are cross-tied in the aisle. The grooms stand on step stools and upturned buckets, twisting sections of mane and lengths of waxed cotton into tight braids. They use the leftover thread to sew the braids into loops at the base of the horses' manes. There are faster and easier ways to braid a mane, but none that look as professional.

Tex, Tailor, and Tigger are watching the braiding with mild interest. ET, whose stall is under attack by Percy, is cowering against the back wall. Percy paces from side to side, rushes to the front of his stall, and stares incredulously at the horses being braided. Bristling with bad temper, he kicks the wall between his stall and ET's. In the aisle, the horses being braided ignore him, standing with their heads lowered so the grooms can reach their manes. They know, Vicky says, that they're "going to a party." With her spiked blond hair, blue eyeshadow, and slick of lip gloss, Vicky looks like she's going to a party too.

Sam is the first to finish, and her braids are perfect: tight buttons of woven hair spaced evenly down her horse's neck. Vicky, who keeps her braiding kit (waxed cotton, little scissors, darning needles, and seam rippers) in a pink faux-fur-covered Barbie case, has only one braid out of place. She's quick to point out that it isn't her fault. *Someone* has trimmed the horse's mane between the ears too far down his neck and it's growing out awkwardly. Max hasn't sewn up Amber's braids yet, and the little red mare has Bo Derek–style cornrows running down her crest. Andi Dees, who came to the O'Connor barn last fall after working with abandoned and rescued horses, is still braiding Joey in his stall. Vanessa's horse has clumps of hair the size of Ping-Pong balls strewn unevenly along his neck. This is the first time she's braided a mane, and the other grooms are conscientiously *not* teasing her about her braids, but she's not fooled. "They look terrible, I know."

One by one, the grooms close their horses back in their stalls and pick up pitchforks. Orlando Betancourt, the "extra hand" on the O'Connor Event Team, has arrived. Greeting the young women and asking how everyone is, he empties muck tubs into a wheelbarrow and carts it off to the manure pile.

Karen arrives at five, whistling for her dog as soon as she gets out of her car. She's followed by Brewster Walker, a professional driver and friend of the O'Connors whom they rely on to drive Blue Thunder when David isn't around. No one else on the team has the requisite commercial driver's license. Compact and energetic, with prematurely gray hair, Brewster is a whistler and a joker and he brags to the grooms that he was still partying an hour ago.

The horses wear lightweight sheets and shipping boots — puffy nylon sheaths that cover their legs from their thighs down to their hooves. Their tails are wrapped to keep them clean in the trailer, and their halters are covered with shearling that protects their faces from rubs. Their puffy boots swish like snow pants as they follow their grooms into the rig, the *boom, boom, boom* of their hooves on the ramp as regular as the reverberation of tires bouncing through a pothole.

Percy becomes even more frantic when he sees his stablemates getting into the rig without him. No longer satisfied just kicking the wall, he rears up and thrusts his nose over it, teeth bared. ET is as far away from that wall as he can get, his face knitted with worry, his ears pinned back so flat that they've disappeared into his neck. His stall, according to Sam, is his private space, about which he's very protective. As Sam points out, it probably never occurred to ET that an attack on his space might come from above. His defenses up, he lunges at her when she walks by, and she raises her arm as if to smack him. "He knows," she explains. "I let him do a lot of things. He can fidget on the cross ties, whatever, because that's just ET. But when he strikes out at me, he gets into trouble." In the back of his stall, ET looks chagrined and worried. "He's such a funny horse," Sam says. "He so wants to be adored."

Someone has wisely closed the iron grating in front of Percy's small stall guard, and as the horses load, he presses his face against it. Watching him, Sam laughs. "Where is that truck going? I've got to get on that truck! You forgot me again!"

The doors of the rig are closed, the bolts fired. Andi and Vicky, who are the only grooms going to the show today, pull themselves into the cab, and Brewster follows. Karen calls out to Sam, "It's gone well for the first trip of the season, don't you think?"

From inside the cab, Brewster yells out that there are no keys.

This is the second time in three days that the keys to Blue Thunder have gone missing. The last time, when they needed to haul the horses down the road to a training session at the United States Equestrian Team's winter barn, the keys were found in David's pocket; he was already at the training session. The grooms freeze. The good cheer evaporates. They spin on their heels and dart into the barn. In the tack and feed rooms, cupboard doors open and bang shut. They shout out possible locations to one another, each more unlikely than the last.

"All dressed up and no place to go!" Brewster yells.

Vicky jumps out of the cab and suggests that someone call David. Why? Karen wants to know. He hasn't been in the rig.

"He was in there yesterday," Vicky says.

"What was he doing?" Karen asks. "Losing the keys?"

The promising season debut is now a disaster. The tempo of slamming doors slows to a halt, and Sam stands in the aisle, shaking her head. "They're not here," she says.

Almost inaudibly, Brewster calls out that he found them inside the truck.

Blue Thunder rumbles to life, summoning Vicky and Andi at a run. With a shudder, the van pulls out of the yard. Karen follows in her Durango. The O'Connors' 2002 season has officially begun, ten minutes late.

Meanwhile, another drama is unfolding in the tack room. Max is sitting on a trunk in tears. She just watched her horse, Amber, leave for the horse trial without her. It's the first time the two have been separated since Jim Stamets, Max's former employer and friend, died.

Max and her red mare are a team within the team at the O'Connor barn. She is protective of Amber, especially since the horse isn't like the O'Connor horses. Amber's barn manners, which Max calls quirky, the other grooms call spoiled, with the implication that Max is the one who spoils her. Her handling of Amber is under constant scrutiny, and the grooms feel that she dotes too heavily on the mare, neglecting her other horses. At thirty, Max is older than the rest of the grooms. She's been kicking around the event circuit for a while, working for lower-level riders. When she started in the fall, she wanted to be part of the O'Connor team, but now she isn't sure. Friends in Colorado have offered to get her a job leading bike tours. The grooming thing, she says, is getting old, and she's openly talked about leaving after Rolex. "When she gets over the Jim thing," Sam says. "I think she'll move on." Max is the fifth groom and the fifth wheel on the O'Connor team, and her little mare, her protector, confidante, and ally, has, for the day, been taken away from her and assigned to someone else.

Vanessa, who is as tall standing up as Max is sitting down, pats her shoulder and mumbles sympathetically.

Sam stumbles onto them when she enters the tack room. Her gaze is slowly pulled to the tableau of the weeping Max and the comforting Vanessa. She slows down, as if the gear that drives her forward has disengaged, leaving her to coast across the room on leftover impulsion. Standing in front of a cupboard while Max, embarrassed, composes herself, Sam says, "Believe me, if I didn't think Andi needed the experience, she wouldn't have gone."

The O'Connors' grooms, like most Three-Day Event grooms, work ten-to-twelve-hour days, six days a week. Their travel schedule and the demands of their job make it difficult for them to maintain relationships away from the barn. Their days off are rotated, one groom at a time, and they mostly spend them catching up on sleep, running errands, and watching videos. The center of their universe is the barn; their time away from it is spent waiting to get back to it.

Sam and her fellow grooms are working for the most visible professionals in their discipline. As husband-and-wife Olympic medalists, the O'Connors are perhaps the only Three-Day Event riders in the United States to have a public identity beyond the confines of their sport. That visibility comes with scrutiny; everything they do is worthy of a magazine article. Their grooms are under scrutiny as well. Riders not as successful as Karen and David are likely to interpret even an offhand complaint from the staff as evidence of the O'Connors' impending tumble from the top of the American eventing establishment. All of this contributes to the grooms' sense of isolation. Even at competitions, the only time they get away from their barn, they stick loyally to one another. Sam knows that people think they are snobs and she defends them, saying that they just have too much work to do; they don't have time to socialize.

In addition to taking care of her horses, part of Sam's job is to keep the pressure and isolation from causing the grooms to turn on one another. Whatever reservations she has about their abilities or their work ethic, she keeps them to herself. She doesn't even share them with David because in her experience he sees exactly what she sees. When the grooms are quibbling with one another, when they're struggling with the demands of the job or even if they're having personal problems, Sam is their confessor.

Andi Dees, whom Sam believes is the hardest worker in the barn, came to Sam's camper in tears one night. "And this was typical," Sam says. "She came to me apologizing." Andi was worried that she wasn't getting along with the other grooms, that she wasn't part of the team. Sam listens to problems but doesn't intervene on anyone's behalf, nor does she take sides. But when someone's confidence flags, she keeps her at her side for a day or two until she is sure of herself again. To cheer Andi up, Sam gave her extra horses to gallop the following day.

According to her mother, Chris, when Sam was in preschool her teachers said that among her peers, Sam was "the best kid there at peacekeeping and getting her way." Sam's "way" at the O'Connors is to have happy, healthy, competitive horses. Achieving that goal means adhering to a system, "the program," making sure that everyone else is adhering to that system, and anticipating and eliminating as many glitches that might occur in the system as possible. She holds herself a little separate from her peers, as if she is constantly appraising the situation. She has a separate camper — one of the perks of her seniority — rather than doubling up like the other grooms. She doesn't join Vicky, Vanessa, and (less frequently) Max when they go out to nightclubs in nearby Gainesville, or go kayaking with Andi on her day off. Her fiancé, Kenny Johnson, doesn't work with horses, doesn't even really know anything about them, and other than the fact that they both live at Stonehall, she keeps that relationship separate from her work ones. On her days off, she sleeps and does errands or watches TV, except on those days that she spends at the barn because David needs her. When the grooms come to her with problems, she is rarely surprised, because she observes them as carefully as she observes her horses. What little she doesn't notice herself, she gleans from her conversations with her grooms. As busy as she is, she always has a minute or two to listen to her staff.

What Sam gets for her discipline, her judiciousness and diplomacy, is a barn where her horses are meticulously cared for and happy. She can trust the other grooms and, in turn, has the full confidence of her employers. Despite their personal differences, the arduousness of their work, and their isolation, the grooms function as a team. They are the best team she has ever worked with. Almost bashfully, she repeats a compliment that David paid her. "People are happy in the barn," he said. "And they love their job."

Max's outburst in the tack room has clearly taken Sam by surprise. Her self-control, her determination to not play favorites, are calculated to keep people from crying at work. She seems unsure what to do: stay with Max or get back to her chores. She takes a half step toward the door, changes her mind, and sits on the trunk next to Vanessa. Max neutralizes the awkward silence by wondering aloud what happened to Orlando. Relieved to have something they can do together, they build a story around her question. Orlando must have gotten locked in the back of the rig. At this very moment, they joke, he's waving frantically at the video camera that broadcasts to a monitor in the cab. The sound of him pushing the wheelbarrow down the aisle is their cue to get back to work, calmed and mollified.

They keep up a steady chatter while they're mucking separate stalls. They spin out their tales, trusting that the other two are still in the barn, that they haven't made a trip to the muck heap at the same time, leaving the storyteller casting her words into the air. They laugh at one another's stories, mostly Vanessa's, of her days off spent flirting with the guy in the video store. Their voices travel the length of the barn as they move from stall to stall, calling over their shoulders when they turn a corner. The horses chew their hay, their ears following the sound of the women's voices the same way they would follow the sound of movement in their herd. Their habituation to their grooms, their constant nearness to them, has taught them that what the grooms are

making are happy sounds, sounds full of purpose and in-
tention. The horses are relaxed, content to follow their
grooms with their ears and eyes, to splash their noses in
their buckets, pick at their hay, or doze with their heads at
half-mast, confident that their role in those intentions will
become apparent soon.

Sunrise, when it arrives, is hidden behind a wet gray fog.
The grooms switch the turnout, bringing in the horses
who've spent the night outside and putting out the ones
who were in their stalls. Percy, still rattled from being left behind, races back and forth across his paddock, skidding to a
halt on the far side, inches away from slamming into a fence
that is almost invisible in the mist. His tail floats out behind
him as he lifts his head and blows a challenging snort. Max
and Vanessa stand at the paddock rail, trying to figure out
what has spooked him. "Listen," Max says, bowing her head.

Muffled in the fog, the sound of the horses galloping
on Lambholm's training track is beating down the hill.
Normally, the O'Connors' horses are turned out after the
morning gallops. The pounding of the unseen racehorses'
hooves sounds like a wild, thundering herd, snorting and
blowing. Percy quivers, tossing his head, and buzzes back
and forth. Sam comes around the corner of the barn and in
a few words indicates that Max and Vanessa need to swap
Percy with a quieter horse in a paddock farther away, the
tone of her voice implying that this is a decision that Max
and Vanessa should have already made. Allowing him to
race around in a panic puts his fragile legs and tendons at
risk. Tiny Vanessa opens the gate, and Percy crowds her,
shoving her backward. "Don't let him push you around,"
Sam snaps. Vanessa shakes the lead shank in Percy's face until he backs up, and then she walks him out of the paddock.

Vanessa and Max's lapse in judgment is a sign of their

lack of experience. Sam's irritability is a sign that she's tired, that she's confronted enough irregular problems for one morning. Once the horses are switched, Sam disappears into the student barn without giving any more instructions. Vanessa wants to know if they're going back to the campers. She points out that she's still in her pajama pants because she thought they would go home after braiding. Max sits on a trunk, the last of the morning's coffee gone cold in her travel mug. Sam doesn't return, and the young women decide for themselves. Vanessa will go back to her camper and change, and Max will start getting horses ready for David, who should be arriving soon to ride before he leaves for North Carolina. They've already been working for five hours, and the real work of the day remains ahead of them. Tired, punchy, and momentarily overwhelmed, they stare at each other across the tack room.

By evening, their work done, waiting for the horses to return from Rocking Horse, their mood has mellowed. The morning outbursts of emotion and temper have left behind another degree of intimacy between them, one more way that they know each other. They're on top of the tack trunks again. Max leans her head against the wall, her eyes closed. Vanessa is lying down, an ankle crossed over her knee, her head resting on Max's leg, a lollipop in her mouth. They're figuring out how to return Karen's seven horses to the show tomorrow morning with a rig that only has six stalls. Unlike today, tomorrow's start times are too close together to send the horses in shifts. Sam buzzes into the room, wheels around, and sits down and crosses her legs in one motion. She has the list of start times in her hand and is thinking out loud. Vanessa is amenable to every suggestion, and Max is a source of endless alternatives, as if exploring possibilities, not coming up with a solution, is the point of the exercise. The inevitable solution, the one they've been avoiding, is that someone will have to drive the O'Connors' aged horse van, called White Lightning (even though it is blue), to the show.

White Lightning has been declared dangerous by Karen and David and it sits on the edge of the property, surrounded by parked cars. Technically, it's for sale, but it keeps being called into service. Max, who likes mechanical stuff, hops into the driver's seat to try the engine while Sam stands on the running board, clinging to the closed driver's door and looking over Max's shoulder. The engine, as they suspected, is dead. Max tries a second and third time, and Sam, laughing, drops her face into her hands. There is some confusion about the location of the battery, whether it is the object under the hood that Orlando is pointing at or the square box accessed through a side panel near the bottom of the truck, as Max believes. Orlando is holding a pair of jumper cables, and there is a spirited patty-cake of Spanish-English translation going through Vanessa, who grew up in Puerto Rico. Max wins, and the rest stand to the side, cringing, as she tries the engine again. White Lightning starts up with a cough.

Stretched out on the grass in the sunshine, grasshoppers whirring, White Lightning chugging away, the grooms sip beers and sneak cigarettes while they wait for Karen to return. They're closet smokers because Karen and David abhor the habit, and the grooms are convinced that they've successfully kept it hidden from them. Calvin, Vicky's monstrous black boxer-chow mix with the sinister underbite, is playing with Karen's tiny terrier, Bizzie. Sam's corgi-husky mix, Ozzie, lies at her side. In Virginia, the dogs are not allowed in the barn. In their efforts to hold on to good grooms, Karen and David have installed electric fencing around the grooms' cottages there so no one has to feel guilty about her dog while she works twelve-hour days. One of the good things about Florida, Sam says, is that "it's a bit of a dog party." Ozzie trots the aisles on his stubby legs, his one blue eye supervising on Sam's behalf. Calvin lingers in the doorways, waiting for someone to stand still long enough for him to lean his ribs against her knees for some patting. The students have dogs, and the vet brings her dog. "If you're not good with dogs," Sam says, "how in the world can you be good with a huge animal?" The women gossip about other grooms and laugh as little Bizzie runs in and out of Calvin's open mouth.

They hear Blue Thunder's gears shifting in time to squash out their cigarettes before Brewster pulls through the gate. Vicky and Andi are out of the rig before he cuts the engine. Vicky lands and opens her arms wide, greeting her dog, who stands before her, his entire body wagging along with his tail. Karen has done well, but not all the news is good. That afternoon, Berringer split open his lip on the metal hook of a bungee cord. It will be weeks before they can put a bit in his mouth. Vicky reports this to Sam, but it was Andi who took the brunt of Karen's wrath. Obviously, it was their fault, Andi says. They left the bungee cord where Berringer could get to it. Andi dryly describes herself trying to lead him quietly off the rig as she was trapped between the spurting blood of his lip and the flying spittle of Karen's invective. It's that assurance and unflappability that Sam is trying to draw out of Andi. She can't figure out how she could so easily handle Karen and yet be undone by the casual bossiness of her peers.

Whatever tension there was during the day is gone as Karen watches her grooms unload her horses from the trailer. "For me," she explains, "I need a groom to decrease my stress, not increase it." Glossy horses follow their grooms to their stalls. Vanessa steers a wheelbarrow to the door of the rig and starts pitchforking soiled shavings into it. Vicky unloads an armful of bridles that covers half her face, and Brewster homes in on any groom who stands still long enough for him to catch up with her. "Look at them," Karen says. "We got here five minutes ago and already that trailer is unloaded."

Sam counts her time with the O'Connors in Florida years. This one is her fourth. In those years she has seen David win an Olympic gold medal on Tailor and win Rolex on Tex, when she was his head groom. She is excited about the World Equestrian Games in Spain in September and she is excited for the big Three-Days, like Rolex. But between Florida and the big Three-Days are a lot of little horse trials. Those are harder to get excited about. For young horses and new grooms, they are places to rack up competitive mileage, but for Sam they just mean more travel, a return to lessons she's already learned. What she is most excited about at her job are the new training techniques she is learning.

Sam's management philosophy, building confidence in her grooms while she lets them puzzle out the challenges of their job, is the same approach David uses with his horses. What he likes best about training them, he says, is teaching them what they are capable of. Like Sam, he does his job quietly. David, she says, "likes to see things for himself." He slips into the barn unnoticed, often startling the grooms, who look at one another nervously, wondering how long he has been in earshot of their conversation.

Over the past couple of years, David and Karen have developed a training relationship with Pat Parelli, a practitioner of the loosely grouped methods referred to as natural horsemanship in which horseman and horse create their relationship by reading and interpreting each other's body language. Working in a round pen with just a rope, a halter, and a long whip (Parelli has designed his own, which he calls a carrot stick), horsemen teach their horses to understand the basic principle of resistance and release. By pushing on the horse and then rewarding him when he steps away, a trainer teaches the horse to respond to as subtle a cue as a wiggled finger or even a glance. Capitalizing on the horse's visual acuity and their obsession with body language, trainers start by pushing on the horse — a pinch on the chest to get him to back up, a tap with the whip to move him forward — and then releasing that pressure as soon as the horse responds, rewarding him. The cues to the horse became increasingly subtle, from a tap with the whip to just a wiggled finger. A horse traveling in a circle on the lunge line, his eye on his trainer, can learn to swing his hind end away from the handler when he ducks his upper body toward it — the pressure *implied* by the visual cue. Learning to respond to slight visual cues makes horses all the more responsive to the cues of leg, seat, and hands once the rider is mounted. David's horses are so sharply attuned to him that he can ride many of them bareback, with just a string around their neck. Part of Sam's job is doing the groundwork with David's horses, especially the younger or newer ones, whom she gets started for him. "I've always been fairly in tune with horses from the ground," Sam says. The formal training helped her "understand where that's going and why. It finally makes a bit more sense."

Pat Parelli, like Monty Roberts, John Lyons, Ray Hunt, and others who have marketed their techniques to a broad audience, learned his skills from a California cowboy named Bill Dorrance. The old cowboy techniques of breaking a horse, of forcing him into submission, are things of the past, these practitioners claim. The new methods are about communication and cooperation. Expert marketers, the

natural horsemanship gurus have developed their own no-
menclature to pitch their methods. Monty Roberts calls his
Join Up; Pat Parelli calls his Horse-Man-Ship.

Regardless of their new packaging, the techniques
themselves are ancient. Alexander the Great, who learned
his horsemanship from the Greek cavalry officer Xenophon
and the Scythians, used them to train his famous mount,
Bucephalus. According to Plutarch, when Alexander was a
boy, he watched his father's grooms mishandling a stallion.
Distraught, he asked to take over the horse's training. The
stallion, Alexander had noticed, was fighting the grooms because he was spooked by his own shadow. His obstreperous-
ness only increased when the grooms fought back. Alexander
took the horse's reins and turned him away from the sun.
Once he was calmed, Alexander was able to mount and he
galloped away. When he returned, his father, Philip, gave
him the horse and wept for joy. "You must go look for a
kingdom to match you, my son. Macedonia is not large
enough for you." On Bucephalus's back, Alexander con-
quered over two million square miles of the ancient world.

Pat Parelli winters in Ocala, and David has arranged for
him to demonstrate his techniques at the U.S. Equestrian
Team's nearby winter training facility. At the facility are two
development programs run by the team. David and Karen
and their peers are part of the Senior Rider program,
where they work with Captain Mark Phillips of Great
Britain, the coach of the U.S. Equestrian Three-Day Team.
The senior riders, in turn, are coaching the Young Riders
program, for eventers under the age of twenty-one, whom
the team is training to take the place of riders like David and
Karen when they retire from international competition.

At the end of a long day in the middle of their week,
Sam and the other grooms close their horses in for the

night and, in growing darkness, meet their bosses at the team facility. Parelli's demonstration includes a barbecue and, like most eventing gatherings, plenty of beer. Sam and the other grooms hit the coolers. Parelli is working a horse in a corner of the front field. In the lighted arena behind the students, the caterers are grilling ribs, the smoky, sweet smell drifting down the hill to the crowd seated along the fence line. As Parelli lectures through a headset he wears under his cowboy hat, his trainers are galloping and jumping their horses over the cross-country fences behind him. Bareback and bridleless, with just a string around their necks, the horses leap over stacked timber, down embankments into water, and over hedges. The horses, Parelli explains, are almost all rescued ones — saved from the slaughterhouses they were on their way to because they were wild and unmanageable. He concedes that they are not the athletes that event horses are, but look: Look what these horses can do. His riders are more interested in training than in competing, Parelli says, and then he asks the crowd how they think the riders would do if they did compete. "They'd kick our ass!" someone in the crowd yells. While Parelli talks, the riders gather on the hill. Then, like a cavalry gone mad, they gallop to the fence line and jump over it. The students cheer and, since the horses are now out of sight, turn their attention back to the lecture. A few moments later, Parelli casually informs a group sitting on a low part of the fence that they might want to get out of the way. The students look up just in time to see a half dozen horses galloping toward them in the dark. Before they can move, the horses jump through a gap in the crowd. A current of excitement buzzes through the onlookers. This is what they want, what they've always wanted. This was the first dream they ever had, the one promised by children's books: riding bareback, bridleless, one being with a horse's body and their thinking brain.

"It's proof of communication," David says about the relationship between the naked horses and their riders. "You take off their bridle, the main mechanism of control. You just take it away and look, you can still do ninety percent of the things. So," he asks "what is control?"

Leadership would be Parelli's answer. Teach the horse to trust you, to choose to follow you, and he will do whatever you ask — without bits, without spurs, without whips.

These are the methods that Sam credits with Tigger's and ET's reform. Despite David's success as a competitive rider, and his success at turning around problem horses, his embrace of Parelli's techniques has been received with skepticism by his tradition-bound peers. "Their initial reaction," Sam explains, "will be that it's just a circus trick, they're just trying to show off. Then, when the horses continue to be successful, maybe people will say, Maybe I can change." Widespread use of these techniques is David's mission. Demonstrating their success has superceded all his other desires. "My whole goal for this year," he's told Sam, "not the Worlds, not anything else; my whole goal is to be warming up at one of the huge Three-Days and be working Tex or Tigger with just a string around his neck."

The myth of the centaur is rooted in riders like these. One theory holds that it evolved when the Greeks first encountered a Scythian on horseback. Master horsemen, according to David Anthony, the Scythians were the first warriors to attack and retreat on command. They mass-produced arrowheads, which made their shots from their innovative short, recurved bows consistent and accurate. They are best known for the Parthian shot, a maneuver in which they attacked their enemies, retreated, and then, when those enemies pursued them, turned and launched a volley of arrows into their faces. This tactic alone was responsible for an estimated thirty thousand deaths. The Greek historian Herodotus found them barbaric and mystifying but was awed by their horsemanship. "Living as the Scythians do . . . in wagons which they take with them wherever they go, accustomed one and all to fight on horseback with bows and arrows. How can such a people fail to defeat the attempt of an invader not only to subdue them, but even to make contact with them?"

Twenty-three centuries ago, in the first book ever written about horses, *The Art of Horsemanship,* Xenophon, who studied Scythian horsemanship, derided forceful training techniques because they stripped the horse of the natural desire to express himself. "For what is done under compulsion," he wrote, "is done without understanding, and there is no beauty in it either, any more than if one should whip and spur a dancer."

Observation and intimate association teaches a horse to understand his trainer as well. In Berlin in 1904, a retired schoolteacher named Wilhelm von Osten claimed that his horse, Clever Hans, could do simple arithmetic and spell. Presented with a problem, Clever Hans pawed out the answer. A disbelieving psychologist named Oskar Pfungst investigated the claim and found that Clever Hans was not actually spelling and adding but responding to imperceptible clues inadvertently given to him by von Osten. Exquisitely sensitized to his handler's movements, Clever Hans was able to perceive as small a motion as one-fifth of a millimeter. A sigh, shoulders dropping, the blink of an eyelid, was all Clever Hans needed to know that it was time to stop pawing. In debunking von Osten's claim, what Pfungst overlooked was Clever Hans's remarkable ability to decipher the wishes of his trainer.

As zoologist Heini Hediger of the University of Zurich explains, "If the simplest thing, the atom, is influenced in its behavior through the human observer, how much more must we suppose then that two living subjects influence each other through observation." It took more than a half century after Clever Hans demonstrated his brilliance before the school of natural horsemanship was able to popularize the use of observation. Clever Hans's legacy to the study of animal behavior was not his demonstration of equine intelligence but the unknowing deceit of von Osten. Among animal behaviorists, the phenomenon of researchers unconsciously affecting their animals' behavior is known as the Clever Hans phenomenon.

In Lane's End's breeding shed, in the midst of what seems to be the last wild act left to the domesticated horse, Kenneth's stallions have learned that while they're eyeing their mate, they need to keep an eye on Kenneth as well. For the past sixteen years, Kenneth has chaperoned the stallions in the breeding shed. Breeding up to forty mares a day requires that the staff work with assembly-line efficiency. Each groom specializes in a single job. Kenneth and the other senior groom handle the stallions. Two grooms handle the mares. The "kids," students on eighteen-month visas who come to Lane's End to learn the business, share the lowly tasks of holding the mare's tail to the side and sliding the rollers, huge Popsicle-shaped cushioned bumpers, in between the stallion and the mare to protect her from his thrusts. There is one groom who handles the teaser stallion and another who checks to see if the mares are in heat and then washes them in preparation for copulation. Bill Sellers supervises and scrapes the last bit of the stallion's semen into a specimen cup, which is passed to the two women in the lab who check its sperm content. What can't be completely regulated are the animals. They have preferences and their own styles in the mating game.

This year, Lane's End expects the early season to be especially busy because a disease outbreak the previous year called mare reproductive loss syndrome caused widespread early fetal losses and late-term abortions in Kentucky's broodmares. Mares that normally would have been pregnant through the late winter are instead clamoring for a breeding date.

Mares have an eleven-month gestation period. The optimal birthday for a Thoroughbred foal is early January, as close as possible to the official birthday for all Thoroughbreds — January 1. Foals born closest to that date will have the most physical maturity when the sales come around. The popular misconception about Thoroughbreds is that everyone is trying to breed a winning racehorse. The truth is that everyone is trying to breed a valuable yearling. Trading on a promise, an expectation of greatness, those who make money in the business do so by breeding and selling horses who represent the most felicitous marriages between bloodlines.

On Valentine's Day, the fourth official day of the breeding season, the grooms start with a communal coffee break in the shed's observation room, digging into the two dozen doughnuts and muffins that Lane's End has delivered every morning from a local baker. The breeding shed door officially opens at 8:30 a.m., and the mares start arriving just before that.

The primary protocol of the breeding shed is first come, first served. The mare owners are assigned to the morning, afternoon, or the evening slot, but not a particular time. Horse vans pull up next to the shed and unload mares onto docks or directly onto the pavement. Their handlers hustle to the breeding shed door, where a member of the Lane's End staff, usually stallion coordinator Jill Mc-Cully, takes their paperwork and assigns them a place in the order. Line jumping is a problem. The mares' people and the stallions' people eye one another suspiciously, the former looking out for favoritism and the latter making sure no one cuts ahead in line. One driver, after losing the battle, settles down in front of the TV in the observation room. "Lane's End," he says with a sigh. "It's a long wait, but at least they got doughnuts."

This jostling starts as soon as the mare owner determines that a mare is in heat. Using ultrasound and old-fashioned palpation, owners can be extremely accurate about when a mare comes into season. Every stud fee that Lane's End collects comes with a live-foal guarantee (LFG). If the foal isn't born alive and healthy, the mare owner doesn't have to pay. A popular stallion like A.P. Indy is booked to about a hundred mares a year, but only about 60 percent of those pay the full fee directly to the farm. The remainder are brokered shares. A.P. has many owners. With their share in the horse they get a certain number of breeding rights per year for their mares. In a year when they're not using all of their rights, they sell them through a broker at a discount. But those brokered shares don't necessarily come with the LFG. If the purchasers of discount breeding rights can't get a date for their mares' first heat, they have to wait for the second. If the mare doesn't get pregnant on her first trip, she has to return on her next heat — about thirty days later. That lost month represents a declining dollar value at the yearling sales. Though it happens rarely, it's possible that a mare might not get a date with a stallion for the entire breeding season. Getting A.P. for $200,000 is a bargain, unless your mare doesn't get pregnant.

After imposing order at the shed door, Jill McCully clips a green plastic tag with the stallion's name on it to the mare's halter. She writes down the order of the morning's stallions on the roster that she carries with her, and then again next to the wash stall and again on a board in the breeding shed. For obvious reasons, they take great pains to make sure a mare isn't bred to the wrong stallion.

Once the mare is checked in, she's led to a stall next to the teaser stallion. Even with all their high-tech diagnostic gear, Kentucky horsemen still rely on the oldest method known for determining if a mare is in heat — observing her reaction to a stallion's advances. Adrian Todd, one of the grooms who usually help handle the stallions, is making those judgment calls this year. Lamed by a fall on the ice earlier in the season, he's still too physically impaired to handle the work in the breeding shed. He pushes a button that opens a panel between the mare and the teaser stallion, a small dark gold quarter horse named Big Mouth. Kenneth says that Big Mouth is the best teaser the farm has had in a long time. Like those of nurse mares and the ponies who escort racehorses to the starting gate, his value is determined entirely by his service to other horses. Good teasers, ones who have enthusiasm for their job and don't get discouraged, are hard to find. According to the farm's vet, when Big Mouth's owner was asked if the horse had a strong libido, he responded, "He'd hump a tree stump if I let him."

Big Mouth snorts and huffs in his stall. When Adrian opens the panel, he rears up and thrusts the entire front half of his body through the opening. Squealing and scrabbling with his back feet, he tries to push the rest of his body through as Adrian closes the panel halfway, blocking him.

The mare demonstrates her readiness by camping out her back legs, expelling urine, and "winking" — exposing her genitalia. "You want somebody you halfway trust," Kenneth says about the groom whose job it is to determine if a mare is in heat. Sometimes it's not that obvious that she's ready. She may have already been teased on her home farm. Her responses then are subtler. If she's not ready, she'll fight the stallion in the breeding shed.

As dangerous as the stallions are, it is the mares the grooms worry about. The grooms know the stallions, and their dangerous behavior, according to Kenneth, is predictable. Last year in Florida a stallion foreman was killed when he was "double-barreled," kicked with both hind hooves, by a mare. She crushed his internal organs and he died instantly. There is a gender difference in horses' use of teeth and hooves as weapons. Stallions bite, sometimes savagely, and strike with their front hooves. Mares kick with their hind hooves. These tools reflect their jobs in the wild. When mares fight, they fight defensively, for status, herd order, and to protect their foals. The double-barrel is used to keep stallions from mounting them when they're not in heat. Wheeling their hind end toward another mare and cocking a hoof keeps that mare away from a foal or from the food, and also establishes the chain of command in the herd. Mares may kick, but they rarely get into battles. Stallions, on the other hand, bite and strike because their battles are head-on assaults — with predators, other stallions trying to steal their mares, or other stallions trying to usurp their position at the head of the band. In the wild, stallions may also spend days courting a mare. A mare who feels rushed gives the stallion plenty of warning, with pinned ears, switching tails, and shoving. In the breeding shed, the stallions don't have days, so the mares' warnings are noted as signs of possible resistance, but they are usually bred anyway.

The first mare of the day is a maiden mare (one who's never been bred) named Kelli Cat. She is booked to A.P. Indy, but before Lane's End risks the safety of their prize stallion, who already has only one testicle, they risk Big Mouth's safety. Thick, heavy leather boots are strapped to Kelli Cat's back feet. Two grooms stand at her head. The chain of the lead shank is over her nose and a chunk of her upper lip is pulled through a loop of rope attached to a pole called a twitch. The groom can twist this as tightly as he needs to. Big Mouth, his neck arched, his small hooves barely touching the ground, his snorts and huffs coming from deep within his chest, dances into the room wearing a leather bib that buckles over his back and presses his genitals safely against his belly. Dave Jefferson, his handler, leads him to Kelli Cat's flank. Her eyes are rolled back and her ears are pinned apprehensively. Big Mouth's entire body quivers. Ears, eyes, tail, everything points toward Kelli Cat. Even the individual hairs on his body seem to be standing up, as if they too are straining toward the mare. He touches her flank with a nostril and she explodes, double-barreling him so hard and so fast that one of her heavy boots breaks its binding, ricochets off the ceiling, and smacks down on the ground with a mulchy-sounding thud. The grooms' heads snap back and then down as their eyes follow the flight of the boot. They stare at it on the floor and sigh.

Kelli Cat's twitch is moved to her ear, where it actually hurts. Her boot is strapped back on and, unfazed, Big Mouth approaches her again. As he rears up, she charges forward into her handlers, shoving them into the wall. Everyone in the shed is shouting "Whoa! Whoa!" and yelling at Dave to get Big Mouth off of her. Big Mouth, so close to victory, ignores him as Dave throws his weight against the lead shank. "Sometimes it's funny," Kenneth says. "Dave's pulling his little heart out and he can't get the stallion down." Because the grooms poke fun at him, so do the mare's people, who watch Dave from the observation room. "I'd like to see them," he says, "come down out of that room and get this teaser off that mare." Kenneth is still outside the shed, waiting with A.P. Indy.

Bill Sellers calls out to the vet, asking her to tranquilize Kelli Cat. "Be easy around her," he warns. "She's scared. Real scared." Nobody likes having to tranquilize a mare. "This is when we become rapists, not breeders," Sellers has said. A tranquilizer masks the mare's reactions. If she isn't in heat, then breeding her is pointless and traumatizing. In the wild, stallions don't breed with young mares; they prefer the older ones. And in the wild, mares don't have to hold to a January 1 deadline. Thoroughbred broodmares are kept under lights that fool their bodies into thinking they've entered the long days of summer. Maiden mares, especially those whose bodies are betraying them, can be physiologically ready to breed but not psychologically ready. Breeders resort to tranquilizers only when they're absolutely sure that the mare is in heat, that her resistance is a result of her youth and inexperience.

The tranquilizer has an almost immediate effect, and Kenneth leads A.P. into the shed. One of the reasons that Kenneth likes A.P. is because of his professionalism. "He knows as much about what he's doing as we do," he says. A.P. enters with the quiet confidence of a dominant stallion, one who, as Sellers says, "knows he floats the boat around here." He doesn't bother to display his worthiness to the mare with the kind of cavorting and squealing that Big Mouth demonstrates. Kenneth backs him up to the hose to be washed. A.P. keeps his eye on Kelli Cat, as if he's evaluating whether or not she passes muster with him. He approaches her with his neck arched, nods toward her flank, touching it with a nostril, introducing himself. He waits until he is fully erect and then rears up and mounts her. On her back is a leather bib with tabs like scales running over her withers. A.P. grabs one of these in his teeth to gain extra purchase as he thrusts into her. His tail flags and he slides off. Bill Sellers is close by with the specimen cup. After squeezing semen into it, he passes it through the window and into the lab, where Jill McCully wipes it onto a slide and inspects it under a microscope. Loaded with busy sperm, the slide confirms that Kelli Cat is officially bred. Jill tosses the cup into the trash. If the sperm count is low, the specimen is mixed with a glucose extender and squirted into the mare. Sometimes the owner of Lane's End, Will Farish, squires some away to breed one of his polo ponies. Mostly, though, all that expensive DNA ends up in the trash. Nearly a million dollars' worth of semen gathers in the Lane's End waste pail over the course of the day.

A.P. and Kelli Cat are led out of the shed through separate exits. "Motherhood should suit her," Sellers says, closing the door behind her.

All that excitement and danger, and Kelli Cat was only the first mare of the day. There are more than thirty left to go.

For every one of the twenty-two stallions at Lane's End, Kenneth has a thumbnail sketch of how that horse behaves in the shed. A.P. is the professional. Charismatic, like most young stallions, is a slow breeder who tries to jump the mare before he's ready. About Roar, Kenneth says, "If you take your eye off him, tchooo! He's gone. On that mare." Silver Ghost needs to be watched, "in case he makes a run at you." And Rubiano, who opened up a fourteen-stitch-long gash in another groom's head the previous year, is just waiting for a groom to make a mistake. "You forget what you've got in your hand," Kenneth says about the dangerous stallions, and you're headed to the emergency room.

Regardless of who he's got in his hands, Kenneth's behavior changes very little. Whatever stunts or acts of aggression the stallions pull, Kenneth responds to them with equanimity. "I can't tell when Kenneth is mad and when he's not," Bill Sellers says, "which is a good thing in handling horses."

When he comes into the breeding shed with a horse, Kenneth stands quietly. Impatient to get started, the stallions grind their teeth, and Kenneth feeds them a length of their own lead shank when they have the urge to bite. Parade Ground, a horse who's so aggressive that he wears a bit attached to his halter and a muzzle, charges in the door. Seeing his mare, he rears up, as vertical as a plumb line. Everyone in the shed freezes, waiting to see in which direction Parade Ground is going to come back down. Kenneth plays out enough line for him to keep his balance and then stands, flat-footed, waiting for him to land on his feet or flip over, as if either consequence were the same to him. It isn't until Parade Ground, from halfway across the shed, tries to jump his mare before he's ready that Kenneth reacts. He yanks the lead shank, pulling the horse's head down to chest level and then charges at him with the force of a linebacker, running the horse backward until he bumps into the wall. Parade Ground trembles, his eye locked on Kenneth, waiting for his permission to move forward. Kenneth prefers horses who are a little aggressive over their courtly peers. They're quick to get their job done. But Parade Ground, he says, is too aggressive.

Kenneth's stout refusal to take anything personally is, according to Sellers, "the reason he's rubbing the horses he's rubbing. His horses in other hands could get bad, could get tough."

"It's something you work at," Kenneth says. "You take anybody that wants to work at it, then they can do it."

Without a background in horses or any formal training, Kenneth learned his trade simply by watching. He watches all the time, discreetly, his chin tilted down while his blue eyes take in the other grooms, the new kids making mistakes, the horses. Everyone at Lane's End learns by watching the horses. When Bill Sellers noticed that Pleasant Tap didn't seem to like the protective leather bib that the mares wear, he removed it. In exchange, Pleasant Tap didn't bite the mares as he mounted them. He hung his head over their sides instead, as if he were embracing them.

The stallions at Lane's End, other than breeding, are asked to do very little. They aren't challenged like competition horses. They don't usually travel. They're never ridden. Kenneth and the other grooms build their understanding of the horses' personalities on countless small gestures, each horse giving them a different meaning. Charismatic, stretching out in his stall for a nap, is behaving normally. When Dixieland Band does it, Kenneth summons the vet. A.P. taking a step back when he's tied for grooming is just taking a step back. When Dixie does it, he's trying to get closer to Kenneth so he can kick him.

Knowing that they're understood makes horses confident, allows their personalities to emerge. For the O'Connors, knowing their horses' personalities, like knowing their grooms', is how they learn to trust them under the perils of competition. For Kenneth, horses with personalities are knowable, and if they're knowable, they're predictable in the breeding shed and therefore safer. When David O'Connor talks about his horses, he so frequently uses the word "personality" and the phrase "like a person" that inevitably he arrives at descriptions for his horses like "He's just a nice person to be around."

If Kenneth's stallions don't know their full worth when they come to Lane's End, then they learn it from Kenneth.

A.P. has grown into his quiet superiority. Sixteen years of good rubdowns from the same man, assiduous attention to his sore foot, and always knowing that if Kenneth has one last peppermint in his pocket, he will give it to him, is how A.P. learned that he is, in fact, a very big deal.

Chapter Four

AMONG HORSEMEN

Orlando Betancourt is the "extra hand" for the O'Connor Event Team, hired to pick up extra chores so the grooms are free to work with the horses. Feminine voices call his name all day long. He is never too busy to put down what he is doing and respond to their requests. He struggles with his English, though he rarely uses Vanessa to translate for him, choosing silence over poor speech. He handles every horse in the barn, including the fractious ET. At the end of the day, he sits on the trunk of his Hyundai and turns his face to the sun. The grooms rely on him, and Karen makes jokes about "Orlando and his harem." But being hardworking, cheerful, and accommodating is not enough for the O'Connor team. Everyone also needs to be a member of the horse cult.

Today, Orlando is having his first riding lesson, on

89

Prince Panache. He rides out with David and the grooms. The women are lithe and easy in the saddle, controlling their horses by reflex. David rides next to Orlando, who has his hands up by his chest and his feet thrust forward as if he is slamming on the brakes. The grooms pick up a trot, leaving Orlando bumping behind at the walk, David at his side coaching him. Prince Panache, his neck low and his nose extended, looks puzzled to find that with an Olympic career behind him, he's now being asked to teach someone to ride.

David needs grooms who can ride. He can't get his horses fit without their help. David is teaching Orlando to ride not because he expects him to ever be skilled enough to take one of his horses out for gallops, but because he likes to share his horses. "We'll be cantering," Sam explains. "We do lots of stuff side by side so he can see how his horse is cantering, and he'll say, 'Open him up a bit,' and all of a sudden you're going like two thousand miles an hour. You have this huge grin on your face and David's laughing hysterically. He knows how much we love it."

David's desire to share his horses comes with risks. Last week, when Sam was schooling Tex over cross-country fences, she fell off and broke her wrist. Now that the season is ramping up, David's head groom is working at half capacity. Though, as Andi jokes, "even with one hand, you wrap faster than I do."

More than grooms in any of the other disciplines, event grooms spend a lot of time in the saddle, and they are usually very good riders. Vicky competed before she came to the O'Connors. Andi competed as well, and had two grooms of her own. Vanessa rode on the show jumper circuit in Germany. The grooms gave up their competitive goals when they took the job, though Sam doesn't think her riding is suffering. "I will never," she shakes her head, "ever ride horses like this again."

Sam started out in her career wanting to be a competitor. Like most little girls who ride, she dreamed of the Olympics. With restricted finances and without the connections of horsey relatives, that goal was simply out of her reach. She could have progressed along her career as she was doing, one horse at a time, ultimately joining the legions of competent and safe trainers who give lessons to support their competitive ambitions. But she would never have gotten her hands on the kinds of horses David provides her by the dozen. And even if she had, she wouldn't have had the skill to draw out that horse's brilliance. World-class horsemen learn their skills from other world-class horsemen. More than anything else, Sam wants knowledge. Training horses and learning about them are far more interesting to her than just competing them. Sam misses competing, and having her own horse. But, she says, "because I've had so much exposure to the higher levels, I still can't figure out if I want to compete advanced or if I would be content to train the younger horses." While she's deciding, she is building her repertoire at the O'Connors'. Problem horses like ET and Tigger help her figure out other problem horses. Tex and Tailor, already trained, are teaching her what a horse can learn and what it feels like to sit on some of the fastest jumping horses in the world.

David shares Sam's quest for knowledge. With a barn full of internationally competitive horses, it seems as if he and his wife know all they need to about extracting brilliant performances. They joined up with Pat Parelli not so much to win more competitions, but to improve their relationship with their horses and, like Sam, to add more skills to their arsenal. In his travels, David has become fascinated by cutting horses, the ones who have an uncanny ability to match their movements to a cow's. When asked what he would have done if he hadn't been a Three-Day Event rider, David draws a blank. Some kind of jumping, he thinks, then suggests, "Something with a cow. I could definitely see a life along those lines." It is a desire to understand what horses know, how they learn, that he shares with Samantha. His goal, like hers, is to figure out the key to each horse. Through riding and ground work, the mystery of equine-human communication is being revealed to them, bringing them closer to the distant goal of all true horsemen: knowing not just one horse but all of them.

David fills the open slots on his grooming staff with horsemen like him. The rest of the grooms on the O'Connor Event Team are on a similar quest — the pursuit of knowledge and the ability to apply it. Karen and David describe their staff as an especially skilled Formula 1 team. On their team, the guy changing tires could lecture on the intricacies of the internal combustion engine, and the guy wiping the windshield can also drive the car. When a horse finishes his round in competition, the grooms surround him following a situational hierarchy similar to that found in wild horse herds. The groom who has the confidence to take control of the horse and lead the other grooms is the one in charge. In addition to training horses, small competitions like Rocking Horse also train new grooms, teaching them to step up to Sam's level of responsibility.

That kind of acquisitiveness, the desire for more and greater knowledge about the horse, seems to have been passed down the human line with the domesticated horse. Evolutionary geneticists Carles Vila and Hans Ellegren of Sweden researched the DNA of equine fossil remains and compared it to the DNA of contemporary feral horses. They expected to find a pattern similar to other domestic animals like cows and sheep. The diversity of DNA in the fossil remains of those animals was reduced to a few main branches as the domesticated animals were bred and the non-domesticated ones died out. The horse, to the researchers' surprise, had almost as much diversity in the contemporary DNA as in the fossilized remains.

That discovery, according to David Anthony, "eliminates the possibility that horses were domesticated in one place and spread from there." Instead, what traveled was the idea of riding horses. "People spread ideas like crazy," Sandra Olsen explains.

The second horse trial being held at Rocking Horse Stables in Altoona at the end of February is David's first competition of the year. He is taking six horses and Karen is taking five. "They just keep piling up," Sam quips. Smaller and more relaxed than a CCI, the competition is compressed into two days, with dressage and show jumping taking place on the first day and cross-country on the second. Since it's still early in the season, David and Karen, like most of the other competitors, are using Rocking Horse for practice. Karen warms up in the middle of the crowd, greeting other riders and commenting on their new horses. David, according to his custom, rides off to a quiet and distant corner of the field. As his ride time approaches, he's nowhere to be seen. According to Sam, he's "off in his own little world." Sometimes she has to trot off and retrieve him in time for his test. Today, he arrives on time, and Sam, trusting that Andi and Orlando are getting the other horses ready back at the rig, stands at ringside watching David's ride. Vicky catches up with riders and other grooms she knows, though she's a little dispirited. Watching riders compete, she says, is painful for her because she misses competing so much. By afternoon, it's too busy to watch the rides as the grooms simultaneously untack horses returning from dressage and tack those who are off to show jumping. The morning's rain gets heavier toward afternoon. Trying to keep her cast dry, Sam wraps it in blue Vetrap, a spongy, self-adhering bandage for horses. There are some jobs she simply can't do one-handed, like setting the rails for the practice jumps. Orlando and a visitor help David in the warm-up, though neither one of them is as good at interpreting David's hand signals as Sam is.

It's still raining on the second day of competition, cross-country day. Even though it's slower, shorter, and smaller than that of a CCI, the cross-country phase at Rocking Horse is still the most dangerous part of the competition, especially with the younger, inexperienced horses, who are unpredictable. The team is noticeably edgy. When the rig pulls in, Orlando drops out of the cab and quickly lines up a row of buckets perpendicular to the trailer to prevent anyone from parking too close to it. The horses peek out the door in their fuzzy halters as the grooms pile the gear outside the rig, covering it with the horses' rain sheets. In and around the rig they stash bridles, a box of extra bits, two kinds of halters for each horse, lead ropes, martingales, breastplates, extra reins, three kinds of saddle pads for each horse, saddles, saddle covers, saddle stands, shipping boots, galloping boots, overreach boots, and a duffel bag full of quilted leg wraps and polo wraps. There are tail wraps, coolers and scrims, and underclothes to keep the horses' sheets from rubbing the hair off their shoulders. There is another duffel bag of towels (all in navy blue), tack cleaning supplies, grooming kits, and braiding kits (including Barbie). A dozen buckets are stacked outside the trailer along with stall guards, extra hay, five-gallon water jugs, sponges, shampoo, bottles of liniment, tubs of poultice, and sweat scrapers. There are plastic bins containing electrician's tape, duct tape, baby oil, hoof polish, extra horseshoes, double-ended snaps, bungee cords with *plastic* hooks, training ropes and halters, bridle hooks, girths, and overgirths. In the rig is a first aid kit and in front of Joey's nose, just out of his reach, a bag of carrot-flavored horse treats. By the end of the day, every single piece of this equipment will be used.

Since Rocking Horse is still practice, no one is paying too much attention to the horses' standings on cross-country day, and as other riders complete the course, Sam and Vicky lose track of those standings entirely. A wrathful rain is pounding the show grounds, as if to rebuke everyone who complained about the weather the day before by showing them a *real* Florida rain. Along with the rain come angry winds that snap the tent flaps and blow the horses' tails up. The O'Connors are surrounded by trailers in which nervous and fidgety horses stomp and kick, their steel-shod feet ringing against the metal sides. The O'Connors' horses stand calmly outside the trailer with their lead shanks on the ground while as many as four people strap them into the gear they need for cross-country.

David discovers that the efficiency of the O'Connor team is not yet perfect. His new mare, Wyndham, is missing her back shoes. She'll have to run cross-country half barefoot, without the traction those shoes would give her. The missing shoes were noted weeks ago by the grooms, and the appropriate people were informed, but somehow the situation hasn't been remedied. Standing at the top of Blue Thunder's ramp, David shouts, "This mare has no brakes!" Sam smiles wryly as she gets his next horse ready. "*You,* young lady," David says, pointing at her, "will not have a job because you won't have a boss."

"I thought he knew." Sam shrugs.

Sam's one-handedness starts to seem like less of a liability as the other grooms' fingers go numb with the cold. Their fingers are too stiff to undo the buckles of the wet, slippery leather straps, and they start pulling them open with their teeth. Andi and Orlando, who Sam says are the best at spotting when she's in trouble, scramble to her side when she gets stymied by too much gear or too much horse. When they arrived, Orlando cleverly rolled one of the water tubs in the parking lot to the front of the rig, but the water trucks never came around to fill it. Absurdly, given the deluge, he has to haul buckets back from the stabling area so the horses can have clean water to drink and for their baths. The grooms are darting in and out of the front of the rig to consult the list of start times. ET and Joey, who are up front in the rig, keep their eyes on the grooms, looking wistfully toward the bag of carrot snacks just out of their reach, but as the rig gets more crowded, ET starts pinning his ears. Sam stands near his head as the other grooms bump into one another and the horses as they dash in and out with pieces of gear. "ET's had enough," Sam warns quietly. Afraid that he'll explode, everyone runs back out into the rain, leaving ET alone with Sam.

The O'Connors aren't the only ones who are suffering. All around them bedraggled grooms leg wet riders into slippery tack. The horses hold their ears out sideways, trying to keep the rain from dripping into them. There is misery in abundance, but no one even considers not running. The sandy footing is holding up in the rain, and they're eventers, the equestrian equivalent of the marines. Nothing short of a tornado or lightning bolts cracking down on the course will keep them from running.

After sending Karen off to the start box on Joey, Vicky returns to the rig and is digging around in the gear, looking for dry blankets. A cry of "Loose horse!" brings her to the doorway just in time to see Joey galloping past, his reins and stirrups flapping. She and Sam race around to the back of the truck and corner him against the fence. Vicky stands still holding Joey, not sure what to do. The loudspeakers are inaudible in the wind and rain, and she's lost track of the start times. She concludes that it's too early for Karen to have fallen off on course; Joey must have dumped her in the warm-up ring. She runs him back out of the parking lot, hoping to get him to the start box in time for Karen to ride. There is a huge puddle at the gate, and Joey spooks at it as Vicky jumps over it. When they come down, Joey lands on Vicky's foot. Just after Vicky limps out of the gate with Joey, Karen is driven through it. She did fall off on course, not in the warm-up. If Joey hadn't run away, she would have been able to get back on, but now it's too late. One of the students bolts off after Joey and Vicky because she needs to borrow Karen's saddle. Other students are popping into the rig to borrow gear. When visitors show up, the grooms sympathetically offer them raincoats, including their own. A visitor gets hot chocolates for the grooms, but they don't even have time to drink them. Andi takes hers with her as she leads a horse to the stabling area for his bath. She has the horse in one hand, the cup in the other, which leaves her none to hold up her pants, which keep sliding off because they're wet and weighed down by the grooming tools stuffed in her pockets.

Despite the missing shoes, David is still alive after his ride on Wyndham. "This one," he says, dropping the reins onto her sweaty neck, "is going to win Radnor." Not Rolex, but a stop on the way, Radnor, which takes place in October in Pennsylvania, is of sufficient importance for the grooms to exchange *their* nickname for Wyndham — Large Marge — for the one she came with — Wendy. Nobody teases Tailor about his long ears or Tex about his jutting croup. As of the second Rocking Horse 2002, they will no longer tease Wyndham about her womanly proportions.

As soon as a horse comes back, the grooms flock to him as if he were the only horse competing that day. They leave him in the care of whoever grabbed his reins first and spin off to get the next horse ready. Karen jumps down out of the rig, and both Vicky and Sam notice that she looks sore, that her fall from Joey was harder than she admits. There are only a few minutes separating the horses' arrivals and departures. The work is twice as intense as it was the day before, but they're also done by early afternoon. They've been working since five a.m. and they've had no lunch break. They never get lunch breaks, ever, under any circumstances. What they have been putting in their mouths over the course of the day is appalling. Back at the barn, in the predawn hours, they started out with good intentions, spooning down yogurt and nibbling on the melon that Vanessa, who is concerned about their collective eating habits, keeps stocked in the fridge. With lots of help from David (according to Sam he would "live on chips and Diet Coke if he could"), they have eaten their way through tubes of potato chips and bags of tortilla chips, pretzels, Twizzlers, and generic snacks like the "Oriental mix" that looks as if it was packaged in the seventies. The horses share their treats. ET and Joey, who are in the front of the rig, nibble on Cheez-Its as well as their own carrot snacks. Every time one of the grooms comes out of the rig, she is chewing.

In the afternoon, Samantha jogs around to the students' trailers to remind everyone who brought an O'Connor horse not to go home without him. She and Vicky make a desperate run to the catering tent, which is already virtually out of food, and buy the very last cheeseburger on the grounds. By the time they get it back to the rig, it's cold and wet. This morning, the grooms looked like any group of twenty-something young women: bright, clean faces and shiny hair. Now, huddling together sharing a wet burger, they look like a newspaper photo of mudslide survivors: dirty, wet down to their underwear, hungry, their clothes and hair plastered to their bodies. Vicky's hands shake with cold as she dispenses the last of the Twizzlers.

The horses, on the other hand, are napping peacefully in Blue Thunder, their bodies as warm and snug as potbellied stoves under their wool coolers. They've had hay in front of them all day, and Orlando has been around at regular intervals with a bucket of fresh water for them to drink from or just imperiously splash their lips in while he waits. In the tight quarters of the rig, the grooms crawl under their horses' bellies and wrap their legs in cooling poultices. All eleven of David's and Karen's horses have competed, and the grooms are waiting for David to return from watching his students' rounds on cross-country. Vicky and Andi, who erupted earlier in a frustrated exchange of hard words when Andi, unable to find one of the breathable warm coolers, risked overheating a horse by blanketing him in a waterproof rain sheet, make amends with apologies and a hug. The shortage of dry coolers was the source of Sam's only snappish moment all day. Someone else's groom had nipped into the trailer to borrow the last one. When Sam was told about it, she bristled. "Oh, she did, did she," she said, speeding out of the trailer to snatch that cooler off the other horse's back if need be.

David finally appears, slouching through the afternoon rain. The grooms start to shut the doors, but he isn't ready to leave. He wants to watch one more student on cross-country. The grooms wistfully watch him walk away until he turns and, with a wave, tells them they can go home.

Orlando crawls into the cab to nap on a cot there. The women pile into a friend's car that is warm and dry and where they find an unopened bag of pretzels and are allowed to smoke. "Heaven," Vicky declares.

She is the only one who knows how to get back to the barn and she promptly falls asleep. Sam, in the tradition of geniuses who don't like to clutter their heads with information they don't need, never bothers to get directions. To make sure she'll always be a passenger, she doesn't even bring her car to Florida. She *is* instrumental in pointing out a huge water slide that she's sure she would have noticed if they'd passed it that morning. Already lost, they rouse Vicky to save them. They spend the rest of the drive complaining about their campers, one-upping one another with stories of cramped conditions and cold showers. Andi wins when she reveals that during her evening push-ups, her face actually dips through a hole in the floor. They long for the first competition that will take them out of town so they can stay in a motel and get their first hot shower of the season.

They don't have a single complaint about the competition — not about Vicky's stepped-on foot, the students who borrowed gear all day long and ate their food, or about the rain. "We love it," they say in unison. Knowing that they're still ahead of David, they take the long route home. The car is steamy; the defroster blows warm, sleepy air. They sneak one last cigarette before the final turn up their road. Vicky drops her head back against the seat. "I wish we could just keep driving," she says.

The first depiction of horses in sport, from 510 BCE, appears on a Greek vase housed at the Metropolitan Museum of Art in New York. It shows three horses and their jockeys in a race. Predating the vase is a description of a chariot race in Homer's *Iliad.* By the time Xenophon wrote *The Art of Horsemanship,* around 400 BCE, the use of horses in sport had long been established.

In a 1996 study, the Barents Group, a consulting firm hired by the American Horse Council Federation, estimated that there were 6.9 million horses in America, over 70 percent of which were involved in showing or recreation. The study valued the equine industry at $25.3 billion, just behind the apparel industry and just above the motion picture industry. The total economic impact of those 6.9 million horses, which includes what the Barents Group calls "induced effects," the overall spending by persons "employed in the industry or its suppliers," was a whopping $112 billion.

The Barents Group study included everybody. Not just the Three-Day Eventers galloping over fences in the rain but also the ambassador to Great Britain who owns A.P. Indy and the son of a tenant farmer who grooms him. Where else would an ambassador and a farmer meet but in the barn, talking about a horse? Competitive drivers, those who race through obstacle courses behind two- and four-horse hitches, were in there with Arabian breeders whose horses compete against the standards of history and sheer beauty. Racehorse owners were there, along with 4-H kids on the aging ponies that are handed down through their siblings as they outgrow them.

The horses who earn their keep were in the study too: police horses, ranch horses, the Morgans and lightweight drafts used for farming, maple-sugaring, and even logging throughout New England. Ponies for parties, park ranger horses, horses for hire by the hour, and the carriage horses who pass their entire lives on the streets of Manhattan are members of the community of working horses. Just like those who have failed the test of athleticism and beauty but whose generous hearts and implacable demeanors have found them a perfect home as therapy horses for emotionally and physically disabled children and adults.

As our horses have passed out of usefulness, their image has lingered in our culture. Their pictures sell us everything from beer to investment services. Our language is replete with horse references, and we use words from our relationship with them to describe some of our most elevated ideas: chivalry and cavalier. They capture a sense of mystery and the unknown for us: dark horse, ringer, horse of a different color. They represent truth and the forthright: taking the reins, straight from the horse's mouth, starting from scratch, and horse sense. Our history with them has been especially useful for describing vigor and excitement: in the pink, hell for leather, feeling our oats, champing at the bit, down to the wire, neck and neck, full tilt, hot-blooded, and wild ride. Even when we replaced the horse with machines, we had to use him to describe his own replacement: horsepower, horseless carriage, and iron horse. Car manufacturers, hoping to instill their vehicles with a sense of power and excitement, name cars like Mustang and Bronco after them.

Back at the end of the Pleistocene, when that early man on the central Asian steppes looked at a horse and decided to climb aboard, the future of Indo-European languages was sealed. Mastering the horse meant mastering travel, agriculture, trade, and warfare. Dominance was so complete that no one else wanted to wait for the domestication of the horse. Once horses were domesticated, everyone wanted a piece of that knowledge — making horsemanship the hot technology of its time. Cultures that didn't master the horse, like those tribes who were shunted to the fringes by the North American Plains Indians, languished and often died. Genghis Khan and his fearsome army literally annihilated entire cultures on horseback. After slaughtering a settlement, they lay in wait for the escapees to return to bury their dead, and then they slaughtered them. The effect of horses on cultures that didn't have them, Sandra Olsen has said, was "something akin to a nuclear bomb." Those that mastered the horse seized lands, won wars, traded their goods, shared knowledge like metallurgy, and, as David Anthony claims, spread their language.

History, it seems, was written by horsemen.

Just down the road from the O'Connors' barn in Florida, on the Reddick-Ocala line, is a pub called the Horse and Hound. The walls, covered with hunt prints and portraits of great racehorses, are an homage to the history of the sport horse. These depictions hang in every pub that caters to horsemen. In places like Gladstone, New Jersey; Middleburg, Virginia; Saratoga, New York; and Lexington, Kentucky, patrons find comfort in their presence, knowing that they are in the company of other horsemen and can speak the horseman's language.

In addition to the predictable artwork, the Horse and Hound has photos of its patrons slipped under the glass tabletops. Happy people holding their horses, their dogs, or the fish they've caught beam from these images of the sporting life. Tucked in with the customer photos are the business cards of professionals whose livelihoods are attached to this sporting life. There are "quality show horses" for sale, stalls for rent, alfalfa and timothy hay for sale, and "farms, land, and acreage" available. On a hot, sunny February afternoon, the horsemen in the bar for lunch aren't talking about the august history of their favorite animal. With the heels of their boots hooked over the rungs of their stools, they trade the mundane stories of keeping horses: the price of hay, lameness, speed, obedience, and genetics. Their hands are battered and gritty and look out of place handling the silverware. Hard-muscled, with prominent veins, they are used to holding reins, or lead shanks, or currycombs, or finding the hot spot on a tendon. The horsemen are oblivious to the tourists in pastels and white sneakers who have wandered in from the highway. Talk and laughter is loud, as befits people who work outdoors with big animals. Their drifting bits of conversation hover above their heads in a cloud that could join an even greater cloud that has accumulated from every time and place in history where people have gathered together around horses.

The second Rocking Horse competition marks the official end of Sam's weekly day off. On Sunday, while the horses snooze in their stalls, Sam is in the rig with David as they head down to Wellington, where the show jumpers are competing — a rare intersection of the two sports, whose participants usually only meet when they compete together on international teams. David and Karen and three of their horses are giving a demonstration of the Parelli training techniques. Anne Kursinski would like to have gone to that demonstration, but she can't because she is doing her own chores.

Most barns have trouble with turnover during the Wellington festival, and Anne Kursinski's barn is having even more trouble than usual. Of the grooms they brought with them from New Jersey, only Brooke is left, and she is out for ten days with an injured knee: Escapade kicked her. "I've been promoted to head groom," Hoffy quips as she trims the whiskers on her horse, Entitled. While Brooke is out, the barn is in the hands of Federico and Martine, Argentine brothers who came to Wellington because they wanted to play polo. One of them confesses that he has never worked with horses before, and the other has only a little experience. "Anne Kursinski has grooms with no experience?" Karen O'Connor shrieks in astonishment when she hears. There is another groom who is having trouble following the no-smoking-in-the-barn rule, and a fourth whose tenure with Market Street was so short that when she didn't show up one day, everyone struggled to recall her name. Anne and Hoffy are angry with Brooke for abandoning the horses to such unskilled care. "I'm trying to show and to teach and to *win*," Anne says. "It's hard to even think about winning when you're wondering if the horses are getting water." They asked Brooke to come in and direct traffic, just sit on a tack trunk and tell the other grooms which saddles belonged to which horses, make sure everyone was wearing the right gear when they went out to the ring. Brooke tried, but the barn was so chaotic that she kept having to do the work herself, so she went back home, afraid that if she didn't stay away from the barn her knee would never heal.

Market Street isn't the only barn in chaos. According to Anne and Hoffy, massive decampments are the rule of the last weeks of the Cosequin festival as overworked grooms abandon their posts and hire into other, seemingly better, abandoned posts before everyone leaves Florida for their home barns. After Wellington, everyone goes to Tampa for three more weeks of competition, and a select few return for the capstone of the festival, the $300,000 American Grandprix Association's Invitational. They are frazzled and spent, and Hoffy is lobbying to pack up whatever staff they have left and return to New Jersey. "Every year, everyone complains about it," Hoffy says of the schedule. "And every year, everyone goes, including us. It's hard on the horses."

The fact that Anne is even considering not going to Tampa is a sign of how exhausted the last standing members of the Market Street team are. Every competition she misses means that her competitors scoop up the points that she might have been able to add to her year-end standing. According to Hoffy, this is one of the worst Florida seasons she can remember. A world-class barn, they've been forced to hire grooms on the spot. "I don't even want to teach them my system because I know they won't be here in a week. Isn't that awful?" The aisle is cluttered, chores drag on into the afternoon, bandages are left unrolled and piled in a tangled heap. Even the chores that are done are done shoddily. The stalls look clean, but a tap with a pitchfork produces the hollow thud of moldy bedding.

Riding boots, especially the elegant custom-made ones that Anne wears, are not meant for walking. All of the aches and pains Anne has endured during Brooke's absence manifest themselves in her feet. Still, "in a funny way," she says, "when Hoffy and I started doing the barn, the horses performed better. They got better ribbons. I enjoyed it very much, other than being exhausted." Hoffy claims that taking care of Eros was more fun than anything else she did. "I like mucking! I like all of it. If that's all I had to do, to take care of three or four horses. You don't have to deal with clients. You don't have to deal with students and their parents." Anne and Hoffy don't have a good explanation for why there has been so much turnover. Their grooms start at $425 per week in Florida. Someone with Brooke's experience makes $600 a week. In Florida and on any other day that they are on the show grounds, they also get a $25 per diem for food and expenses. That amount is fairly typical of most professional barns, except for those that are privately funded, where grooms can make more money and often have less work. The show grooms, at least to start, make more than their peers in eventing or on the stud farm. Pay there is far less standardized, and most event riders are loath to reveal their grooms' salaries. They generally start around $18,000 to $20,000 a year. But, depending on the experience a groom brings with her, that amount can vary wildly. Because event grooms (like show grooms) burn out so quickly, many riders are willing to pay quite handsomely for a groom who stays the course over many years. Stud grooms also start at around $18,000 to $20,000, and tend to top out at around $40,000.

The benefit packages are similar in all three disciplines. Stud grooms may not be offered housing to start, but once they develop seniority, it's usually provided. Housing the grooms in individual cottages, as the O'Connors do, is a little unusual (as is installing invisible fencing for their dogs). Most event and show grooms share a house, though there is often a separate apartment for the senior groom. Professional barns with good reputations, like Market Street, the O'Connors, and Lane's End, offer insurance and 401ks. In addition, the grooms of horses who are competing can expect to take home some of the prize money if their rider wins and part of the commission if one of their horses is sold.

Since no one is getting rich, most grooms stay in the job for the intangibles: a winning rider, high-quality horses, affection for their coworkers, extreme loyalty to their employers. That last reason is why Samantha thinks that some grooms stay in the job too long. Loyal to the riders they work for and fueled by that rider's efforts to get them to stay (more pay, better housing, more riding, a horse of their own), grooms continue to work long after they're burned out and end up hating the very horses they took the job to care for.

Anne and Hoffy suspect that their high standards are what has caused the massive decampment from their barn. "They're totally supervised," Hoffy says of the Market

Street grooms. "I know that doesn't happen at all barns and I know some of them don't like that." An easy solution to the turnover problem would be to do what many of the other riders have done: hire Mexican immigrants who work illegally. Anne doesn't hire illegal immigrants, and she is reluctant to turn the care of her horses over to an entire staff of people with whom she does not share a language. "Some of the barns," she says, "you don't even know how much the professional knows is going on."

There are so many illegal immigrants working at Wellington that one show official revealed that the previous season a code word was read over the loudspeaker whenever immigration officers showed up at the gates. Hearing it, the grooms handed off their horses to the nearest white person, leaving ringside, she said, "lily white."

Anne and Hoffy use the word *professional* often. That's what they are and that's what they want to hire, but they can't pay as much as the barns that have independent wealth. Anne understands why a groom would rather work for the "millionaires," who don't supervise them as closely, pay them better, and assign them fewer horses to groom. She also thinks the problem rests with the expectations of many grooms. "They don't want to be grooms," she explains. "They want to be you." Like Brooke, the grooms they hire who have professional aspirations are frustrated by the lack of riding opportunities. Even Karen O'Connor, who needs her grooms to ride to help keep her horses fit, acknowledges that the ideal groom is one who doesn't really want to ride, just wants to take care of the horses. Grooms who are more interested in riding than in developing their overall horsemanship, Anne believes, are part of the culture of the horse show world.

It is a world in which wealthy riders can simply buy their way to a ribbon, rather than earning it by putting in hours in the saddle and in the barn. That creates a throwaway ethos. If one horse doesn't work out, he can be sold. If the rider isn't good enough, he can spend up to a million dollars to get a horse with a proven record, one who can win competitions for him. This is especially true in the hunter and equitation divisions, which are subjectively judged and where the course design emphasizes stylish rides over athletic ones. This is a cynical and bitter view, but one echoed in the equine press. Old-school trainers rail about the lack of discipline among their students. Top riders complain about wealthy amateurs buying the best horses out from under them, and everyone points their fingers at the unscrupulous trainers who allow it to happen — without, of course, naming names.

Growing up in California and riding at the Flintridge Riding Club, Anne trained in multiple disciplines. From the legendary Jimmy Williams, she learned to do the "kooky things" he did, like teaching a horse the Spanish walk, laying one down with a running W (the device used on Hollywood stunt horses to make them fall realistically), and even riding bridleless. Much of it, she says, she wouldn't do today, but it was part of her repertoire, as was her training with international dressage competitor Hilda Gurney. All of that work taught her to respect horses. "I rode everything and I rode and I rode," she says. "If they reared, or they stopped, or they bucked, I rode." From the grooms at Flintridge, she learned how to groom and how to braid a mane. Because it was part of her education, she learned to drive Jimmy Williams's big rig. When she moved to the East Coast to work with the majordomo of American show jumping, George Morris, she learned about nutrition and fitness. All of those skills helped her to get inside the horses' heads, inside their brains: "*That* was fascination." And that fascination fueled her desire to ride ever more talented horses for higher stakes. What she, like many of the other old-school professionals, sees around her in Wellington are riders who overestimate their own skill and underestimate the abilities of their horses.

Underestimating horses is almost universal. People who've never ridden, never picked up a brush or led a horse to the paddock, offer their weighty opinions about the horses running in the Kentucky Derby as they gather around the television set. A summer at camp riding horses whose intelligence and trusting natures have been dulled into oblivion by a lifetime of insensitive handling leads many people to conclude that all horses are stupid. We condescend to them, claiming that everything they do is a result of punishment or praise from their riders, assuming that they have no capacity to experience the joy of their own athleticism. Six thousand years of horsemanship, an estimated forty thousand books written on the topic, and still the best horsemen out there, like Anne Kursinski, approach every horse as an individual, a brand-new enigma who needs to be puzzled out. "They have so much to teach humans," she says. "They're brave and they're noble and they're honest, whether you like it or not."

Pat Parelli has an explanation for the profound misunderstanding of horses. They're not like us, he says. We're predators; they're prey. We're better with dogs because they're predator animals like us. They hoard food, build dens, accumulate possessions. Horses, on the other hand, loathe being confined because then they can't flee. They're not territorial and they're not interested in "stuff" unless their lives are so bereft of stimulation that they turn to toys out of boredom. Not understanding those differences, we approach horses with whom we have no relationship and ask them to trust us by allowing us to pat them on the face. Misled by the popular mythology of children's books, we throw our hands into their blind spot, trying to scratch their ears. We insult them by blowing into their noses. We clap them loudly on the neck, which, as Parelli jokes, "women and horses hate, dogs and men love." When our overtures are rebuffed, we call the horse flighty and stupid. We ask them to understand us before we have tried to understand them. All that misunderstanding forces the horse to withdraw into a protective, mindless obedience or, in the case of spirited horses, into defensiveness and aggression. What David O'Connor finds most compelling about horses is that even after all that misuse, they still have the "ability to trust and to gain trust even when they have not always had perfect lives."

That trust is Anne's goal. She understands that earning it through the inglorious job of being a groom is a hard, thankless endeavor. She's unapologetic, though, about her standards: "Anyone who's any good at anything works hard." What is available to the grooms through taking care of the horses are the same opportunities that are available to Anne when she rides them — figuring out their needs and their skills, and knowing them intimately. "It's all the same stuff as life," she says. "What is life about and what does it mean to be a winner?" For Anne, life is about structure and discipline. Like the beauty within the rigid form of the sonnet, the structure and discipline of impeccable horsemanship produce, as Anne says, "the lightness and the total freedom of the horse."

By the end of Wellington, less interested in philosophy than in finding relief from the pressures of her job, Brooke hands in her notice. The level of care that she was happy to provide earlier in the season is, she now believes, unrealistic given the inexperience of the staff. She is tired of working with grooms who won't listen to her and whose ineptitude creates more work. "They don't even make more work for themselves," she says in frustration, "because they're not doing any of it in the first place." She is tired of being blamed for their mistakes and was hurt when one of those mistakes led to her being yelled at by Anne in the schooling ring, in front of all the professionals gathered there. In the end, Brooke wants to ride. Grooming, she says, "isn't going to get you anywhere." She bears no ill will toward her employers, despite the tensions and the yelling, and she's the only groom of the whole season who gives notice instead of just not showing up after payday. "They're very good horsewomen," she says of Anne and Hoffy. "I want to ride in a clinic with Anne, and if they're ever desperate and are going to the Olympics, I'd like them to call."

Given the breadth of the industry, there are plenty of places that Brooke could have gone, especially now that she's put in her time at the barn of an Olympic competitor. Her new job is at a barn in Illinois that has about sixty clients. Brooke will be riding and teaching all week, and there are plenty of other people her age with whom she can go dancing on her nights out.

These are the lives of professional horsemen. Orlando, who wants to be near horses even if he can't ride them; Samantha, whose desire to know as much about them as she can compels her to sell her own horse and commit to the role of servant; and Anne, who finds the meaning of life in her relationship to horses. They all share the same fascination for the animal that compelled the first horseman of central Asia to choose one horse from the herd as his own. It is the same fire that inflamed Alexander when he first met his great partner, Bucephalus. And it is the same sentiment expressed by a sign hanging in the ladies' room at the Horse and Hound: "I've spent most of my life riding horses. The rest I've just wasted."

Chapter Five

ON THE ROAD

By the middle of March, it is time for the O'Connor dog and pony show to hit the road. Before they leave, the horses need to have complete physicals. At one end of the barn, the O'Connors' vet Christiana Ober sits on an overturned bucket, her ultrasound machine on the floor next to her. With her hand on a horse's leg and her eyes on the screen, she scans the gray matter for telltale signs of tendon problems. At the other end of the barn, their farrier, Paul Goodness, makes the aisle ring with his hammer and anvil, releasing acrid clouds of smoke as he singes red-hot shoes into the dead tissue of a horse's hooves. The dogs circle him, darting under the horse to snatch up the crescents of trimmed-off hoof, their favorite snack, as soon as they fall to the ground.

The ancient practice of farriery, the vet inspecting

the horse's legs, the separate workstations, the horses on cross-ties and being ridden, give the barn the atmosphere of a medieval market day. All this activity is preparing the horses for the six-week run of competitions that start with the Southern Pines Horse Trials in North Carolina this weekend.

Every step the horses take now is part of their training. Vanessa is untacking a big gray with a charming pink nose whose job at this stage of his career is to "go straight and stay chill." Andi is trying to bathe a gray she has just finished riding. He balks when he approaches the hose, and she circles him for a second approach. He plants his feet and tries to fool her into thinking that he's following her by stretching out his neck. She circles him again, and he plants his feet even farther away. Methodically and unemotionally, she shakes the lead shank in his face, backing him up until he lowers his head submissively and follows her to the hose. The grooms never fight with the horses. They don't lose their patience with them or raise their voices, because by now they are well versed in bringing out cooperative behavior.

It's a good afternoon for misbehaving grays. Samantha takes Verona, a four-year-old stallion who has been sent to the O'Connors for training, out of his stall. He is just reaching his sexual maturity and is being victimized by his own surging hormones.

Competition horses normally have their hormones controlled. Mares' diets are supplemented with hormone suppressors, equine birth control pills that prevent them from coming into heat. Stallions are usually gelded before they start formal training. Even in the macho environment of the racetrack, trainers admit that geldings often make better runners. They are able to focus on their work instead of sniffing out estrous mares and battling with other stallions. Owners generally don't geld racehorses because of their potential value in the breeding shed, but the alchemy of a great show horse is so hard to reproduce that breeding stallions simply don't command the same kind of stud fees as racehorse stallions. Most trainers admit that they prefer a horse with heart and willingness to a brilliant athlete who is combative and willful.

Without warning, Verona leaps and kicks in the aisle. With one arm still in a cast, Sam shakes the lead shank in his face and sends him scrambling backward, then leads him forward. He is complacent for a moment and then bucks again, this time into Joey's stall. One-handed, Sam hauls Verona onto the lawn, where she ducks her head toward his hind end, spinning him in one direction and then the other. Unnerved by the force of her actions, Verona's eyes lock on her, trying to anticipate her next movement. The other grooms stand in the aisle watching. Sam's actions have so much authority that none of them interferes, even though it's unwise for her to be pitting her will against this stallion when she has one arm in a cast. "If he hurts her, I'll kill him," the farrier's assistant mutters, as if Verona were some guy who had bested him for Sam's affections.

Karen strolls over from the office and stumbles on Sam and Verona's game of feint and dodge. Sam walks him to an empty paddock, leaves him with Karen, and joins the other grooms, who are inspecting Joey's stall. Mysteriously and luckily, someone had closed the iron grating over Joey's door before Verona kicked it. His hooves hit that instead of Joey's face. Bloody clumps of gray hair cling to the wire and the door latch.

Happily, Verona is not one of the horses the O'Connors are responsible for hauling back to Virginia. He is eventually sent back to his owners, who end up extracting his semen, freezing it, and gelding him.

From the road, the activity at the O'Connors' barn is almost invisible. The farms around Ocala are fronted by broad paddocks full of broodmares napping under the shade of the oaks, their babies tucked up against their bellies or sprawled on the cool grass nearby.

In the middle of the state, Ocala is an hour away from everything that most people go to Florida for. In her four winters here, Sam has never been to the beach. She tried last year. Her fiancé, Kenny, flew down with Nicole's boyfriend, and the two couples planned to spend a day at the beach. When they woke up, it was raining. The women slept until two in the afternoon and then joined their boyfriends in front of the VCR and watched movies for the remainder of their holiday. This year when Kenny came down they went to SeaWorld, because what else does an animal trainer do with her time off but go watch other trained animals? Now, days before her departure, it is clear that she won't get to the beach this year either.

Because of her cast, Sam is missing out on gallops too. In the midst of their packing, the grooms also have to keep up with the increasing intensity of the horses' workouts. David is shorthanded and tells Samantha to get one of the students to gallop his horses. "I can't," the student cries. "I know you have like a million horses and I only have two. But I can't! I don't have the time!"

The grooms are doing their own interval training as well. To check for soundness, Christiana Ober is watching all the horses jog. When the grooms aren't riding or packing, they're sprinting up and down the road in front of the farm, jogging horses. Vanessa, gasping for breath, jokes about how winded she gets, and Max, who wears clogs to work because she has back problems, wipes out, sprawling facedown in the road, losing the horse and twisting her ankle.

After jogging the horses for Dr. Ober, they have to jog them again for David, who arrives after Dr. Ober has gone.

As they hurry through their chores, the grooms count every piece of gear in the barn. The horses are headed to three different destinations with two departure dates a week apart. Every time the grooms use a piece of gear, they have to decide where to pack it: with the horses going to Southern Pines in North Carolina, with the horses going to the Plantation Field Horse Trials in Pennsylvania, or with the horses going directly back to Virginia. They have vague, distracted expressions on their faces. When someone interrupts their counting, they stare blankly, as if they no longer understand any language but numbers. They're avoiding the staff member who works in the office and keeps appearing in the barn with fluttering lists in her hand, asking questions. Vanessa sits on a tack trunk, counting out vials that contain individual dosages of the horses' joint supplements. Next to her is a box of syringes; she needs one per dose. She is counting and sorting them into piles when one of the students interrupts, asking if there is an extra vial that she can borrow and replace when they get back to Virginia. Vanessa's head is bobbing with her count, and the student takes that as a yes. Vanessa tries to subtract, loses count, and has to start all over again. The other grooms wander the aisle, stray pieces of equipment in their hands, trying to gather a consensus about where they will next be needed.

Finally, it's the night before departure. The grooms sprawl over trunks in a nearly bare tack room. The trunks with plastic lids bear indentations from their butts. Vanessa and Andi are staying behind and leaving a week later with the second load of horses. This assignment suits both of them because they like Florida better than Virginia, where there is less to do. Vanessa has made friends in nearby Gainesville.

She makes friends easily and is an avid letter writer. Andi is leaving behind a new boyfriend. "She's been getting laid for all of us," Max jokes. From the other side of the room, Sam clears her throat loudly. "Oh, right," Max says, as if Kenny doesn't count anymore because he and Sam are now engaged.

They're passing around snacks, joking about getting a sponsorship from Frito-Lay. "This is dinner on O'Connor Island," Vanessa says with a laugh when David walks through the room. They're going over their lists one more time. They've been so involved with the minutiae of getting the O'Connors' twenty-five horses and their equipment to three different locations that they've lost track of the total number of horses leaving. When asked what that number is, they start at the beginning of the list, ticking off the horses on their fingers, as if adding up a final number would make their heads pop.

Christiana Ober is there too. She has nine health certificates left — exactly enough for the horses in the barn. She and Sam are giddily filling them out. If they make a mistake, Dr. Ober won't be able to get a replacement book from the Virginia Department of Agriculture in time to get the horses out of the state for their competitions. Someone comments that with all the plain bays in the barn, the agriculture officer at the Florida border couldn't tell them apart anyway.

They have a brilliant plan for moving the horses, one that they've been developing for two weeks. Karen joins them and they reel it off. David will leave first at five a.m. in White Lightning, hauling all the gear they need for Southern Pines but no horses. Max and Orlando will go next, Max driving her Escort wagon and Orlando towing his ailing Hyundai behind Karen's Durango. In those three cars, they'll pack all the buckets the horses need, because they have to have water as soon as they step off the rig. At six, the professional driver they've hired will haul ten of the horses; the remaining three will hitch a ride along with the students. Vicky and Sam will follow the rig in Vicky's Bronco, nicknamed Jim Bob. Karen will leave last, in the camper that she and David live in at competitions.

All those nicknames, for one another, for the horses, for the vehicles, and even for the competitions, would make it impossible for even an informed visitor to the O'Connor barn to eavesdrop on a conversation and understand what they are talking about. The nicknames create a private world within the public commodity that is the O'Connor Event Team. There is Custom Made, the horse with the gold medal, who is also Tailor, the horse who has never taken a lame step. The grooms' nicknames for one another are androgynous shortenings of the names their parents wish them to be known by: Samantha is Sam; Vicky, Vix; Eleanor, Max; Vanessa, Ness; and Andrea, Andi. It's as if they're trying to reconcile their feminine selves with the bodies that can toss hay bales, lift engorged wooden trunks, and still the panic of a twelve-hundred-pound animal. Naming the vehicles actually makes organizing easier, eliminating potential confusion about which truck everyone is talking about. Among themselves, they speak a secret language, one that separates the hangers-on from those whose talent, work ethic, and professionalism have initiated them into the team.

Meticulous to the end, the grooms go over their plan one more time. In a week, David or Brewster Walker will return to drive the horses to Plantation Field in Blue Thunder and the remainder will be shipped back to Virginia with a professional driver. The washer and dryer and the heavy rubber stall mats have to be shipped along with the stall guards, the wheelbarrows, the bulletin boards, and the little refrigerator. When Vanessa and Andi close the doors on the barn a week from now, there will be nothing left behind but the walls.

They lean the horses' shipping boots outside their stall doors and place the tail wraps on top. They check feed and water and, with a last glance over their shoulders, they turn out the lights.

By five a.m. the next morning, the team is on the road. David pulls out in White Lightning, Max and Orlando behind him. The professional driver, Robert Sloane, has parked his truck on the road overnight and in a cloud of patchouli oil, he and his assistant driver load up the horses according to a carefully prepared seating chart. For the eight-hour drive north, it's important that all the horses in the rig are riding next to someone they like. Lined up outside the rig, in the dark, talking quietly, the grooms look as if they're stealing the horses. Sam and Vicky hug Andi and Vanessa goodbye and the convoy pulls out of the gates.

Riding in trucks when they're asked to is just one of the many ways that horses have learned to inhibit their natural instincts. Trucks are big, loud, and confining, and once the truck is on the road, the ground moves under the horses' feet. Everything about them would cause a wild horse to flee in terror. But riding quietly is expected of show horses, and through habituation and their desire to cooperate, they've quelled their fears.

Whether the horse was first ridden or driven is a subject of much debate among archaeologists. The nomadic lifestyle of the steppe inhabitants would indicate that horses must have been used to haul possessions around as the tribes moved. Moving horses from depleted to fresh grazing land would have been impossible to do without other horses to herd them. The archaeological record, though, indicates that some tribes traveled less than others — a sign, according to Sandra Olsen, who has uncovered manure pits and fence post holes at upper-Paleolithic dig sites, that the nomads had a supply of food that would carry them through the winter. Horses alone among grazing animals use their hooves to paw through snow. Cattle need human assistance. Sheep and goats forage with their noses. In her research into the pasture management of contemporary Kazakhs, Olsen found that horses are the only animals capable of pawing down through ten inches of snow or more, which would have been necessary in an environment with a mean snow depth of twelve to twenty inches.

Lacking evidence of yoke, harness, or bridle, what eludes researchers is the moment when these nomads went from keeping and eating horses to riding them. David Anthony's research into the first bit is his attempt to pinpoint that moment. He concedes that it is possible to ride a horse without a bit, and indeed, the evidence of natural horsemanship indicates that horses can be trained to respond to visual cues and body language, forgoing the need even for a halter. The leap of imagination that may have changed the course of history might not have been slipping some means of control over the horse's head, but the astute observation of a central Asian nomad, sympathetic to the animals he was keeping, who first befriended a horse and then could not resist sliding onto its back.

Driving horses, not riding them, was the original symbol of the elite. David Anthony believes that the reason driving horses are depicted in ancient art was that driving was the occupation of the elite — riding was for the lower orders. Historian Mary Littauer suggests that there was something repulsive and unseemly about contact with the horse's sweat through loose, filmy garments. (We have the Scythians to thank for the innovation of trousers.) Before they were ridden to war, horses hauled chariots there.

Without stirrups, which first appeared in China in the fourth century CE and then in Eastern Europe by the seventh century CE, safe riding would have been limited to only the most accomplished horsemen. Once the stirrup was invented, whole armies could go to war mounted, and the highly stylized riding that is the foundation of modern-day dressage was abandoned for a more utilitarian style.

As transportation, horses were more practical in front of a vehicle. They could only carry one person comfortably, but in front of a cart they could pull up to half a dozen. Adding horses to the harness enabled them to pull heavier loads, though the skill of the driver also had to increase. The Teamsters union, to which most professional horse transporters belonged, was originally formed as a brotherhood of the elite drivers who could handle up to eight horses carting loads through narrow urban streets.

According to author Juliet Clutton-Brock, the first public carriage appeared in Great Britain in 1564. In the ensuing four hundred years, before horses were replaced by machines in the early part of the twentieth century, a staggering amount of abuse of those horses was recorded. Economically marginalized drivers tried to save money on overhead by demanding that their horses pull ever heavier loads. Fashionable Victorians severely restricted their horses' heads with check reins that forced a high head carriage and left them unable to lean into their harnesses. In 1877, Anna Sewell, a Quaker, published *Black Beauty* in an attempt to educate readers about the suffering of horses. As Black Beauty narrated his life, almost every one of his companions came to a bad end at the hands of ignorant and vain handlers. They broke their necks in the hunting field; they were ridden into the ground by drunks; they were incinerated by careless smokers; and, most often, they broke down in front of some kind of vehicle. Fallen on hard times because of his blemished knees, Beauty ended up as a cab horse, a hack for hire. He was well cared for by his working-class master — an unusual presentation at the time. According to Keith Thomas, author of *Man and the Natural World*, the first legislation in England against animal cruelty was part of "yet another middle-class campaign to civilize the lower orders." Sadly, Black Beauty's childhood friend, when he saw her on the street, hadn't been as lucky as he. "It was Ginger! But how changed!" Beauty said. "The beautifully arched and glossy neck was now straight and lank and fallen in, the clean straight legs and delicate forelocks were swelled: the joints were grown out of shape with hard work, the face, once so full of spirit and life, was now full of suffering."

The English and Irish Thoroughbreds like Tex and Tailor who dominate the sport of eventing probably have some of those humble cart horses in their ancestry. But in the mere eighty years since horses ceded the way to motor vehicles as the main form of transportation, the traces of servitude were left behind. Tex and Tailor ride now, and they ride in style.

On the way to Southern Pines, though, the beautiful plan for the road trip falls apart in South Carolina when Max's car breaks down. The vehicles of the O'Connor team are strewn up and down Interstate 95 between South Carolina and Florida, and Max's distress calls ring cell phones along that route like a southerly wind. She is searching for her AAA card, which is in Reddick, in Vanessa's pocket. One by one the students whizz by, going too fast to stop, their faces staring out of the windows at Max, their mouths forming perfect Os of surprise.

Orlando is waiting with Max and he has a plan. He wants to drop off her car, unhitch and drive his Hyundai, and give Max the Durango. "It's a good car," he insists of the Hyundai. No one on the team considers that option for even a second. Sam and Vicky, in Vicky's Bronco, Jim Bob, are less worried about Max than they are about the horses, who are going to arrive in North Carolina before the grooms. They find David not at the front of the pack, where he is supposed to be, but at the end. He stopped at a military museum on his way north. "I've been driving past it for fifteen years and never stopped," he says with a shrug. When the cumbersome White Lightning looms into view, Max shouts, "Go, go, go!" at Orlando, who speeds off, trying to catch up with the horses.

This is the second time that David has waited with Max on the side of the road. On the way down, her bicycle flew off the top of her car and caused an accident. David kept her company while a state trooper wrote her a ticket. "It's part of the job," he says with a shrug.

There's an extra driver in the entourage and Max ends up leaving her turquoise blue Escort with a mechanic whose parking lot is full of cars with out-of-state plates, as if they were driven there to die. In ten minutes, she sorts through the plastic bins and garbage bags that contain all of her worldly possessions and decides which ones she can live without, in case she never sees her car again. She's surprisingly sanguine when she calls the friends she's staying with in Southern Pines. She'll get there, she says, reminding them to have her cocktail ready.

She arrives just forty-five minutes after the rest of the team. Sam's dog, Ozzie, is patrolling the stabling area, and Max spots him and follows his stout figure through the parking lot to the O'Connors' tent. It's overcast, and the dim light is giving way to darkness. The grooms haul heavy trunks out of White Lightning and into an empty stall they'll use as a tack room. They throw shavings over the grass floors of the tent and tie stall guards over the doorways with baling twine. David notices that ET is stretching out awkwardly. There's no manure in his stall. Instead of the normal grumblings of digestion, there is ominous silence from his gut, which is as tight and still as a kettledrum. ET is colicking.

Like a cold for humans, colic is dead common in horses. It can pass on its own in a matter of hours or, like the transition from a cold to pneumonia, it can turn into a fatal condition. Horses have seventy-two feet of intestines, small and large, which are narrow and twist around in their bellies like a go-cart track. The intestines are lined with nerve endings, so when horses have trouble with their plumbing, the pain is severe. David puts a training halter on ET, squirts a paste sedative into his mouth, and takes him for a walk, which can sometimes loosen things up. In the growing darkness, David and ET pace slowly and uncomfortably in the aisle between the tents. At its worst, colic requires surgery in which the horse is anesthetized and flipped over on his back, and his stomach is cut open and the intestines pulled out of his body. An incision is made at the site of the blockage, which is then squeezed out. Once the intestines are empty, the incision is sutured closed and the intestine rapidly stuffed back in. Recovery takes months, and often the horse never returns to his previous competitive level. Vicky, standing at Sam's side, nods her head silently when Sam asks her to empty out White Lightning in case ET has to be rushed to the hospital.

The horse's digestive system, sensitive and finicky under domestic conditions, is the reason he survived through the Ice Age, when most of his large-animal peers died out. Most grazing animals like cows and sheep have multiple stomach chambers that allow them to repeatedly digest the same meal until all its nutritional value is extracted. Scientists used to believe that these animals, ruminants, make better use of poor-quality nutrition. The horse's system is pretty ineffective at extracting nutrients. Instead of multiple stomachs, horses have a cecum, seventy feet long, fed by the small intestine on one side and emptying into the large intestine on the other. The cecum is full of highly active enzymes, and when horses eat, those enzymes help them grab what nutrients they can as the food flies by.

High-cellulose, poor-quality grasses, the kind that began to take over the planet as it cooled and the forests died out during the Ice Age, actually worked to the horse's advantage. The big ruminants were victimized by their own thoroughness. Unable to process more food until their stomachs were done with what they'd already eaten, they died waiting to digest. Horses just kept eating and eating. As author Stephen Budiansky explains, horses can survive on grasses that would starve a cow to death. Archaeologist Marsha Levine believes that upper-Paleolithic nomads domesticated the horse because he had brilliantly evolved into an animal that could convert poor-quality food — high-cellulose grasses — into high-quality protein — his own flesh.

As much as horses love their grain, its high protein content and its delivery, in bulky meals, are exactly what make it difficult for them to digest it. Factor in the stress of travel and the restricted water, and driving a horse to a competition is asking for trouble. What is surprising is not that ET is colicking, but that the rest of the horses are not. Which is why no one on the O'Connor team is bothering to speculate why ET got sick.

The grooms busy themselves, staying out of the way, as Sam squats against the tent wall watching David. The walking and the sedative don't bring any relief, so David calls the Southern Pines vet. Karen isn't on the grounds yet because the camper blew a tire tread and she's stranded at a truck stop, waiting for a replacement. Max wants to go to her friend's house, but she doesn't have a car; Vicky wants everyone to leave except her and Sam, but there are no extra drivers. David's cell phone rings, and Sam jumps to her feet and takes ET off his hands. It's dark, the vet hasn't arrived yet, and David decides to get some dinner, leaving ET in Sam's care.

The vet's truck pulls up while David is at dinner. Sam circles ET back into his stall and holds him still, waiting for the vet to inject him with a sedative to ease his pain and calm him. Instead, the vet appears in the doorway, sees Sam, and starts booming out instructions. ET, startled by the vet's loud voice, lurches forward, shoving Sam into the wall. One-handed, she is only able to hold him still for a few moments at a time and she's telling the vet to be quick, to inject ET on the fly. The vet lingers in the doorway, afraid to enter. He tells Sam to get the horse under control, to put a chain shank over his nose. Sam shakes her head. The O'Connors don't use chain shanks, and introducing one to ET in his present stressed-out state could cause him to rear up and flip over in panic. ET's eyes are rolled back in his head and he's trembling. The vet won't come into the stall, and Sam is furious. Her brown eyes are huge, her lips are pressed together, and bright red spots appear on her cheeks. At this worst possible time, the vet is questioning her ability and her knowledge of the horse. Sam holds her temper. She knows that in the vet's eyes, she is just a groom. Sam thinks he's a chicken, willing to let ET thrash around and batter her into the stall wall rather than follow her advice.

They're at an impasse. The vet won't enter the stall, and Sam won't put a chain over ET's face. Luckily, David arrives. Two-handed, he has more control over ET, and perhaps because he is David O'Connor, or perhaps because he is a man, the vet stops booming out instructions and gives ET his shot.

It is only recently that women have begun to appear at the top level of horse sports in numbers that reflect their interest at the lower levels. Equestrian Olympic competition opened to women in 1952, the first year that it was open to riders who were not part of the United States cavalry. The first female United States rider, Jessica Ransehousen, competed in 1960 as part of the United States Dressage squad; 1964 was the first year that women competed in the disciplines of eventing and show jumping. Men had been borrowing horses from women for years. By 1964, the best horses and the best riders, even if they were women, were able to compete. Today, the equestrian disciplines of the Olympic Games are the only sport in which male and female athletes compete against one another as individuals. Still, given the number of girls who compete as juniors, the representation of women at the professional level is still disproportionately low. David O'Connor believes that there is actually a disproportionate number of girls at the lower levels because girls mature faster than boys. Maureen Fredrickson, a social worker who lectures on gender differences in pet ownership, explains that boys express their affection for animals by tinkering with their physical environment, like building cages and doing chores. Girls, on the other hand, are more interested in grooming and handling the animal. "It's all about relating and talking about relationships," she says.

This evidence seems to coincide with Carol Gilligan's findings that showed that girls judge their life by the quality of their relationships. Based on the relationship-building skills that Gilligan identified, what girls have to offer in abundance is exactly what horses are looking for — someone who is as motivated as they are to explore every nuance of their social connections, even if those connections are to another species. And no wonder girls are drawn to horses.

At precisely that time in their life, early adolescence, when the cooperative playing that they are so good at has been replaced by competitive sport and the hierarchies of academic accomplishment, there is the horse, the animal that shares their values. And because they are so good at understanding the horse — better, in fact, than most boys their age — they are able to marshal his strength, his athleticism, to their command.

Among adults, the number of men and women in the sport starts to even out, but at the upper levels, David O'Connor believes, women drop out of the sport to have families and then find it impossible to return to their previous professional level. "They go on and do something else," he explains. If boys have crossed the line into professionalism by the time they are twenty-one or twenty-two, they are more likely to stay with it for life.

A less felicitous explanation for the disproportionate numbers is that the owners of the horses, unlike the horses themselves, have gender preferences. "Karen is just as established as David is," Sam says. Yet David "always gets the catch rides on the horses. Always."

Those attitudes are changing. The show jumping team at the Sydney Olympics was entirely composed of women. As more women owners control their own money, they have more say about who rides their horses. Likewise, as women in the sport become more savvy, they've become better at creating the business partnerships they need to accumulate buyers for their horses. As women have caught up to their male peers, they've ushered in new thinking about training methods as well. Dr. Robert Miller, the veterinarian and keynote speaker at the American Veterinary Association's 2000 convention, called the rethinking of traditional training methods a "revolution," one he attributed to the dominance of women in the industry overall. Women, he explained, are more likely to adopt "persuasive rather than coercive" methods for controlling their horses. Even though natural horsemanship techniques are largely taught by male ex-cowboys, it is women who've made them popular.

The vet at Southern Pines apparently missed out on all the enlightenment. He assumes that his methods are more effective than Sam's, even though she knows the horse better than anyone else. His next suggestion causes both David's and Sam's eyebrows to raise in unison. He wants to manually probe ET's rectum. While not an unusual procedure, it isn't a necessary one, especially for a fractious animal who is already on the edge of panic. Sam and David build a hay bale barrier between the vet and ET. Everyone who doesn't have a reason to be in the aisle is sent away. Vicky finds a volunteer to drive Max and Orlando home. ET, to Sam's and David's surprise, initially tolerates the vet's probing until the vet, emboldened, abruptly forces his hand up ET's rectum. The hay bales save his gut.

The O'Connors' hometown vets, Christiana Ober and her boss, Kent Allen, would have been more sensitive to the horse and to Sam. For big competitions, the O'Connors bring their vets and their farriers with them, but at these smaller shows, they are at the mercy of the local talent. Despite what David refers to as the vet's "ego problem," ET is fully recovered in the morning. The solution to his problem was what Sam and David would have recommended from the beginning: a mixture of water and castor oil poured down his throat.

Southern Pines is the beginning of the dog-versus-show-official wars that will continue for the rest of the year. The competitors and their grooms spend half their lives in tents and they treat the temporary stabling as an extension of their home barns. At home, the dogs roam free. At competitions, the officials want them tied up. The dogs side with their owners. Horse shows are part of their work, and if they are tied, they have no reason to be there. By late Thursday, Ozzie has already been very productive. An escaped horse wandered down the aisle. Ozzie ran to his front and barked. Taking a cue from the Parelli training, he dodged his head toward the horse's hindquarters and stopped him in his tracks. Calvin raced up from the side and boxed the horse against the tent and held him there until his rider came along to retrieve him.

One of the older horse trials, Southern Pines is the traditional start of the season. Most East Coast eventers winter in the area or not far away. The tents look cheerful under the bright sunshine and blue sky. In addition to the professional riders, there are amateur riders with one or two horses and their moms, dads, and siblings along as grooms. One of them is in the O'Connors' row. She and her mother look slightly awestruck, like kids on the local basketball court who've suddenly discovered that Michael Jordan has popped in to shoot a few hoops. They speak quietly to each other and glance around furtively, trying to comprehend the precision of the O'Connor eventing machine.

While the riders cross the road to the schooling field, their families kick back in lawn chairs, catching up on news and showing off their new dogs. Like conventioneers, the riders' families know one another almost exclusively from these competitions. As the season progresses, they will spend more time with these other supporters from distant states than they will with their neighbors from nearby barns.

In the schooling field, a hundred or so riders are walking, trotting, and cantering in schooling figures. From a distance, it looks chaotic and willy-nilly, as if crashes are imminent. Yet there is such precision to their movements, and the riders are so skilled at judging a horse's stride, that in fact it's like a well-rehearsed choreography. Horses who've never seen each other stay focused and calm as they brush past each other, stirrup to stirrup. Asking a horse to behave in this kind of a situation is as counter to his instincts as asking him to get on a truck. Some animal-rights activists argue that asking horses to spend their lives traveling from show to show is abusive. A recent study revealed that there is a high rate of ulcers in show horses. But their cooperation could be seen as part of their role as domesticated animals, a domestication in which, equine behaviorists believe, the horse has always been complicit.

Six thousand years ago, horses were on the brink of extinction. Their comeback to their current worldwide population of 60 million, Stephen Budiansky speculates, occurred because they proved so useful, first as food, then as mounts, worthy of feeding and protecting. But it wasn't just their usefulness to humans that led to the domestication of horses. The horses, Budiansky holds, sought us out as well. Horses and humans found each other on the margins of established societies. Humans eking out a living on poor farmland could strengthen their diets with the horse. Horses who were losing their natural habitat to human expansion found that they could rely on humans for their survival. Horses developed a new niche, according to Budiansky, "one that exploited the grain fields and garbage dumps of human habitations."

Once they'd made contact, horses' inherent tamability made it possible for humans to exploit them. They possess many of the same care-soliciting behaviors that human babies use to get their mothers to take care of them. Horses are naturally curious. They crave social interaction and will seek it out even from different species. They're playful, skilled at deflecting aggression, and submit willingly to their dominant companions. Preserving these attractive juvenile characteristics into adulthood is part of a constellation of adaptive behaviors known as neoteny. They have excelled at communicating with us because they are so accomplished at communicating with one another.

Zebras, the horse's near relations, are not tamable. Even though they also live in social groups, they are not curious about humans or interested in creating relationships outside their species. Throughout history, and sometimes hilariously, people have tried to domesticate zebras, only to be met with kicking hooves, biting teeth, and stubborn recalcitrance. The horse's suitability to sport, Budiansky writes, might be because our sports are analagous to their own play behavior. This confirms the unscientific and anthropomorphic evidence of generations of horsemen: there is something about games that horses like. As David O'Connor explains: "People say that the horse doesn't have a choice. Well, they do. If they don't want to jump, they won't jump." Even the structure of the horse's mouth suits him to human use. In between the front and back molars is a gap of exposed gum. Unique to horses, that space, called the bar, makes a perfect place for a bit to rest. Without it, the bit would rest on teeth, where the horse could clamp down on it and render it useless. Their relationship with us may have saved them from extinction, and their contemporary relationship with us is rich with the kind of social interaction they crave. "Their life is interesting," David says about his competitive horses. "It has variety and yet it has consistency at the same time. There's safety in that." They cooperate with our training endeavors, habituate to a life on the road, learn to stay focused on their riders when they are experiencing the equivalent of being thrown into a strange herd, all for the purpose of maintaining the quality of that interaction. In exchange, as David says, "they have a life, instead of just, . . . " He shrugs. "You know."

There will be a string of six competitions that the riders

at Southern Pines will be traveling to together — Poplar
Place in Georgia; Morven Park in Virginia; Fair Hill in
Maryland; and Plantation Field in Pennsylvania — all horse
trials; the Foxhall Cup, a CCI three-star in Georgia; and finally Rolex in Kentucky, America's only CCI four-star.
The competitions don't run themselves. Administrative responsibilities are ramping up at Southern Pines. Throughout the day before the competition starts on Friday, the
loudspeaker pops to life announcing meetings. Around sun-
set, the riding done, the late arrivals just pulling in, the
grounds are turned over to the grooms as the riders gather
for a meeting. They return with beers in their hands. David
is besieged by official business. The two governing bodies
of American horse sports, USA Equestrian and the United
States Equestrian Team, are in the midst of an ugly and
complex legal battle over the control of those sports. David
has publicly sided with USA Equestrian, and together they're
strategizing about how to win the fight.

The chores finished, the horses tucked in, Sam, Vicky,
and Max head out for dinner. They're returning later to
braid. This is the only competition all year where they'll
braid the night before, and that is only because they have
thirteen horses and two and a half braiders. On Sam's cast,
Karen signed, "Sorry about your arm. Can you braid by
Tuesday?"

The temperature drops after the grooms leave, and
Karen stops by the barn to throw sheets on all the horses.
She asks a visitor if she's noticed that "all my horses are nice
and all of David's are mean." Nice or mean, Karen's or
David's, they're all buckled into their jammies — Wendy
(aka Large Marge) a little stuffed into hers. Across the way,
the riders have returned to their campers. Festive strings of
colored lights hang over patio chairs as the riders stretch out

in them, their muscled legs released from the sweaty confines of tall boots.

In the barns, the lights glow through the yellow tents, infusing the grass with neon brightness. Grooms walk up and down the aisles, lugging water buckets and moving gear around. Clutches of family members who are staying at area motels linger in the night, gossiping and finishing their drinks. The dogs are loose again, prowling the grounds and uncovering the day's stories with their noses. By eight p.m., the stables are almost quiet, just a handful of people left finishing chores, including grooms who are cheating by braiding the night before. By next weekend, this competition will be writ into the history books, and these same people will gather in another field. In another quiet, rural corner of the east, tents will pop up, loudspeaker wires will be laid, Porta-Potties will be trucked in, and a field will be ruined by parked cars as this equine circus gathers for another event. Some of the horses will change, as will the officials and the spectators, but the riders, the grooms, and their dogs will be the same. Sam and the rest of the grooms will hold to their rituals, repeat their unpacking and packing procedures, loving their horses whether they win or lose. There are worse lives of labor for a horse. As the aging Sir Oliver said to Black Beauty when he was still a colt, "We horses must take things as they come, and always be contented and willing so long as we are kindly used."

Chapter Six

WINNERS AND LOSERS

It's the last week in April, and the Kentucky Derby is less than two weeks away. The *Lexington Herald-Leader* carries daily reports about the workouts of the horses who will be running. Liquor stores are stocking up on Kentucky bourbon, and the local markets are building displays of souvenir glasses. Derby Day, the first Saturday in May, is the one day of the year that horses are part of the national sports dialogue.

None of the horsemen at the Kentucky Horse Park in Lexington this last week of April are thinking about the Derby. They are thinking about Rolex. Competition starts on Wednesday with the first official vet inspection. The riders have been training for this competition for a year and preparing for it even longer than that. There is no future; there is only the Rolex

CCI four-star. From now until the last show jumping round on Sunday, there is nothing else in the world but this competition.

The O'Connors arrived late on Monday. On Tuesday morning the grooms are off to a leisurely start. They've come directly from Georgia and the Foxhall CCI three-star — a competition that David says was okay and that Sam characterizes as a disaster, with abysmally low placings for all the O'Connors' horses. It's sunny and cool, and the grooms are relieved to be away from the heat of Atlanta. The O'Connors have brought seven horses. Karen has Regal Scott, Bally Mar (Amber), Upstage, and Grand Slam. David is competing Tailor, Tigger Too, and ET. For those seven horses there are five grooms: Samantha and Vanessa at the head of David's string; Vicky at the head of Karen's, with Max along to take care of Amber and a fifth groom who works for the owner of Grand Slam. As the grooms amble through their chores, the O'Connor entourage trickles into the stabling area. Over the course of the weekend, family and friends will arrive, as will former grooms and former students. An equine massage therapist and an equine acupuncturist will be on call, along with two vets and two farriers. The horses' owners are here for the weekend, along with their friends and families. Almost all of them are sporting navy blue baseball caps with the O'Connor Event Team logo. This is a hat whose possession, a columnist for *The Chronicle of the Horse* wrote, would "make your friends writhe with envy." Most of the people in the entourage are here to help. According to David, he and Karen can count on as many as thirty people to come to their aid for big events. That's the whole point of the team concept, he explains. Plus, it's kind of fun. "They just appear," he says.

The entourage doesn't have much to do before the start

of the competition. They've dragged lawn chairs into the middle of the lane between the barns and are leaning back in them, their faces tilted toward the sun, drowsily holding the horses' lead shanks while the grooms brush them.

David and Karen need to ride every one of their horses twice a day before the first dressage test on Thursday. When the horses are not being ridden, the grooms have to beautify them. Out of the trunk they pull the special grooming tools. With tiny scissors, Sam is trimming every single hair that pokes over the top of the horses' hooves. Small battery-operated clippers take care of the fuzz around their jawbones. She and Vicky use Nice 'n Easy hair coloring to dye ET's and Upstage's tails, which have gotten bleached by the sun. ET has a skimpy tail, and the fake extension that will be used for his vet inspection and his dressage test hangs in the tack room, looking like a brunette sister of Cousin Itt.

The horses are bathed and the sensitive skin around their noses and eyes is baby-oiled. Stray long hairs are yanked out of their manes and tails. With time on their hands and unable to stop themselves, the grooms turn on the dogs. Vanessa scrubs up Ozzie's thick, dirty fur with a long-toothed currycomb. He looks a little embarrassed at first and then gives in to the pleasure of it, rolling over and offering Vanessa his white belly. Calvin gets a bath and a spritz with the horses' coat conditioner. His underbite gleams white against the shiny black of his coat and he's pleased to be told how handsome he is.

Sam takes Tigger out to a quiet, unused paddock that is thick with long grass. She sits in the middle of it while he grazes around her. In addition to having a temper, Tigger is a little needy, according to Sam. Even having her stand at the rail is too far away for him. Cross-legged, she chats on the phone with her fiancé, Kenny, while Tigger grazes in a ten-foot circle around her. He passes so close to her that the top of her ponytail brushes up against his belly. When she stands to leave, he races to her side, fearful of being left alone.

In the stabling area, more of the entourage has arrived. Brewster Walker is there with a full cooler of beers that he's passing around. The horses' massage therapist has shown up and, with nothing to do, she works on the grooms, whose bodies she describes as "corpses that haven't fallen down yet." Every one of them is aching. Max is rubbing horse liniment into her feet. Vanessa groans as the knots are worked out of her neck, and Sam's shoulder is so tender that she winces and ducks away from the massage therapist's hands.

Two hours before the first vet inspection, the stabling area is in the kind of cheerful frenzy you would normally associate with elves. Karen and David are back at their camper, changing into sport jackets and slacks. The grooms have changed into clean shirts. The horses stand quietly as every last bit of dirt and stray hair is flicked, whisked, buzzed, snipped, plucked, and spritzed. Roll-on dyes cover up their nicks and blemishes. Special whiteners are used to brighten their markings. With a black Magic Marker, the grooms color any white hairs in the horses' manes and tails. Just before the horses head up to the jog, the grooms comb a checkerboard pattern on their hindquarters, and on their thighs, using a dampened brush, they swoop a jagged pattern called shark's teeth.

Stone-faced, in sport coats, pants, and skirts, the judges stand behind a row of potted geraniums, their severe attitude indicating that they are not going to be fooled by appearances. As Sam leads Tailor, in his plain bay wrapping, up to the tarmac to wait his turn, even the most experienced horsemen stop talking to watch. Winner of the Badminton four-star and Olympic gold, third-place winner at this competition last year, Tailor is the horse to beat. Seen from behind, the muscles of his hindquarters slide smoothly over his frame. The joints of his hips, shoulders, knees, hocks, ankles, and stifles move so smoothly that his limbs seem to swing without friction. As Tailor pushes each foot down into the ground, the opposing joints of his legs — stifle and hock, knee and ankle — compress his energy into the ground and then spring it back up to his body with compounded force. The ringing of his steel shoes on the pavement is in perfect four-beat time, the rhythm of his gait as steady as a metronome. The judges will be looking at that gait, listening to the force of each footfall, scrutinizing the plane on which Tailor's head travels. Any bobbing of that head, one footfall sounding weaker than the others, any leg that doesn't swing as evenly as the rest, will be counted as evidence of unsoundness, and Tailor will be spun from the competition. Unlike human athletes, who are allowed to compete as long as they can stagger onto the field, every one of the sixty-three horses competing at Rolex has to be perfectly sound to pass inspection.

In front of Tailor's hindquarters, in the space just behind his rib cage, are his flanks, abdomen, and barrel. Underneath his ribs, the yards and yards of his intestinal tract are calmly digesting Tailor's food, delivering protein, vitamins, and minerals to his body.

Just in front of all his plumbing are Tailor's lungs, the source of his awesome ability to seize oxygen and pump it into his blood. Six times larger than David's, Tailor's lungs hold about thirty quarts of air. Tailor is so lean that the muscles of his diaphragm, just under and behind his lungs, are visible.

Between Tailor's left and right lungs is his heart. Tucked safely behind his sternum and rib cage, his heart pumps blood throughout his body, delivering the nutrients and energy he receives from his food, which has been specially formulated by equine nutritionists at the University of Kentucky.

Heart is the word that horsemen use to describe willingness, courage, bravery, and desire, the emotional characteristics of great horses. When Secretariat, the greatest horse of his century, was autopsied, his heart was found to be three times the normal size. Not pathologically large, just a perfect heart three times bigger than other horses'. That finding suited the imagination of his admirers. It explained not only his speed but, for them, his desire to pull ahead of the rest of the pack, even after he'd already won. It explained how he won the Belmont Stakes by *thirty-one* lengths. Television viewers who were lucky enough to have tuned in for that race saw Secretariat blaze over the finish line and then, astonishingly, breathtakingly, seconds of empty screen before the rest of the pack thundered through.

At the front of Tailor's body is his head, with the finely chiseled bones of the Thoroughbred face. His nostrils, which he can distend to almost twice their usual size, allow him to take in those thirty quarts of air at a breath. His eyes, as beautiful and kind as the eyes of all the horses who have been inspiring artists for fifteen thousand years, will deceive him on cross-country day. His limited depth perception will show him only the first fence of a two- or three-jump combination. He'll compensate for this deficiency by using his brain. When he lands and suddenly discovers that there is another solid, imposing obstacle just a few strides away, his brain will quickly measure the distance, enabling Tailor to check or expand his stride to get over it. It is also Tailor's brain that will keep him from panicking, that will keep him calm and focused on dressage day, when his nerves and fast-twitching muscles are forced into containment by the rigid demands of the dressage test.

And it is Tailor's brain that is keeping him calm now. With one yank, he could be free of Sam's hand. Given his size, speed, intelligence, and fitness, there isn't an animal in North America that could best him, and yet Tailor still chooses to follow this young woman out of the barn like a puppy. Sam has been his companion almost every day for the past four years. Before he knows he's hungry, she is feeding him. Before he knows he's frightened, her voice is calming his fears, and before he knows he's hurt, her hand is soothing his pain. She knows his quiet emotional side better than anyone else in the world. As the gathered horsemen look at this animal, who is one of the most accomplished athletes in the history of his sport, Tailor lowers his head, his ears level with Sam's shoulders, and quietly follows the groom he trusts and, in his own horsey way, loves.

All seven of the O'Connors' horses pass the first inspection, as does every other horse in the competition. The grooms are excited. Their horses are fit, relaxed, and ready to compete.

Every sport has its pinnacle: the World Series, the Ironman Triathlon, the Super Bowl, the Kentucky Derby. For Three-Day Eventers, that pinnacle is a CCI four-star. Rolex is one of only four in the world and the only one in North America. With Badminton and Burghley, both in England, it is part of the Grand Slam of Eventing. Any rider who wins all three in the same year (though not on the same horse, since Badminton and Rolex are a week and an ocean apart) takes home a purse of $250,000. The Grand Slam of Eventing is only a few years old, and so far no one has won it. Compared to racing and show jumping prizes, $250,000 is not very much money, especially since, according to David, the starting cost of maintaining a horse at the two-, three-, or four-star level is $25,000 per year. But it's a lot of money for eventers who choose their discipline not for its purses but because they love the sport. Of the thousands of riders in North America who have chosen eventing, only forty-five of them, on sixty-three horses, have accumulated enough credentials to qualify for Rolex, and most of those are hoping merely to finish respectably, not to win. From the moment a rider realizes that the horse she's sitting on *could* be a four-star horse, every step of that horse's training will be one more pixel added to the rider's picture of herself galloping over the Rolex finish line.

For riders who dream of representing the United States on an international team, Rolex is the gateway. From the top finishers at Rolex, the U.S. Equestrian Team, which selects and supports the teams in all equestrian disciplines for the Olympics, the World Equestrian Games, and the Pan Am Games, will compile its long list of horses and riders for the World Equestrian Games in Spain in September. The O'Connor grooms are excited because there is every reason to believe that the winning horse might be in their stable. For five years, Rolex has been the O'Connors' competition. In 2001, David won it on Tex and was third on Tailor. In 2000, he was second on Rattle and Hum. Karen was third that year on Prince Panache, the horse on whom she won the competition in 1999, when she was also second on her horse Regal Scott. In 1998, Karen was fifth, and in 1997, the year the competition moved up from a three-star to a four-star, she was first on Worth the Trust. Despite their past successes and their serious firepower, Karen warns a visitor to the barn that their position on the World Equestrian Games team is not yet certain. "We could tank this weekend," she warns.

David rides Tigger one more time and then he and Karen are done for the day. The grooms, who've been working since five a.m., are still in the barn twelve hours later. ET has turned his butt to the stall door, signaling that his day is over. The massage therapist works on Upstage, and the acupuncturist has stuck needles all over Regal Scott. Sam hears the massage therapist calling for help and ducks into Upstage's stall. The other grooms are sitting on the trunks and discussing their dinner options with Brewster, whose job, in addition to driving the horses and keeping the cooler full, is to pick out the restaurant for dinner. As with getting directions, Sam never bothers to even develop opinions about restaurants, much less offer them. Her thoughts are entirely about her horses. She has little to say even about the plans for her wedding, which, even though it's a year away, her mother has already started working on. She is the first one to respond to someone else's needs and the last one to sit down for a beer at the end of the day. "She will be part of our group for the rest of her life," David says.

To document the beginning of Rolex 2002, the company poses for a photo. Laughing, they arrange themselves in a half circle, their arms slung around one another. Sam sits on an overturned bucket in the middle, her cell phone to her ear. As everyone around her, even the dogs, mugs for the camera, beers in their hands, their cigarettes hidden behind their backs, Sam finishes her last chore of the day: getting an update from the Stonehall barn manager on the horses who've been left at home.

In the parking lot, the grooms are divvying up into separate cars when there is a thunderclap of metal against wood. Max, pulling out in Karen's Durango, has hit the support beam of the farrier's station and drastically rearranged the bumper and taillight. Max, her eyes wide, a high wheedle of desperation in her voice, explains to everyone that she couldn't see the post because the spare tire was in the way. The grooms speculate about whether she is going to get into trouble. Max decides not to call Karen.

Worrying about her car the night before her dressage test, Max says, "is the last thing she needs." For the next two days, until Max confesses, the grooms collect stories from former students at the competition about the O'Connors' likely response to the damage. Contrary to what Max hopes, David and Karen are definitely not cool about the destruction of their property. One former student recalls an awful and terrifying lecture she got from David when she drove through one of the Stonehall fences, which was repaired in the time it took her to go to the lumber yard and get replacement boards. Their fear of Karen and David, their urging of Max to come clean, and their gratitude that they aren't the ones with a secret to confess make the grooms seem less like the O'Connors' employees than their children.

The Kentucky Horse Park is twelve hundred acres of green, rolling terrain. It houses the International Museum of the Horse and administrative headquarters for USA Equestrian, the United States Pony Clubs, and a couple of breed registries, among other equine associations. Famous racehorses like Cigar live in the Hall of Champions and are led out for regular public showings. A life-size statue of Man o' War graces the main entrance. In the days preceding the start of the competition, tourists rolled around the lanes in horse-drawn carriages. Truckloads of grounds crews mowed lawns, ran weed whackers against fence lines, trucked stadium seats to the main arena, and staked down tents. After Rolex, park officials hope that they'll also have visitors wandering in during Derby Week.

By five a.m. on the first of two days of dressage, the park is ready for the 85,000 spectators the organizers are predicting. It is still dark; the statue of Man o' War is lit by a ring of floodlights. He faces away from the barns and seems to stare out beyond the boundaries of the park, beyond the bluegrass, to the point in history when this sporting relationship between people and horses began.

By six-thirty, the skies are at last brighter than the barn lights. In the stabling area, the sounds are muffled: the murmuring of the grooms, the horses shifting their weight, and the soft *whoosh* of brushes. The security guard at the entrance to the stabling area grins hopefully as an army of lean, athletic, and pretty young women pass him, flicking out their wrists to show him their red security bands, as if that's what he's looking for.

Sam and the grooms are taking the horses out to hand-graze them. Even though they're only going to a grassy knoll overlooking a schooling arena a few hundred yards away, the shavings are brushed off the horses' rugs, their manes are wetted over, their feet are darkened with hoof polish, and they're outfitted in matching blue blankets with the O'Connor Event Team logo embroidered on them. With Styrofoam coffee cups in one hand and the horses' lead shanks in the other, the grooms are dragged from one luscious patch of grass to the next. Conversations are started, interrupted, and returned to as the horses bring the grooms together, change their minds, and then drag them apart again.

Among fans of eventing, the O'Connors are as popular as NBA stars, and Karen and David feel very responsible toward their audience. They are accessible and friendly, and when probed about how their competitiveness affects their marriage, they are outspoken about their mutual support. When asked whom she most admires in the world, Karen says her husband. (David mentions Pavarotti.) As their ride times approach, spectators fill the arena seating. Young girls point out David to their mothers and then blush when their mothers, somewhat incredulously, say too loudly, "Oh, that's him?" Others hold up hand-lettered signs that read,

"We ♥ You David!" The girls are enamored not with David, in his anachronistic costume of breeches and hunt coat, but with the greater thing that David becomes when he sits on his horses. "A horseman afoot," Thomas McGuane wrote in his book *Some Horses,* "is a wingless, broken thing, tyrannized by gravity. A crumpled figure in every discernible way, a defeated aging little crone where moments ago a demon or a fire queen filled us with obsessive attention." Without their horses, David and Karen seem hardly worthy of a second glance. With them, their images hang on the walls of these girls' bedrooms, next to those of movie stars.

"It's our time right now," David says about his own and his wife's popularity. "It won't be our time forever." Spectators hush as they ride into the ring. They trade bits of information about the O'Connors as if they have received it personally from them when, in fact, it is published in the program. Even Sam has been asked for her autograph. "I'm only the groom." She laughs.

On the second day of dressage, David and Karen are the last two riders. Karen is in eighteenth place on Regal Scott and thirty-fourth on Grand Slam, and the affectionate and fiery little Upstage is in a disappointing forty-sixth place. ET, whom Jimmy Wofford, the handicapper for *The Chronicle of the Horse,* described as "quite possibly the fastest horse here," is in twenty-ninth place. Wofford predicted that with a good dressage score, ET could end up with a top-ten placing. David isn't as optimistic about the little black horse: "He would rather do something easy than something hard." Which is fine with David. That's simply who ET is. Winning at the three-star level has been easy for ET, and in doing so he has already exceeded the expectations that David had of his problem child. The challenge of a four-star, he worries, might unnerve ET, rattle his confidence and make him afraid enough to stop on course. He is more optimistic about Tigger. An ex-racehorse like ET, Tigger is anxious and prone to fits of pique. When David first started competing him, Tigger used to rear and buck in his dressage tests. His dressage test at Rolex has put him in fourteenth place, well within the reach of a top-ten or even a top-five placing, which would put him on the list of horses for the World Equestrian Games in September. David's best ride, on Tailor, is still ahead of him, and Karen is going last on the storied Bally Mar (aka Amber). "What a terrible weight of sadness will settle over Karen," Jimmy Wofford wrote, "as she turns down the centerline on this horse. She knows how much her late friend Jim Stamets, who had the ride on Bally Mar, wanted to ride at Rolex."

The horses are as polished for dressage as they were for the jog. Tight braids run down their crests. Their coats gleam; their white markings are bright. Karen and David are dressed up too, in top hats, white breeches, white gloves, and shadbellys — riding coats with tails. Karen warms Amber up in the schooling ring, and David is behind a tent on Tailor. He aims Tailor for the field next to the schooling ring, inadvertently cutting through a throng of spectators. Realizing who he is, and who he's riding, the fans surge toward him, dangerously crowding Tailor. They remember their etiquette and check themselves, but David and Tailor still have to pick their way through the crowd. They both look down, trying not to step on anyone. With bowed heads, surrounded by hushed and awestruck fans, they look like humble returning warriors accepting the gratitude of those they have been defending.

The entire O'Connor Event Team gathers at the gate of the large ring that encloses the foot-high white fence marking the dressage arena. David turns down the centerline on his best horse, and Sam steps away from the rest of the grooms. They are nervous, and Brewster's joking has created a burst of giggling. Sam stands apart, her wide mouth pressed into a line of fierce concentration. Two hours later, she can replay every hoof beat of Tailor's test.

Sam stood at the side of this ring last year, watching Tex win the competition and Tailor come in third. Even though she used to compete herself, that experience, she claims, didn't come close to what she feels when David wins "on one of these horses that I love to my soul." On the videotape of the 2001 Rolex, at the show jumping round, as David went clear on Tex, the camera caught Sam hugging Karen and then turning away, the back of her hand wiping tears out of her eyes. When the first-placed competitor knocked down a rail, ceding the win to David, Sam heard the rail fall before anyone else did. When David turned to her to confirm what he thought he saw, she already had her arms around her horse. "I was bawling," she said.

David's score on Tailor puts him in fifth place, and at the edge of the ring he leaves through his swarming entourage. Karen passes him on her way in with Amber. The only groom not in David's entourage is Max, who stands alone at the rail, watching her horse. The last dressage ride of Rolex 2002 belongs to the quirky chestnut mare with the dramatic story, and as Karen enters the arena, the crowd cheers and applauds, spooking Amber. Karen pats down the air next to her with a small white-gloved hand, and, chagrined, the crowd falls silent. But it's too late; Amber is rattled, and her performance puts her in thirty-third place.

Phase one of the four-day ordeal is over, and the grooms are giddy. Tomorrow is the longest and most grueling day of competition, but before they can get some rest, they have to attend the demonstration that Karen and David have arranged to give with Pat Parelli. Ambitiously entitled "The Future of Training," the demonstration lasts four long hours. The grooms' attendance at the Parelli demonstrations is compulsory, and they've begun to tire of them. They're still enamored with the techniques, but the hype, the overlong demonstrations, and hearing the same anecdotes, which were funny the first time, again and again are wearing on their nerves. Tex and Prince Panache have been shipped to Kentucky just for this demonstration, and Sam stands at the entrance to the arena, with their reins looped over her arm. The rest of the grooms sit on the stairs along with Christiana Ober, the vet, joking and giggling. Vanessa runs to get Sam and herself some drinks from the concession stand. Seeing a huge line, she simply elbows her way to the front of it. She and Sam drink their Cokes in one gulp. Discouraged by the line and afraid that if she cuts in front again she'll get yelled at, Vanessa sucks on the ice cubes. Sam is more than tired; she's angry. Tomorrow is a long and dangerous day, and it is far more important to her, and to David and Karen, than this demonstration. It's after ten o'clock and way past everyone's bedtime before the horses are put away. The grooms still have to eat, get back to their motel, and shower so they can return before sunrise.

When cross-country day opens, the grooms are running on reserves of nervous energy. They fuel up on doughnuts that the massage therapist and the acupuncturist have provided. In the tack room are bags of snacks that the horses' owners and Sam's mother have brought for the grooms, knowing that there will be no time all day for them to get something to eat.

Outside the Kentucky Horse Park, state police have lined up traffic cones on the road outside in preparation for the 85,000 spectators and their cars. David describes Rolex as a destination event, one that not only riders but spectators plan their year around. One group of women friends claims that they have been coming to Rolex for ten years, their annual pilgrimage outlasting marriages, career changes, and cross-country moves. Scattered over the four-mile length of the cross-country course, fans huddle over their programs, picking out the differences in course design since last year. Families who mark the growth of their children in Rolex years lug beach chairs and coolers to the water jump (called the Head of the Lake), which is the most complex and spectator-friendly jump on the course. College equestrian teams and Pony Club groups cluster in their matching jackets, their trip to Rolex the culmination of a year's worth of fund-raising. There are hundreds of tents at the trade fair where vendors hawk everything from custom saddles to horse trailers to chocolates in the shape of running horses. There are dog agility competitions, Pony Club contests, and more Parelli demonstrations. There is even a pack of dogs from the local animal shelter wearing kerchiefs that say, "Adopt Me!"

What David loves about Rolex's cross-country course is the big galloping fields. The course designer, Englishman Michael Etherington-Smith, is not afraid to build huge fences — tall, wide, imposing — the kind that encourage horses to gallop forward bravely. For David, riding horses to fences is like running across the street at an intersection. You have to adjust your stride to the distance between the two curbs so that when you jump up onto the sidewalk, you don't land halfway there. At the four-star level, it's even more complicated. Not only are there those two curbs, but the street is rutted with potholes and there is a speed bump with a big puddle after it that has to be cleared. And before you are safe on the curb, there is also a little pile of trash that has to be jumped, and all of this has to be completed before the lights change, which they do after a scant few seconds, forcing you to sprint at top speed. On the cross-country course, after you've gotten through that first intersection, there are thirty more, all with different challenges, stretching ahead for the next four miles. You know the course; your horse doesn't.

Bold, forward riding makes it easier for the riders to calculate their horses' striding. Course designers have been improving the safety and rideability of their courses since the Barcelona Olympics in 1992. NBC's coverage of that event showed a horrifying spectacle of falls and crashes. After almost a century of obscurity, the sport of eventing found itself in the public eye as animal-rights activists cried foul and started picketing competitions. Even their peers in other equine disciplines suggested that eventers needed to look at what they were doing. The changes enacted were so sweeping, challenging the very premise of the sport, that other disciplines now look at the eventers' model when they want to enact changes in the safety and equine welfare of their sport. Their collective soul-searching initiated changes in course design, empowered organizers to add mandatory halts on course, gave volunteer fence judges the power to eliminate horses on course, and required more training for technical delegates; even the definition of a refusal was parsed, all to make the sport safer for the horses. The carnage of the early days of the sport, when the winner was the last horse standing at the end of the competition, is largely a thing of the past. But eventers still have a reputation for being crazy, and the sport is still defined by its danger, both to horse and rider.

In fairness, though, horses are lamed in all equestrian disciplines. "You can't make the sport safer than life itself," David argues. He points out that athletes die in all sports, even on high school football fields. Anything, he adds, that involves speed involves danger. Across the horse world, the most egregious criticism one rider can level at another is to question the quality of his horsemanship. In the internecine and competitive world of professional riders, that charge is leveled with discouraging frequency, sometimes for as mild a cause as trying something new. When it bears weight is when a horseman asks too much of his horse — pushing him into performing a job that the horse is clearly unhappy about or afraid of performing, and crossing the line into abuse. To the eventers' credit, the horses at Rolex appear to be happy doing their job. They jig and bounce in the start box, and seem eager to get onto the course. They stretch out in their gallops and turn to the fences, ears pricked, nostrils flared, demanding to be let loose to attack them. Along with the cheers of the spectators are spontaneous bursts of laughter as the fans are swept up in what can only be described as the horses' joy — their reaction to discovering just how powerful and courageous they really are. Ultimately, David says, "You can't explain why they do what they do."

The word *attack* figures largely in the pregame-strategy discussions of event riders, and as Karen readies herself for the first ride of the day, the stabling area looks like a command center. There are extra trucks loaded with veterinary supplies lined up next to the barns. Additional helpers have arrived for most of the riders, including the O'Connors. There are extra officials monitoring the activity on course. Outside the ladies' room a line of competent and severe-looking volunteer fence judges has formed. Joe Silva, of the Massachusetts arm of the ASPCA and the director of the equine ambulance program, is suddenly twice as visible as he has been for the past two days.

The tension in the stabling area is almost unbearable. This is an altogether different group of young women than the ones who've been giggling and joking for two days. Today their horses will complete four phases of speed and endurance. Phases A and C, called roads and track, require several miles of trotting. They bracket phase B, the five-minute steeplechase. Phase D is the cross-country phase. The horses will gallop over four miles of rolling terrain at speeds up to thirty-five miles an hour and jump almost fifty fences designed to not fall down.

In the tack room, her voice shaking, Vicky admits that she's scared. Sam is mute. The braiding kits, coat conditioners, and hair dyes have been packed away. Today, the grooms roll three layers of protective bandages onto the horses' legs. From a small case of shoe studs — cleats that screw into the horses' shoes—David picks the ones he thinks will give him the best traction with the same attention he would give to choosing diamonds. The bridles are sewn into the horses' manes, the loose leather flaps secured with electrician's tape. In the wee hours, the grooms lugged extra equipment to the two places on course where the horses are required to stop and rest: the C-halt, between phases B and C, and the vet box, the halt before cross-country where the horses are evaluated by a veterinarian before they are allowed to continue. The riders' shadbellys and top hats have been put away, replaced by crash helmets and body protector vests. The members of the entourage, including Sam's mother and David's father, are on hand in empty stalls during these preparations, ready to help but staying out of the way.

Karen, who rides first in the day's order, leaves the stabling area on Regal Scott, and David, who's riding fourth, follows later on ET. Sam softly wishes him good luck, and he smiles. Some competition days, she says, those are the only words she speaks to him all day. As soon as David leaves, Sam and Vanessa race for the grooms' shuttle that will take them to the C-halt. The shuttle they race to, though, is not the grooms' shuttle but the one for the spectators. For a few wild moments, they literally run in circles, Vanessa several steps behind Sam, until Sam spins around and bumps into her as she races off in the other direction, Vanessa at her heels. They look like Laurel and Hardy as they try to figure out where *their* shuttle is. Sam is so accustomed to figuring things out for herself, to never asking for help, that several minutes pass before it occurs to her to get directions from someone in the secretary's office, the building they've been running around.

Vanessa retrieves the minibike from the barn while Sam learns that the shuttle is on the other side of the stabling area, and they race off, weighed down by coolers and halters. Karen's three grooms are already at the C-halt when they arrive.

There is so little drama in the first three phases of speed and endurance, just horses trotting in a field, that most of the spectators don't even know where they're located. Samantha stands outside the tape with the O'Connors' two farriers. There are no spectators anywhere, just grooms and officials. David appears at the top of the hill, signaling her to slip under the tape and hand him a water bottle.

In the C-halt, ET is nervous and half wild, dragging Sam and Vanessa around at the end of his lead shank while David rests, watching them from a folding chair. After the mandatory ten minutes, he trots out for phase C, and Sam, Vanessa, and one of the farriers scramble into the bed of the shuttle — a pickup truck with the rear gate down — that takes them to the vet box, where they will wait for him. Deep layers of clouds have been gathering all morning, and in the back of the shuttle, everyone is cold, wishing they'd brought their jackets. The farrier huddles up against the sexy and lighthearted Vanessa, sharing her warmth.

David trots into the vet box just as Karen trots out of it. ET is sweaty and blowing lightly, his head up and ears pricked. The farrier stoops to inspect ET's shoes and studs. Before cross-country, ET's legs need to be greased, to help him slide over any fences he knocks, but he's not interested in grease. He rolls a hind leg all the way up to his hip socket and lashes out at the helper holding the grease bucket. Every time she gets close, his hoof flies out with bone-shattering speed. Sam looks mildly amused, like the mother of a disobedient child who is nonetheless impressed by the strength of her child's will.

The British accent of the Rolex announcer, Nigel Casserly, contributes to the Anglophile atmosphere that the organizers like to perpetuate, in emulation of the spiritual home of the sport, Badminton, England. Nigel's job is to call the rides and provide droll color commentary. He calls Karen clear, clear, clear over those first few jumps of the course visible from the vet box. Everyone cheers except Sam and Vanessa, who are getting knocked around by ET. Just as David stands up after his rest, Nigel announces that Karen has fallen at the Head of the Lake. The O'Connor team stops, tilting their heads toward his voice, waiting for his announcement that she's back on. It arrives at the same time as the distant cheer from the spectators at the water jump. She is safe, but she has just accrued sixty penalty points on her best horse. With only a few points separating the leaders of the competition, Karen is out of a top placing unless everyone else falls off too.

The vet box and the finish line are both located in an area the size of a high school football field. There is also a yellow tent housing TV monitors and two-way radios that officials, riders, and the horses' owners use to follow progress on course. Miles of video cable link up cameras at each fence that broadcast to the tent, the vet box, the announcer's booth, the press box, and to a mammoth TV screen set up for the spectators in the middle of the course.

David's foot is in the stirrup when Karen, soaking wet from her dip in the water, crosses the finish line. He turns away from ET and jogs across the box, calling her name, his voice tight with worry. Karen reassures him with a wave, and he mounts up and rides out.

Vicky leads Regal Scott between two parallel rows of buckets full of ice water. His tack and leg wraps, which took twenty minutes to strap on and adjust, are ripped off as if they are on fire. His entire body is covered with an oily layer of sweat. White lather, frothed up by the friction of his galloping, coats the insides of his back legs and lies in a band across his chest where his skin rubbed against his breastplate. Veins have popped to the surface of his skin, throbbing, trying to cool the blood that races through them. Vicky and her helpers frantically sponge ice water on him, wicking it off on contact because the heat of his body warms it instantly. Scotty's eyes are glazed, and his sides heave as he tries to catch his breath. He looks intoxicated. Vicky is trying to walk him so his muscles don't seize up, but the vet needs to get his temperature and heart rate. Vicky dances from foot to foot, muttering, "Hurry up! Hurry up!"

Scotty is only the first of Karen's four horses, and she's already taken a bath. Every time she is on course, Nigel reminds the spectators that over the span of the day, Karen will gallop forty-four miles. She will also make almost two hundred jumping efforts — more than any other rider here, a feat that doesn't surprise her competitors. When she was still Karen Lende, she had as brutal a fall as a rider can have when she was competing at the Seoul Olympics in 1988. Her horse, suffering from some kind of optical illusion, perceived two separate jumps when there really was only a wide space between the front and back poles of a single jump. He dropped his legs into it. She was launched over his shoulders, her head the pivot point of a full-length body flip. Traveling at twenty-five miles an hour, she slammed into the ground flat on her back. Miraculously, she re-mounted and, dumbfoundingly, her horse made the same mistake again, slamming her into the ground a second time. She was clearly bleary-eyed as she remounted a second time, stabbing her toe into the air next to the stirrup. On her third approach, her horse obviously decided that he'd had enough of this fence that was springing to life and grabbing his legs. To everyone's relief, he slid to a stop and they were eliminated. Fourteen years later, Karen is still just as tough.

As David disappears from sight, Sam listens to Nigel. Earlier in the week she walked the course and now has a picture in her head of every jump as David goes over them on her little black horse. Almost halfway through, ET ar-rives at the water jump where Karen fell and skids to a stop. Nigel announces that David is raising his hand and with-drawing ET from the competition. Sam lingers in the vet box and then, realizing that ET won't be crossing the adja-cent finish line, sprints out the gate and across the field to the barn.

In the stabling area, she cools out ET and puts him away. She's relieved that David pulled up. "He has always been a cross-country machine," she says of ET. When she saw him struggling over the first few fences of the course, she says, "he just didn't seem like my horse." Patience and careful training have transformed ET from a loser into a winner at the three-star level, but David's prediction is right. He isn't a four-star horse. Sam responds to that assessment with a shrug. "We'll see." She smiles.

The rain starts to fall just before lunch, as Karen is run-ning the course on her second horse, Grand Slam. As spec-tators hurry to their cars, Nigel reminds them that the trade fair has rain ponchos for sale. ET is sulking, his butt turned to the stall door. David heads out on Tigger Too, the horse the team has pinned its hopes on. He has turned in his best dressage score ever, and the U.S. Equestrian Team has always been interested in him. He's never had a fault on cross-country, according to David. He has risen through the ranks of nameless, faceless failed racehorses to prove his worth in another discipline, a transition that few ex-racehorses ever accomplish. Tex and Tailor, the stars of the barn, are, at sixteen and seventeen, in the twilight of their careers. It is Tigger, the bright chestnut with the freckled face, who is the rising sun of the O'Connor Event Team.

The lunch break has emptied out the vet box. Only a few officials are there, waiting for David, the first rider, to arrive. When David appears on the hill, they are not expecting a rider for several more minutes. One of the entourage members, sitting in a chair under a tarp, looks at her watch. "What's he doing here?" she asks. The officials come to the doorway of the tent, looking at their watches and asking the same question. It's too soon for David to be here. Coming alongside the course, Sam pounds on the window of the grooms' shuttle, begging the driver to hurry up.

David is arriving too early because he missed a flag on phase C. He has gone off course and has turned up the hill too soon, skipping the last several minutes of the phase. He doesn't know it yet, but Sam does, because she saw it happen from the back of the truck. She says nothing as she leaps out and takes Tigger's reins from David's hands. She'll let the officials tell him that he's eliminated and won't be allowed to complete the rest of the course. They gather around him in the rain as he stares at his feet. "I got wrapped up in the moment," he explains, "because Tigger went ballistic on me. Just thinking more about him than what I was doing." For the second time that day, Sam's route back to the barn starts at the vet box instead of the finish line. Grim and unsmiling, with time on his hands he hadn't planned on, David stares down the hill at the flag he missed.

Karen arrives in the box on Upstage and, without looking at her, hands him off to Vicky. She and David meet in the middle of the box. Two heads shorter than David, Karen tilts her chin up, her hands on her hips in the universal symbol of a woman who expects to be answered to.

"I'm not the kind of person who makes that type of mistake," David says later, but he almost made a similar mistake at the 2000 Sydney Olympics. Just a few jumps away from a gold medal — the prize his to keep or lose — David nearly went off course in the final show jumping round. He and Tailor landed over a jump, and then David looked around the ring, clearly lost. Tailor, ears pricked, turned his head left and right, mirroring David's. He switched leads from right to left as he tried to figure out where David wanted him to go. The crowd gasped as those precious seconds threatened to tick over into time penalties. Then, his brain returning from wherever it had gone, David pointed Tailor at the next fence. That year, he won the gold medal anyway, so it was easy to tease him about his near disaster. For months, Sam says, everywhere they went, his fellow competitors offered to get David a map.

Tigger's elimination is too bitter a disappointment for comment. Nothing will be said about it until later that evening, when a tipsy fellow competitor waves away the mistake. "I've got to cut him some slack," he says. "I wanted to skip that flag too. Who wants to go all the way out there and come back?"

David has one horse left, Tailor, his veteran and best friend, who can do anything that David asks of him except memorize his course in advance.

Karen is just about to mount up on Upstage when a

dozen officials come flying out of the tent. Joe Silva, the ambulance driver, has his two-way radio to his ear as he races to his truck and trailer. Grooms in the vet box jump onto minibikes and zoom over the hill. What they've seen on the video monitor, even before Nigel announces it, is that Mark Weissbecker and his horse Titleist have fallen at fence ten. Everyone in the vet box is straining to hear Nigel's voice through the wind and rain. He calls the ride of the competitor on course ahead of Titleist, and when she finishes, the loudspeakers go silent.

Karen is pacing while Vicky walks Upstage. Trying to fill that terrible silence, Nigel and his fellow announcers gamely interview one another. Minute after minute of horrible emptiness ticks by. They fill it with a distracted interview of a retired official. There is more silence, and then the hold that was called, stopping the horses behind Titleist from going forward after he fell, is lifted. Karen trots out to the start box on Upstage.

In the stabling area, no one is saying anything about Titleist, but Sam knows what happened. He broke his neck. The groom who tells Sam this also asks that she not say anything to David and Karen, because no one wants the other riders to know yet, although many do.

A soft wall goes up around eventers when a horse dies in their midst. The only official record will be a terse press release issued at the end of the day. Nigel doesn't announce the fatality, nor does he ask for a moment of silence from the spectators to commemorate the passing of an equine soul. Quietly, the riders glean the details from one another, but too much talk feels unseemly, as if they are dwelling on the tragedy or, superstitiously, inviting it to happen to them, which is always a horrible possibility. "I put it the same as a person dying," David, who has never lost a horse, says about Titleist's death.

The riders are vulnerable when a horse dies, fragile in the face of the evidence that what they are doing is asking their horses to risk their lives in pursuit of athletic glory. Pointing out that most fatal injuries happen to horses when they're in their paddock or stall, or that until they break down in competition, sport horses receive the most tender and exquisite care in the world, seems like defensive posturing. Instead, the riders mount up and kick on.

The rain only gets worse over the day. All but the hardiest spectators leave. The trade fair empties. The riders who complete the course rack up time faults; in the deep, slippery footing others simply withdraw and trudge home at a walk. David's ride on Tailor is the second to last of the day. Karen will be last on Bally Mar. About ten horses before David is scheduled to head out, he suggests to Samantha that maybe he shouldn't run. This is the first time, he says, that it occurred to him. Tacked up, taped, bandaged, and sewn into his gear, Tailor stands under the eave of the barn, his reins looped over Sam's arm, ready to go. Nigel announces seventeen and twenty time faults on the steeplechase phase for the horses in first and second places. "Nope, nope, not running him." David laughs later when he describes Sam's resolute response to the news that even the best horses are running too slowly to win. She is already pulling off Tailor's gear when David tells her to wait. She is scared to death. Sick to her stomach. "Anything could happen out there," she says. "As small as a tendon or as big as flipping over a fence and killing himself," which, no one needs to point out, has already happened today.

"If we're having some kind of conflict," David says of his grooms, "if somebody doesn't agree with what we're doing, we have to deal with that after the competition." The only person who can stop David from running the horse is the horse's owner, and he isn't there. While David

changes, still considering whether or not to run, Sam turns
to her mother. "This might be his last four-star," Sam says,
weighing in against running Tailor in the torrential rain.
"He doesn't need to do this." The coach of the U.S. Equestrian Three-Day team tells David the same thing. They
know what the horse can do; he's already on the list for the
World Games. Like an incantation, Nigel calls time faults,
refusals, and horses being withdrawn as riders bail out on
the cross-country course.

David rides out to start phase A. Sam's mother and
Vanessa pat her arm, reassuring her that David will take care
of her horse. "He knew how scared I was," Sam says later.
He promised her that he would stop if it was dangerous.
"David makes good decisions," she says. "He would never
hurt one of these horses if he could help it." Of the final
fifteen horses of the afternoon, thirteen are withdrawn, retired on course, or eliminated. In the vet box, David includes Tailor in that group of thirteen, then Karen rides in
on Bally Mar, the last horse of the day, drops the reins, and
throws up her hands. Smiling and patting Tailor on the
shoulder, Sam takes his reins and leads him back to the
safety of the barn.

The riders who have withdrawn their horses gather in
the tent with the officials and the owners. The last rider still
on course is Bruce Davidson, aboard Little Tricky. At fifty-
two, still competing at the four-star level, still trying out for
the U.S. team, of which he has been a member off and on
for over twenty years, Bruce is the far out old man of
Three-Day Eventing. A veteran of every competition in the
world, he isn't going to let a little rain stop his run at Rolex.
Little Tricky's ears are pricked, and water splashes up under
his hooves as if he's galloping through surf. In the tent, the
riders and owners hold their breath and release it collec-
tively as Little Tricky nails his striding and launches himself

neatly, cleanly, and bravely over fences that he can barely see in the torrent. Bruce, tall and wiry, folds up his body at each jump, balanced and light in the saddle. As Little Tricky turns to the last fence, those people who aren't already standing are on their feet, waiting to see if Bruce and his game little horse will pull it off. As he clears the last fence and turns toward the finish line, raucous cheers fill the tent as the riders, who could officially call themselves the day's losers, cheer Bruce and Little Tricky all the way home.

Given the outcome of the day for the O'Connors, it is the grooms and not the horses who are in need of pampering back in the stabling area. They're cold and drenched as they tuck the horses in for the night. Regal Scott's knee is swollen from his crash at the water jump; he won't be competing in the show jumping round of the competition. Tigger Too is having his feet soaked in a pan of Epsom salts. The drinks are going around, and Vanessa jokes about raiding the stash of Maker's Mark that the distillery supplies for one of the riders they sponsor. A team of veterinarians that includes Christiana Ober and Kent Allen is watching the O'Connors' other horses jog. Dr. Allen has brought along his teenage son, who chatters incessantly, intoxicated by the presence of all these young women. The massage therapist and acupuncturist are slipping in and out of the stalls. The horses' legs are smeared with poultice and then bandaged in soft, comforting standing wraps. Drenched, riders are sitting on the tack trunks all over the stabling area, babbling about the rain, which has finally stopped.

Snug and dry in their stable rugs, David's horses are ready for bed. He walks down the aisle, saying good night. He pats Tigger's face and tells him he's sorry. At Tailor's stall, David has no words and down the line, he wags a finger at ET's delicate face. "You," he says, "were bad." ET responds by offering David his butt.

Out of the seven horses the O'Connors brought to the competition, only two will compete in show jumping, and their placement is so low that the final phase is merely a completion exercise. Sam giddily jokes about having nothing to do, while Vicky prepares Grand Slam and Upstage, who finish the competition in twelfth and twenty-fourth places. There are no consolation prizes for the horses whose day was taken away from them by the rain. The winners are the horses who ran early in the day. The spectators cheer anyway. They have returned in droves to slough through the ankle-deep mud at the trade fair, taking advantage of last-day sales, and they line up at ringside to see Kim Vinoski take her victory gallop on Winsome Adante.

Rolex 2002 is a terrible disappointment for the O'Connor team. Looking at his career, David says, is like filling in a list of check boxes. Along with the ones that include his first four-star, his first team competition, and winning an Olympic gold medal, is a new one for missing a flag on the endurance phase. The good news is that Tigger made the long list for the Worlds in Spain anyway, joining Tailor, who was also added. Their stablemate Tex was listed even before Rolex. There is good news for ET as well. "He won't be sold," David says. He is too difficult and challenging a horse to sell to a less experienced horseman or to partner a young rider through the start of her career. David's quest, more than winning Rolex or any other single competition, is to be a better horseman, and ET has helped him along that path. He is going home to Virginia. "We'll just enjoy him," David says. "He's got a life with us."

On Monday morning, the O'Connor grooms pack the rig early and wait for the final "in-barn," the last official inspection of the horses by the U.S. team. Discovering that

they're last on the list, they leave for lunch. When they return, the sun is out, though it's still cold. The horses have
obviously been napping while the grooms were gone, but
they poke their heads out of their stalls expectantly, as if the
grooms might have brought them a doggy bag or might be
organizing some game they would enjoy. With his teeth,
ET grabs a lead shank and flings it onto the ground. Not
getting the reaction he wants, he picks up his halter and,
like a baby throwing toys from a high chair, tosses it out
into the aisle for Sam to retrieve. She ignores him. He grabs
the last thing left he can reach, the index card with his name
on it stapled to his stall. Sam glares at him from across the
barn. He waves the card in the air cheekily until she laughs.
When she approaches him, he drops it on the ground and
pretends he doesn't know how it got there. She pats him
and coils up his lead rope, clipping it to his stall so he can
chew and tug on it all he wants.

The grooms throw stable rugs on the ground in the sun
and then curl up back to back, two per rug, and try to nap.
The grounds are quiet. The grooms, the horses, and the officials are the last souls left in the Kentucky Horse Park. A
blustery wind, the remainder of the weekend tornadoes that
touched down outside Lexington, blows up and down the
empty aisles. The trees, whose new buds looked so tender
and hopeful in the warm days before the competition, now
seem bare and vulnerable in the flat afternoon light. The
groundskeepers who buzzed around with weed whackers
and flowerpots in the days leading up to the competition
seem happy to let the dead leaves and paper debris blow
across the grounds and gather in the corners of the empty
tents. The vendors are gone, leaving behind trampled grass
and deep mud. The leaderboard is still up, though it looks
as if it has been there since last year — the information on
it already very old news.

On fence ten of the cross-country course, identified in the program as Rails, Ditch and Rails, although it is traditionally known as a coffin jump, there is a wilted grocery-store bouquet of flowers turning brown, the cellophane wrapper crinkling in the wind. Stuffed in between the rails are some crumpled marigolds. The flowers were placed there by a ten-year-old girl whose aunt gave her the trip to Rolex as a gift. They were standing at the fence together when Titleist crashed into it.

Somewhere on course, Titleist threw a shoe. His rider, Mark Weissbecker, thought he felt something off in the horse's stride, but when Titleist boldly and sure-footedly tackled fence nine, he seemed fine. Between fences nine and ten, Titleist threw a second shoe. As he galloped down toward the jump, Titleist planted his front hooves for take-off and went skidding. If he hadn't been a giving and generous horse, he would have skidded into the fence just like that — flipping both himself and his rider over it. But he did the dead-honest thing and with his eleven-hundred-pound body skidding at almost twenty-five miles an hour, he lifted up his front legs and tried to clear the jump, catching his hind legs instead. His rider was thrown clear and was unhurt. Titleist fell and broke his neck. Dead within two minutes of hitting the ground.

What Titleist saw as he galloped through the rain was the next two fences and then beyond it a broad, grassy field that swept uphill until it met the tree line. The spectators were behind the tape, and after fence ten, there was nothing between Titleist and fence eleven but a fast gallop. Just him and his rider and the firm ground his legs would have devoured as he sped on to his next fence. What a fast jumping horse would call heaven.

Chapter Seven

PRODUCTION LINE

The Rolex fans clear out of their motels just in time for the Kentucky Derby fans to fill them up again. For the grooms at Lane's End, Derby fever means that in addition to being stud grooms, they have to double as tour guides as Derby fans arrive by the busload at the gates of the farm. After the morning breeding session, the grooms tuck in their shirts, smooth their hair under their baseball caps, and escort their assigned groups around the stallion complex. Ideally, the stallions are in their paddocks, where their fans can admire them from afar, instead of in their stalls, where the tourists often make the mistake of feeding them their fingers. "Every year," one of the grooms says after waving goodbye to his group, "someone gets bitten."

The tourists are as diverse as those you'd see at any

national monument. A group of Japanese businessmen arrives, on an annual pilgrimage to see Kingmambo, a horse whom the Japanese breeding industry has offered as much as $30 million for in the past. There is a group of thirteen young women from Colorado State. Ever the matchmaker, Jill McCully assigns them to the most adorable agriculture student. Nervous about his first tour, he turns his stud catalog into a crib sheet. Over the stallions' foaling dates, he writes their current ages, double-checking his math with the other grooms. There are breeders here as well, separated from the large groups and escorted through the barns in twos and threes, their voices soft as they conduct their preliminary business. The breeders are probably the only visitors who really understand what they're looking at. Each name in a horse's pedigree actually means something to them: sprinting speed, potency, precocious development, or late blooming. Their knowledgeable eyes travel over the horses' bodies, noting minor conformation flaws that are often invisible to even experienced horsemen. Preparing for her third tour of the day, Jill McCully wishes aloud that everyone would stop at the nearby Kentucky Horse Park first for a Horses 101 course. Historically, most breeding farms only allowed members of the industry to visit, but the National Thoroughbred Racing Association (NTRA) has been encouraging greater inclusion of racing's dwindling fans. Jill McCully would love to talk about pedigrees and breeding, but she ends up trying to hide her annoyance with questions like why aren't there any geldings on the farm.

Some of the fans are here because they love horses. Quiet and respectful, they linger at paddock rails or outside the horses' stalls, unable to tear themselves away; no amount of time could satiate them, and the grooms clear their throats and wait impatiently. For others, like the group that sets up a tailgate picnic in the driveway, the trip to Lane's End is just another way station in a weeklong bender of food and bourbon that will culminate in Saturday's race at Churchill Downs in Louisville. They make the trip to the stud farm for the same reason that conventioneers in Detroit, stuck with time on their hands, might visit an auto manufacturer — because this is the birthplace of a singular American product: the Thoroughbred racehorse. They scan the immensity of the grounds. Their heads tilt upward the vaulted ceilings of the barns. They run their hands over the gleaming brass and wood of the stalls and discover that there is not a single corner that has been left undusted by the grooms, who stand like uniformed footmen in attendance on their horses. Those clues are an indication that *somebody,* and somebody with very deep pockets, values these horses highly.

Numbers provide meaning in the Thoroughbred industry. Individual horse's résumés are evaluated by stud fees, number of stakes races won, percentage of winning foals, number of starts compared to number of wins. Kentucky horsemen rattle off these numbers, as versed in their meaning as stockbrokers are with the Dow average. The *Jockey Club Fact Book* and its Web site are compendiums of pie charts and bar graphs. The obsession with numbers is partly the universal search for data to support a gambler's hunch, and partly just the language of production.

Making money in Kentucky has less to do with producing winning racehorses, all of whom combine some alchemy of DNA and desire, than with the sound business practice of producing the right product at the right price. According to *The Blood-Horse,* an industry publication, two thirds of Kentucky's breeding farms make less than $75,000 per year. Without the funds to buy the services of popular stallions, they survive by producing a quantity of yearlings in the low to middle price range. "What I think we have at the moment," says Geoffrey Russell, director of sales at the Keeneland auction house, "is an overproduction of commercial horses." Commercial horses are not the ones who run the Kentucky Derby, they are the ones who populate the race cards of small-time tracks in places like Boston, Oklahoma, and West Virginia. The success of these tracks is more often linked to slot machines than the thrill of racing. The Thoroughbred industry is struggling to hold on to its audience with the legalization of riverboat gambling trips and Indian reservation casinos throughout the country, and if slot machines are more of a draw than horses, racetrack owners want them.

The stakes are high for Kentucky. Horses are the state's number one agricultural crop. In 2001, the Kentucky Derby alone brought $92 million to the state. This is a heavy financial burden for a product that Geoffrey Russell calls "a very luxury item."

Ultimately, the winning racehorse, who bests his peers in high-quality races like those of the Triple Crown, is the product that drives the entire industry. NTRA's national advertising campaign shows an impassioned young woman in a fetching hat at a crowded ringside screaming, "Go, baby, go!" A more accurate image of the contemporary race fan would be a gnarled, down-on-his-luck senior citizen who is just as likely to be watching a simulcast of a distant race as the one taking place before his eyes. For those fans, the horses are not "baby"; they're not even named, they're numbers. What all the fans share, though, is an experience of the sublime. For his two-dollar bet, the railbird can buy a small piece of the risk that is shared by the jockey, the trainer, the superrich owner, the horse, and the comely young woman in the hat.

Perhaps their proximity to the horses, their actual day-to-day knowledge of them, is what makes the grooms at Lane's End rather uninterested in the Derby, other than for the fans it brings to the farm. There is some mild speculation about the race at the barn, but the biggest reminder of the Derby is Charismatic taking even longer than usual in the breeding shed. "He's remembering the Derby," Bill Sellers jokes. "Remembering D'Wayne. Remembering being sore."

For the grooms, Louisville on Derby Day is a good place to get run over by a drunk. Kenneth has never even been to a Derby. The grooms don't have any hot tips; they're placing their bets according to the same advice everyone else is using. They're not even excited about Came Home, the horse running in the Lane's End colors. For the grooms, Derby day is another workday, one on which their schedule is light so they can get home in time to watch the race on TV.

Jill McCully likes to say that Lane's End emphasizes quality, not quantity. Even though they have fewer horses than their main competitors, in 2000 and 2001, Lane's End was the leading consignor of yearlings at Keeneland's prestigious September sale. At each of those auctions, they also sold the highest-priced filly and colt. In 2000, the colt set a world record, selling for $6.8 million. Aside from grabbing the front page of the *Daily Racing Form,* a sale that high also skewed the averages. The average price of a yearling at that sale was $54,000, but the *median* price, what most farms were trying to achieve, was just $11,500. In 2001, it dropped to $9,000. Lane's End represented only the very top echelon of the 30–35,000 foals that were part of the North American registered crop that year.

The winner of the 2002 Kentucky Derby, War Emblem, was sold for $20,000 as a yearling. Just weeks before the Derby, he was sold again, for $900,000, to Saudi Arabian breeder Prince Ahmed bin Salman, who didn't have a

Derby contender that year. Along with his trainer, Bob Baffert, bin Salman was sourly accused of having bought the Derby. Everyone buys the Derby, bin Salman responded, according to a *Harper's* magazine article written by John Jeremiah Sullivan. "If you tell me who is going to win [next year]," he said, "I'll buy him again." While not a popular image of a horse owner, his was a truthful one. Racing may be called the "sport of kings," but it's also a business, one that refers to broodmares as factories and the annual arrival of foals as a crop. "Back to Economics 101," Geoffrey Russell explains when pointing out the difference in value between pregnant and barren broodmares. "You're selling a factory. You want to be sure she's in production."

This cynicism, coupled with industry insiders' inclination to compare contemporary horses unfavorably with their predecessors, gives the impression that the heyday of American racing is in the past. It has been twenty-five years since a horse has won the Triple Crown. And no contemporary horse has created the excitement that the racehorses of the seventies, Secretariat, Seattle Slew, and Affirmed, did, or equaled the enthusiasm and hype surrounding the match race between Kentucky Derby winner Foolish Pleasure and the glorious, doomed filly Ruffian. In 1975, two years after Wimbledon champion Billie Jean King beat Bobby Riggs in the "Battle of the Sexes," Ruffian and Foolish Pleasure met for a match race that was quickly characterized as an equine battle of the sexes. Fans could declare their loyalty by sporting T-shirts and buttons advertising the Great Match Race with one of two horses' names underneath. New York's Off Track Betting printed 200,000 of their own buttons, each with a single word, *Him* or *Her*. The horses' jockeys, Jacinto Vasquez and Braulio Baeza, appeared on *The Tonight Show* and were given special awards from the New York City Athletic and Community Task Force. Then, on

July 6, in front of 50,000 fans at Belmont Park and an additional 18 million watching on TV, Ruffian shattered her leg after opening up a lead on the colt. Fans stayed glued to their televisions and radios, waiting to hear that the veterinarians had saved her, only to wake up the following morning to the news that she had been euthanized overnight. Her death was the low point in what many people believe was the greatest decade in American racing.

In the eighties, even though there was a massive bubble of investment in racehorses that coincided with the economic prosperity of the time, no one horse captured and held the public's attention. Geneticists Barry Gaffney and Patrick Cunningham from Trinity College in Dublin have offered an explanation. Evaluating the race times of every three-year-old racehorse in Britain between 1966 and 1985, they found that the winning horses had gotten no faster during that time. Packs ran closer together as the speed of the average horse improved, but the elite runners were racing at the same speeds they had for thirty years. Northern Dancer won the Kentucky Derby in two minutes in 1964, and nine years later, Secretariat broke that record by coming in under two minutes. (Such was the excellence of the sport that year that the second-place finisher, Sham, also broke the two-minute record. He and Alydar, who made a career out of coming in second to Affirmed, are the patron saints of the also-rans.) Until Monarchos in 2001, no one came near Secretariat's Derby record, and no one at all has come close to his victories in the Preakness and Belmont Stakes. In a 1997 article in *U.S. News and World Report,* Stephen Budiansky summarized the search for a faster racehorse in an article entitled "Too Fast to Get Faster." Horses, unlike humans, he explained, have evolved as superb running animals. Their starting aerobic fitness is so high considering their body mass that there simply isn't much room for improvement. Additionally, horses have anatomical limitations. Their breathing and their movement is coupled. When a horse's front feet hit the ground, his head and neck lower and the rib cage moves up and to the rear, squeezing the lungs. When the horse lifts his forelegs off the ground, the movement is reversed: his head and neck come up, his rib cage slides forward, and his lungs expand. The linkage between stride and breathing means that horses can only run faster by lengthening their stride. Physiologically and mechanically speaking, horses have reached the limit of their ability. It would make sense, then, that breeding for the longest stride would produce faster racehorses. But, as Budiansky points out, equine social psychology is a huge part of why a horse wins. Breeders breed to winners because racing lore is full of ugly little horses who made it to the winner's circle.

The hope for the industry lies in the fact that the diehard fans who can actually compare one year's Derby to its predecessors are a very small group. Racehorses don't have to get faster; they only have to be faster than the horses they are running against, all of whom come from the same gene pool. According to Budiansky, it's a gene pool in which any two horses have 13 percent of their genes in common, more than that between half siblings.

The Jockey Club stud book has been closed to new blood since 1791, restricting innovative breeders from bringing new blood into the Thoroughbred line. Compounding that problem is the fact that most races, unlike those of the Triple Crown, are sprints — under a mile long. To fill the race cards at the majority of tracks, many of which are too small to run long races, breeders of commercial horses are producing not distance runners but sprinters, who peak early in their careers and then retire to the breeding shed, where they can start returning some of their owners' investment.

There is a whisper of change in the business. Owners interested in buying broodmares want to see them win more than one or two races before they invest in them as breeding stock. One breeder has revealed that one of his owners asked him to breed a horse that could do two turns (over a mile) and do it for five years. These demands, Bill Sellers believes, will be good for Thoroughbreds, as breeders will respond by producing long-term soundness over precocious speed.

While War Emblem was winning the Derby, Lane's End stallion Summer Squall ran a Derby of his own in the breeding shed as he struggled to get a mare pregnant. Her van driver, waiting in the observation room, counted thirty-one covers before Summer Squall ejaculated into his mare. The following day, Summer Squall is so tired that he is unwilling to perform his signature trick, offering to shake hands in exchange for a peppermint.

Luckily for him, there's a more interesting performance to watch. As guests of the Farishes, Pat Parelli and his wife, Linda, are at the barn. Lane's End is trying to incorporate the Parelli methods in the training of yearlings, in hopes that more obedient babies will bring higher prices at the sales. They've made the almost unheard-of decision to hire an outside trainer to work with their horses. Parelli is also there, along with one of his trainers, Hanze, to work with Parade Ground.

When Parade Ground arrived at Lane's End from the racetrack, he was "not a bad horse to fool with," as Kenneth says. For reasons they can't explain, Parade Ground has "gone south" on the staff. He is now so dangerous that it takes two grooms, each holding on to the separate lariats that the horse wears, along with a bit and a muzzle, to lead him to and from the breeding shed and in and out of his paddock. The lariats are never taken off. When he is in his stall or turned out the lariats trail behind him. They've called in Parelli, Jill McCully says, because they're worried that the horse might kill one of his grooms.

Parelli believes that aggressive horses are reacting out of fear and insecurity. His theory is supported by the research of Katherine Houpt, who writes in her book on domestic-animal behavior that horses who are high in the equine hierarchy are usually the least problematic for handlers, as are the horses at the bottom of the herd — in other words, horses who know their place are easiest to deal with. Confident stallions, those like A.P. Indy who have dominated their herds, can be trusted, once human leadership is established, to behave themselves around humans. Smart, insecure horses like Parade Ground renegotiate on a daily basis. They don't know where they fall in the herd, so every social interaction is a battle for them as they try to figure out their place. The more intelligent a horse is, the craftier those negotiations become. "Most humans," Parelli says, "want a dumb horse — one without the brains to complain." Samuel Johnson, the eighteenth-century lexicographer, made a similar observation when he described what men looked for in women: "Men know that women are an overmatch of them, and therefore they choose the weakest or the most ignorant. If they did not think so, they could never be afraid of a woman knowing as much as themselves." Parade Ground's current groom thinks that the horse is very smart. He makes the same observation about him that everyone makes of A.P. Indy: that he's always watching, always has his eye on the grooms and what's going on in the barn. It is precisely this intelligence, combined with his insecurity, that has made Parade Ground such a dangerous horse.

Hanze has already been working with the stallion for a week. In that time, the horse has shed his two lariats and his muzzle, and on Sunday morning, Hanze leads him into the breeding shed single-handedly. When it comes time for Parelli to demonstrate his techniques to the Farishes, their family, their friends, and the jockey Chris McCarron and his wife, as well as the Hollywood production team of Laura Hillenbrand's *Seabiscuit* movie, Hanze hands off a rehabilitated horse. In his cowboy hat and Wrangler jeans, Parelli lunges Parade Ground in a small clearing next to the breeding shed.

David O'Connor partnered with Pat Parelli because of all the methods of natural horsemanship, he says, Parelli's are the easiest to teach. Parelli has condensed his system to a boilerplate that he calls the Seven Games. He starts riders off with the Friendly Game, one in which they accustom the horse to their touch. While the horse gets used to being touched, the handler learns where the horse is sensitive and what gestures make him nervous. From there, the horse learns to move away from pressure, which is counter to his instinct to push into pressure, as he would do if he were being attacked by a predator. Ultimately, as the rider becomes more adept at interpreting the horse's sophisticated body language, the horse will learn to trust the rider and look to him for what Parelli calls leadership, in much the same way the horse would look to a dominant member of his herd. Parelli's methods differ from traditional training methods in that they rely more on rewards for good behavior than on punishment for bad behavior, and the onus of understanding is on the rider, not the horse. Parelli likes to emphasize that his techniques can be mastered by anyone, distancing himself from those trainers who refer to themselves as "horse whisperers." He has good reason to highlight that difference. Horses whisperers are derided among most horsemen as charlatans preying on frustrated and unknowledgeable horse owners. As Verlyn Klinkenborg writes in his book *The Rural Life:* "There's no such thing as a horse whisperer. There never has been and never will be. The idea is an affront to the horse."

Most of the people in the crowd gathering to watch Parelli have no idea how dangerous Parade Ground is, or even that horses sometimes attack their human handlers. One of Kenneth's former charges, a stallion named King Pelinor, once grabbed a groom by the throat, flung him to the ground, and buried his teeth in the man's chest, opening up a hole that required the groom to wear a drainage tube for six months. "These horses," Kenneth says, "any time, they could take a man out. No problem." A week after King Pelinor attacked the groom, Kenneth went into his paddock with him, and the stallion charged him as well. Kenneth managed to escape. "My mistake," he says, "was thinking the horse wouldn't do it to *me*." Parelli makes no such mistake with Parade Ground. Parade Ground, he says, is one of the five most dangerous horses he's ever seen. The horse looks cooperative enough, but when Parelli takes him to the round pen, he doesn't go inside with him. He stands on the back of a farm cart parked outside the ring, holding Parade Ground's lunge line from behind the safety of the fence.

What if, Parelli asks the crowd, your horse *steered* better than the horses he was running against? What if your horse could win races not because he was the fastest horse but because he was the most responsive, the most willing to follow the jockey's suggestions? Given that elite runners don't appear capable of getting any faster, and that the middle-of-the-pack runners are closing the gap between themselves and the leaders, superior handling sounds like a winning strategy. Ambassador Farish and Chris McCarron wear expressions of studied blankness, as if this idea is either the most ingenious one they have ever heard or the most ridiculous.

There's more than just obedience at stake for Parade Ground. At only $7,500 per session, he's not the most spectacularly bred horse in the barn. He is well-known in the area for his aggression, and Farish worries that the horse's reputation might keep breeders from sending their mares to him. Without intervention, Parade Ground's future is bleak. In his current condition, he is useless as a pleasure or show horse. No one is going to fall in love with him and make him a pet. He has to prove himself as a breeding stallion or he's destined for the slaughterhouse.

The grooms skip the demonstration. Parelli's jolly overtures to them in the breeding shed earlier this morning did not win them over. While he's wowing the crowd, they gather in the front barn, suspicious and resentful. The techniques he's demonstrating are articulate versions of what they do with their horses every day. "When one comes in off the track," Kenneth says, "you have your problems and you deal with them then. If you get him going in the right direction and he understands that, then you don't have any more problems." What the grooms don't have is Parelli's marketing language — his Seven Games shtick. Kenneth has accumulated his skills through observation and practice. "You just watched how everybody did it," he explains. "Then you picked up how it was done the best way." Without Parelli's gift of gab, Kenneth can't explain how he keeps his horses in line. "Well, I don't know," he says. "Everything comes naturally."

The grooms are suspicious because Parelli's showmanship makes a very difficult task look easy. If he were to hand

Parade Ground off to someone in the crowd less skilled than he, not only that person but the entire gathering would be in danger. The methodology of his Seven Games is available to anyone who buys his videos, but without attending his very expensive clinics, most horsemen would find that his level of success eludes them. The innate qualities of good horsemen go unaddressed. Without the maturity to see the horse as a separate individual, one whose reactions are guided by his own hardwiring and not personal animosity, all the training in the world isn't going to turn someone into a true horseman. Challenging horses require ever more innovative approaches to their training, and horsemen develop their arsenal of techniques one horse at a time. Those showy skills are what the grooms at Lane's End possess, and the lack of recognition for their skills is what has driven them into the barn in resentment. They're feeling slighted because their contributions to keeping most of the horses at Lane's End from getting like Parade Ground in the first place are not being recognized. Handling breeding stallions is one of the most dangerous jobs in the business. Bringing in an outside trainer as a celebrity guest is like indicting their horsemanship just because out of all the horses they handle, one slipped through their fingers. Even Parade Ground's groom, who supports Parelli's methods and volunteered to take on the horse, is lingering at the back of the crowd, looking out over the paddocks. Parelli jokes that the biggest incentive for learning his program is that you don't have to pay him $20,000 a day to fix your horse for you. This claim does nothing to smooth the ruffled feathers of the grooms in the barn. "He knows there's money here somewhere," one of them jokes. "He can smell it."

Parade Ground is returned to his stall, still wearing his bit but without the weight of the lariats and muzzle. The afternoon breeding session starts, and what's left of the VIP tour wanders in to observe. They ask questions that the grooms ignore. They ask them again, and the grooms still ignore them, compelling another visitor to answer them, if only to keep them from asking the same question yet again.

Once everyone is gone, the grooms are back in good cheer. One of the benefits of the annual importation of the agriculture students is that they give the older grooms, the men who've been working side by side for years, new people to talk about. Their favorite subject of conversation this year is the rather hapless young James. Despite the guidance of the senior grooms, just this week he horrified them by stooping behind a mare's hooves to retrieve a dropped wad of cotton. During a tour earlier in the week, he returned Dixie Union to his stall and then turned his back to him and stood in the doorway to answer questions. Behind him, Dixie Union stared at his back, his ears flicking as if he was thinking, Bite? Not bite? Bite? "See that?" Kenneth grinned. "That's bad. Turning your back on them like that." Most of the kids, Kenneth thinks, take too many chances. "They'll learn," he says. "They all do."

As they stand in the sun at the entrance to the front barn, one of the older grooms beats a path to them from the breeding shed, grinning so wide his molars are showing. Young James, it seems, just walked in on Ambassador Farish in the bathroom. Even worse, he didn't know who Farish was. The groom telling the story, Kenneth says, is the groom who most likes to stir up trouble. "I guarantee you," Kenneth says about him, "first thing in the morning, he'll tell Bill."

Kenneth groups the Derby-season visitors and the break in the routine they bring with them into a category of events he calls "something different." When he first started handling stallions, he was excited about it because it was different than handling broodmares and yearlings, which is where he started. Then the stallions became routine. The tours were fun at first, but after all his years of leading them, he'd just as soon pass them on to the kids. He thinks it's good for them and they usually get a tip, which the older grooms always ask them to account for. "How much did you get?" one of them asks a kid who just spent fifteen minutes tracking down a map so he could direct his group to the next barn on their tour. "Five bucks?" he says. "That ain't hardly worth all those directions."

Inevitably, the tours come to rest in Kenneth's aisle, because that's where the Derby winner lives. He takes Charismatic, his coppery chestnut coat gleaming from twice-daily grooming, out of his stall. The tourists excitedly tell one another their piece of Charismatic's hard-luck story, expanding its mythology. The braver ones reach out tentatively to touch the shoulder that won the Derby. A.P. Indy watches patiently. With more charisma than his so-named stablemate, more, for that matter, than most Hollywood celebrities, he seems to know that the force of it will draw the fans to his stall even though he's not a Derby winner. (The problems he has with his feet were what kept him out of the Derby, according to Sellers.) Kenneth takes him out next and holds his lead shank loosely. A.P. lifts his head and pricks his ears when the tourists raise their cameras to their eyes. When they reach out to pet him, he arches his neck imperiously, reminding them that it is he, not they, who is the result of three hundred years of selective breeding. As they whisper among themselves, he rolls his white-rimmed eye toward them from under his thick forelock. He seems to be appraising them one at a time, perhaps puzzling over how such a sorry-looking bunch of animals can believe that they are dominant to him. It is as if A.P. has read the Koran and taken to heart its promise that the horse "shall be favored above all other creatures, for to thee shall accrue the love of the master of the earth."

Busy ogling the horses, the tourists don't notice the grooms, seemingly interchangeable in their khaki uniforms. They are the voiceless laborers of the racetrack and the production line. Veteran race writer William Nack once described the grooms as the horses' rightful owners. They are the "bivouacked army of men and women who make and remake the straw beds in the horses' stalls, who turn off the lights at night for them, who scold and succor and curry them. Who brush, rub, massage, bathe, feed, water, stroke, graze and bandage them. Who pick their feet and sing to them." As attached as racetrack grooms are to their horses, there are possibly only two who have ever reached public attention. One was Will Harbut, who groomed Man o' War, and the other was Eddie Sweat, whose love for Secretariat, whom he called Big Red, was so well known that the statue of the horse being erected at the Kentucky Horse Park will have Eddie Sweat at his side. "I been on the racetrack thirty-four years," Sweat said in a *Time* magazine interview with Nack, "and I ain't ever gonna give up. I think they'll take me to my grave with a pitchfork in my hand and a rub rag in my back pocket." In *Secretariat: The Making of a Champion,* Nack revealed that Sweat died "virtually penniless," in 1998. His last years had been spent battling leukemia. He had so little money that the Jockey Club paid for his wife and daughters to be flown to his funeral. To the end, Nack said, Sweat was hoping for another Secretariat.

Racetrack grooms work for day wages with no benefits or insurance and live in substandard housing, half a dozen to a room, with deplorable toilet facilities. By comparison, stud grooms, with their salaries, their benefits, their regular workdays, have jobs that seem almost cushy. Their concerns are those of the ordinary workingman: security, pay, benefits, and retirement. "Well, I can't really complain," Kenneth says. "Though I like to." When he worked at Nuckols Farm, his younger son came to work with him. "He still tells his wife that all the time," Kenneth says. "'When I was little . . .' He was a little fellow, he'd feed for me. He liked doing it." Between the choices Kenneth had as a young man, the factory or the stud farm, he thinks the factory would have given him more time with his family, so he wasn't disappointed when neither of his sons followed him into the business. He hopes that Lane's End will let him move into the night watchman's job when the work becomes too much for him, but he suspects they'll be reluctant to take him away from the horses, because it is hard to find grooms as skilled as he is. He's learned to be patient, though, and it has stopped bothering him that outside the industry few people, including his friends and family, understand how good he is at his job. Despite the grooms' resistance to Pat Parelli, Kenneth took away a bit of wisdom from the clinic. What was wrong with the horse business, Kenneth remembers him saying, is that the people who know the most about the work aren't always the ones in charge.

By Monday morning, the grooms' lives have returned to normal. The visitors are gone. The Derby is over. The breeding shed is filled with the sounds of squealing stallions, neighing and grunting, the scrabble of back hooves, and the jingling of the lead shank chains. They're back to producing Thoroughbreds. It is hoped that out of one of these matings will come the horse that everyone has been waiting for for over a quarter of a century, the next Secretariat.

★ ★ ★

In November of 2001, the Keeneland bloodstock sale begins with the exchange of $4 million for one prize broodmare. During the first two days of the sale, when the best horses are offered and attendance is at its highest, the sales pavilions' cafeterias are crowded, forcing top buyers to share their tables with mere spectators. Outside the glassed-in arena, the air is filled with cigarette smoke, and the three bars are crowded. During after-school hours, entire families camp out on the outer benches, their heads bowed over the sales books, exercising their birthright as Kentuckians — developing opinions about the values of horses. The garbled incantations of the auctioneers are broadcast via loudspeaker everywhere in the pavilion, their rolling spiel of gibberish bracketed by dollar amounts that rise in hundred-thousand-dollar increments. The constant trilling of cell phones has buyers, sellers, farm managers, trainers, breeders, and reporters patting their pockets so compulsively that it looks like a contagious tic has spread through the sale. Big-money players, like those from the Thoroughbred Corporation and Coolmore, move through crowds that part before them with a hush. There is no public listing of what the horses are expected to sell for, yet mysteriously, the seats in the arena fill in advance of the highest bidding. Agents for the top buyers leave their reserved seats to the spectators and hide themselves in the crowd, hoping to cloak their bids. The cues to the bid spotters are absolutely invisible to the audience, signaled only by the spotters' abrupt cry of "Whoa!" and the theatrical waving of their arms. The air is filled with the scent of nervous horses and money.

In the final two days, the select sale reaches the bottom of the barrel. The cafeterias are nearly empty, and the bathroom attendant is bored enough to volunteer, in detail, her pumpkin pie recipe. The sheikhs and the princes are gone. Polo shirts and Italian loafers have been replaced by flannel shirts and work boots. The assistants and sycophants that crowd around the buyers are gone too. In their place are workingmen, sitting alone and in pairs. They make no effort to hide their bids for horses who are selling for as little as a thousand dollars apiece — the minimum bid set by Keeneland to discourage slaughterhouse agents, who make their profit on the price per pound. Lane's End and other big consignors like Taylor Made and Eaton Sales are gone. With a credit line no bigger than what most people have on their credit cards, a hopeful buyer could now take home a bargain from one of the world's most prestigious bloodstock sales. Even the horses look a little duller, blandly eyeing the seats as if they know that their transfer from one owner to another will excite no one.

These horses aren't headed for Churchill Downs or Saratoga or Santa Anita; these are the ones headed for small-time tracks. Whether any of them possess dark horse speed will probably remain undiscovered. Their better-bred cousins are headed to innovative training programs, to barns that have the resources to hire a Pat Parelli to tease brilliance out of them if need be. The lucky ones of this bunch will end up in another discipline or as someone's pet, skipping the track entirely. The unlucky ones will be crassly handled, raced with injuries, and misunderstood for their entire careers. Like that of every horse since their kind was delivered from extinction by human hands, their fate lies with the men and women who buy them. As Black Beauty's mother warned him: "There are a great many foolish men, vain, ignorant and careless, who never trouble themselves to think. I hope you will fall into good hands, but a horse never knows who may buy him, or who may drive him; it is all a chance for us."

Chapter Eight

OLD SCHOOL

D r. John Steele graduated from Cornell Veterinary School in 1946. Until 1961, he says, he did everything. Then, just horses: standardbreds, Thoroughbreds, show horses. For the past twenty years, he's done "just this." He waves his hand in an arc over the entrance to Anne Kursinski's barn, the gesture meant to incorporate Anne, her staff, her horses, and other A circuit show barns like hers.

He's patted a New York Yankees baseball cap over his gray hair. Arthritis has bent his hands into the shape of chevrons. One hip is permanently cocked and the big toe of his right foot doesn't quite touch the ground, but he is serviceably sound for the work he does, and what he has to offer is not the shape but the knowledge of his hands.

The home barn of Anne Kursinski's Market

Street, Inc., is in Frenchtown, New Jersey. Halfway between New York and Philadelphia, it's a part of the state that is losing ground to suburban sprawl. The highway exit ramp ends in front of a Wal-Mart, and McMansion developments are elbowing their way into the farmland. When Anne gives directions to her barn, she uses the landmarks that horse people see: farms, paddocks, black fencing.

It's May, the beginning of Anne's push toward qualifying for the World Equestrian Games in Spain. She's just completed a two-week tour that included the $45,000 Garden State Grand Prix, in which she took first place on Eros, second on Indeed, and third on Great Point. Eros placed tenth at the Keswick Horse Show in Virginia. The Devon Horse Show is next week; one more show after that, and she'll head out to Spruce Meadows, in Calgary, and then down the West Coast to California for a series of selection trials for the World Equestrian Games. She's been through so many staff turnovers since the beginning of the season that she's lost count of how many employees she's had this year. She and Hoffy have hired a barn manager, Christy Merkley, who they're hoping will bring some stability to the barn, even if the grooms keep coming and going.

Dr. Steele is here on this chilly May day to evaluate Anne's horses. Tens of thousands of dollars' worth of high-tech therapeutic and diagnostic equipment is stashed around her barn, but she trusts this old man's hands more than anything that science has to offer her.

Anne and Doc Steele stand shoulder to shoulder, an elderly gentleman and a slender female athlete with a blond bob. Their affection for each other is palpable. Chuy is back, having returned to Anne and Hoffy after Florida. The job he had left them for, taking care of ponies, was easier, but what he really wants, Anne says, is to take his horses to the international ring. While Anne and Doc watch, Chuy jogs

Indeed, whom Doc describes as a "diesel truck," up and down the wide cement aisle. He's a massive bay, but his broad white blaze and thick black forelock give him the adorable demeanor of a pony. Indeed thinks jogging is exciting and he tosses his head, practically yanking Chuy, who's never seemed small until now, off the ground.

Christy Merkley has been around the A circuit for years, and when Doc spies her coming around the corner, he smiles and extends his hand. "What handshake?" Christy says, opening her arms. "A hug." Their down vests poof as they embrace, and Doc holds on to Christy's arm, telling her just how good it is to see her.

Anne announces that Christy has moved in. "Old school," Hoffy says. Anne nods. "Old school," she echoes, "like us."

Doc lets go of Christy and after a pause extends his hand anyway — an old-school gesture of professional respect.

"Whatever you're doing," Doc says to Anne as Indeed is passed back to his stall, "is working." Indeed is recovering from the split hoof that kept him out of competition for the entire Florida season.

Anne and Doc move on to the next horse while Christy and Hoffy compare notes about the condition of the stalls. Hoffy suggests that somebody, meaning one of the new grooms, needs a lesson in the art of mucking out.

On his cell phone, Doc Steele politely though scathingly dresses down the person on the other end for calling in another vet to consult on a horse he was working on and then closing him out of the loop. Now the person is back, several months into the horse's treatment, asking for his advice. His assistant, Bill Stanton, raises his eyebrows at Anne and Hoffy. "I'm glad that's not me," he says.

Chuy runs a rub rag over Sincere, shining him up for

Doc's exam. Sincere shifts and fidgets on the cross ties, and Doc prods him into place. "C'mon, son," he says. Holding a short plastic pipette, he presses it into the muscles of Sincere's crest, the muscle at the top of his neck, under his mane, following it with the flat of his knuckles. He drags it down Sincere's spine and then draws a grid pattern over the top of the horse's hindquarters. At Sincere's head again, he traces the pipette along the side of Sincere's neck and draws another grid pattern, then pulls a line over the area where Sincere's girth lies. He repeats the procedure on the other side. Sincere will tell Doc where it hurts by flinching. Doc's hands will tell him whether that hurt is in the horse's muscles, nerves, or soft tissue. A bit of acupuncture, Doc recommends, but other than that, Sincere is fine.

Christy is out in the paddock, trying to catch East Bay, who should have been ready. Anne hates it when Doc has to wait, but it gives them the chance to admire Chuy as he grooms Sincere. They stand together, silent, their eyes locked on Chuy's firm, quick gestures.

When Doc gets to East Bay's hindquarters, East Bay swats him with a hoof. Doc slaps him on the butt. "Don't get any ideas," he growls. East Bay drops his head, knitting together the space where his eyebrows would be if he had any. "You don't do that to Eros," Anne points out with a laugh. "Because Eros would do it back," Christy says.

Bill Stanton helps Doc work on a student's horse, a big gray Thoroughbred who seems to have topped out at his current competitive level. Anne thinks that the horse is sufficiently talented to continue into the higher ranks and suspects that something is hurting him. Doc's preliminary diagnosis is that there's a problem in the horse's stifle, the joint in the horse's back leg that connects it to his hip. Bill starts at the horse's front end, pulling each leg out to the front, back, and side, turning them in exaggerated, unnatural-looking circles, as if he means to pop the legs out of their sockets. The gray stands quietly while he's being yanked on until Bill finds the problem in the horse's hock, the bulbous joint halfway down his hind leg — a rearward-facing elbow. Bill feels the problem at precisely the same moment that the horse tosses his head, resisting. "I'm gonna have to disagree with you, Doc," Bill says. Everyone turns to Doc, waiting for his answer. He looks at the horse and, with a nod, silently defers to Bill's diagnosis.

As educated and experienced as Doc is, he still believes that his best diagnostic tool is a good groom, one who can pinpoint the precise moment that something went wrong with a horse and whose hands are knowledgeable enough to direct Doc to the source of the problem. In the past decade or so, he says, good grooms have become rare. Despite the proliferation of college degree programs in equine studies, he believes that the "kids these days" are more interested in showing and winning ribbons than in developing their horsemanship. From a man who's been in the business for over fifty years, these sentiments are not surprising. But they're echoed by Anne and Hoffy, who are in their forties, and even by the O'Connor grooms, most of whom have only a few years of legal drinking under their belts.

Anne calls the Devon Horse Show and Country Fair an "old-fashioned" horse show. In 2002, it is 106 years old and it has some old-fashioned problems — not enough parking, for instance. The competitors' lot is full by eight a.m., and if someone has to run an errand, she loses her spot. For ten bucks she can park in the spectator lot, but even that runs out of room, leaving the driver at the mercy of neighboring businesses and gas stations and whatever they choose to charge. Instead of the eight show rings and accompanying schooling rings of Wellington, there is one show ring, the Dixon Oval. A second ring doubles as a schooling and show ring. The old wooden barns have windows only on one side, and they're stuffy and airless during this last week of May. Heavy rains fell overnight, and there are big steamy puddles throughout the grounds.

With Anne at Devon are Chuy and a new groom, Kym Champagne. Anne's enthusiasm for her is a little tempered by her disastrous turnover problems. Kym is very good, so good in fact that the meticulous Hoffy snapped her up as soon as she saw her working with the horses. At twenty, Kym has been working professionally for two years. She came to Anne from California, where she spent the winter on the Indio Desert Circuit. Kym was raised by her mother; she doesn't know her father. Though she's always loved horses, she didn't get to ride until high school. "Finances," she explains simply. In high school, she badgered her mother into sending her to a boarding school that had an equine program. At that school, Kym said, "I was never anywhere but the barn, even on holidays." By the time she graduated, she was managing the barn, and though she was offered scholarships to equine studies programs, she skipped college because she already had good jobs lined up.

Kym loves to ride. At her last job, she had five or six horses to ride a day and some that she was showing, but she gave them up to work for Anne. She didn't expect to do any riding at all at Anne's and she was thrilled to find that Anne lets her ride almost every day, taking the horses out for a trail ride or a little light work in the arena. "If I ever get a day off," she says, "maybe I can go get a lesson with Anne or somebody," though she thinks that Anne might be a little on the expensive side for someone living on a groom's wages. When Kym arrived at the barn, she was terrified of making a mistake. "It's so intimidating to work for Anne," she says, "because she's been there and done that." As she gets more experience, she also gets more confident, and the payoff of working for Anne is that the horses she grooms might actually win.

Which is what Escapade did on Sunday night when he won the Open Jumper class, kicking off the second week of competition at Devon. Hoffy's two hunters, who competed the first week, have returned to Market Street, which is only about an hour away. They're down to five horses for the second week: Eros, Indeed, and Great Point, who are in Chuy's care, and Escapade and Sincere, who are with Kym. They've got enough extra stalls so that Chuy and Kym can each have their own grooming stalls, which is the best way to get along with Chuy, who is possessive about barn tools. Earlier in the week, Anne remembers, laughing, she reached for a pair of magnetic boots only to have Chuy snatch them away. "Mine," he said. "No, Chuy," Anne reminded him. "They're mine. They're all mine."

Only two arenas means that the pace at Devon is slow and the classes go late, sometimes starting after nine p.m., making a very long day for the grooms who arrive at six a.m.

Unlike the hunter / jumper exclusivity of Wellington, Devon has a little bit of something for everybody. Pleasure driving, saddle seat, coach races, family classes for which organizers have been compelled to list seventeen different definitions of what constitutes a family. There are classes for light and heavy farm horses and competitions for police horses — shown at the walk, trot, and canter, not, as you might imagine, eluding bullets and giving traffic tickets. On the Thursday morning before the $75,000 Budweiser Grand Prix, the Dixon Oval is held hostage by a series of nineteen breeding classes divided by gender, age, and breed. All over the show grounds young horses competing in the classes are twirling at the end of their lead shanks like kites, buffeting their handlers, planting their feet, and screaming whinnies to their companions in the barn. They're here because in 1896 the local businessmen who founded Devon started the show to coerce farmers into breeding them stylish hunters who were suited to galloping and jumping in the hunt field. The prize money went to the breeders of the most attractive and suitably conformed horses.

Anne wants Kym to get Great Point out for a walk, but the frantic, spinning colts and fillies, screaming out forlornly to their friends, have spooked every adult horse on the grounds. The few riders who have ventured out can be seen between the barns or behind the bleachers, reeling in their bolting, leaping horses. Great Point, it is decided, will have to wait until afternoon.

Despite their feisty disobedience, the babies temporarily turn into polished performers in the ring. Escorted by sportily dressed handlers, they walk and jog in hand, then they line up for the judges, one sweltering in his sport coat, the other turning red under her hat and along the edges of her linen dress. Like toddlers at a long church service, the horses reach their limit during the lineup. They spin around the handlers and rear up, and their tender bodies quiver and their nostrils distend with their effort to trumpet a grownup horse's neigh. Most of the spectators are there because they came early to claim the nonreserved seats before the evening's Grand Prix, and they look delighted to have stumbled on such a vigorous display of equine willfulness.

The Devon country fair, which at most shows would be called a trade fair, is studiously old-fashioned. Little white cottages with blue trim and thatched roofs are selling equestrian products, but also handmade sweaters, crafts, and antiques. There's a raffle for a PT Cruiser. One of the snack stands sells only tea sandwiches. Volunteers lovingly cut circles and squares of white bread between which papery slices of cucumber or sprigs of watercress have been layered. There's a candy stand doing a brisk trade in lemon sticks — whole lemons that have been pierced by a sugar straw. The stand is child-sized, the countertops within the children's reach. Dragging their parents behind them, the kids zero in on penny-candy baskets as their parents whack their heads on the eaves. At the hamburger stand, volunteers, mothers apparently, call children back for their change, which they count out slowly into small, sweaty palms.

On the far side of the country fair is a midway. Children with painted faces revolve in lazy circles on carousel ponies. Heels down, eyes up, they display perfect equitation. Unlike most contemporary horse shows, Devon is a family event. Prices are reasonable ($2.75 for a burger). The stands are a bit run-down, like the wooden barns. The grandstand seats smell like the locker room at a public pool. Sprinkled in with the behatted ladies and bow-tied gentlemen are T-shirted, overweight, normal Americans. Devon exudes an atmosphere of tarnished glamour.

By lunchtime, the breeding classes are done, the last baby whinny silenced. Kym takes Great Point to the schooling ring for a walk. She's a strong young woman with the robust athleticism of a rugby player and she is firmly planted in Great Point's saddle, which is good because around her the horses who are competing in the local hunter class are warming up. Evidently, the only qualification for the local hunter class at Devon is geographic proximity. Horses of all shapes and sizes, whose riders exhibit the entire range of athletic ability, are trotting, cantering, and jumping little fences. "Watch the gray," Kym says. "He's about to be loose." His rider doggedly points him over a small jump, which he clears, but not without leaving her hanging off the side of the saddle.

After bathing Great Point, Kym ambles drowsily through her chores in the afternoon heat. In the kind of move that drove Brooke nuts, Chuy has disappeared. Market Street's staff problems are not resolved. "We bicker a lot," Kym says. "I try to stay out of it." Her attitude toward her work is that of a hired hand. Regardless of her skill or her love of the horses, she's there to follow directions. "I do what I'm told. I sit down and I shut up and I try not to complain. I just try to get done what needs to get done." She's happy to follow Anne's instructions because the horses are so well cared for. Her work ethic has endeared her to Anne, who relies on her even though she's only been there a month. "It's such a comfort to know you're home when we're gone," Anne has told her. Kym has also, if not endeared herself, at least ingratiated herself enough to get along with Chuy, who, she reports, is unwilling to help out anyone in the barn except her. "It's a task to get him to help," Kym says, but when she asks him, he does.

She seems happy to have the barn to herself this afternoon. The horses are damp and sleepy in the heat. She putters through her chores, sipping on a bottomless cup of Coke. "I'm a junk food addict," she admits, though she doesn't look like one. Of the horses she takes care of, so far Escapade is her favorite. "He's neat and hard to understand." Because it's important not to rush around him, she starts grooming him early. "He's so neurotic," she says. Chuy arrives, having gone back to the motel to shower and change for the Grand Prix. The stuffy barn now smells like his aftershave. In his grooming stall, Eros is pinning his ears and gnashing his teeth. A cover, Kym says, because he doesn't want anyone to know that he's "secretly nice."

After the low-grade activity of the afternoon, the air filled with the sound of desultory cicadas, the excitement of the approaching Grand Prix sounds like the arrival of a swarm of bees. Fat burgers, hot dogs, and sausages sizzle loudly on the grill in the Groom's Kitchen, the snack stand next to the barn. At this hour, it's empty of actual grooms, who are getting their horses ready, and full of spectators who've figured out that the stabling area is more exciting than the midway. The Groom's Kitchen isn't just a name. Taped to the soda machine is a price list of items that cater to the barn staff: No-Doz, Extra-Strength Tylenol, LifeSavers, and lighters.

Historically, the Devon Horse Show was *the* summer event for Philadelphia Main Line society. What's left of that society is arriving at the gates to take their reserved seats in the grandstand. Women in delicate sandals, their pastel dresses swirling around their ankles, step discreetly around piles of manure, their hands tucked under the elbows of gentlemen in linen and seersucker. A pediatrician from Philadelphia, in dress slacks and tassel loafers, is poking around the barns, "the pits," as he calls them, bumming cigarettes and trying to weasel gossip out of the workers.

Christy arrives from Frenchtown with the horse van. Escapade will be going home tonight after the Grand Prix. Kym is hoping that she can go home as well. Hoffy is staying in New Jersey. Her parents are in town and she wants to finish up some paperwork before the West Coast trip. When Christy checks in with her on her cell phone, though, Hoffy confesses that she spent the entire afternoon looping over the lawns on the riding mower. The warm-up ring has been dragged, but Christy grabs a rake anyway, to scrape away a few hoofprints that the tractor missed in front of a jump. She jokes with the ring stewards who are policing the warm-up, on the lookout for cheaters who've put sharp objects or caustic substances in their horses' boots, which will hurt them if they rap a pole and cause them to be extra careful about tucking their legs up.

★   ★   ★

Like Three-Day Eventing, the hunter / jumper world has had problems with its image over the past decade. In 1991, according to Ken Englade's true-crime book *Hot Blood*, a sting operation set up by the Chicago district attorney's office and animal welfare officials in Gainesville, Florida, caught two men, Harlow Arlie and Tom Burns, trying to break the leg of a horse named Streetwise by whacking it with a crowbar. They had been hired by Streetwise's owner, who was hoping to collect insurance money on his fatally injured horse.

What led the Chicago DA to Gainesville was not an overwhelming interest in equine welfare, but the 1977 disappearance of candy heiress Helen Brach. Before she disappeared, the DA believed, she was preparing to rat out a con man named Richard Bailey who had been selling her cut-rate racehorses for top dollar and pocketing the difference. The investigation into Bailey led to Tommy Burns, who had killed not just Streetwise but many more horses. For an up-front fee and 10 percent of the insurance payout, which he complained was hardly ever forwarded to him, he would creep into a barn at night, split an extension cord, clip one end to the horse's ear and the other to his rectum, and then plug it in. In his defense, he claimed that the horses died instantly. Without knowing to look for burn marks, veterinarians concluded, though not always without suspicion, that the horses had died of colic. Streetwise had his leg broken, according to Englade (and it was Arlie, not Burns, who wielded the crowbar), because he had a history of colic, so his insurer would only pay for other kinds of accidental death.

Once he was bagged, Burns proved to be a loquacious

and cooperative witness. Killings in the horse business, he said, were widespread. When the investigation was over, twenty-three of the hunter/jumper world's top trainers and owners were indicted, a number that investigators believed was only a fraction of those who were guilty, according to Englade. Included in that number was George Lindemann Jr., heir to a cellular phone fortune, who had received $250,000 in insurance money for the death of his horse Charisma. Along with him, his barn manager, Marion Hulick, was indicted, as were Donna Brown, the wife of former Olympian Buddy Brown, and Barney Ward, one of the most successful jumper riders on the circuit. Ward was convicted of arranging four horse killings.

Most of the accused confessed immediately, hoping for leniency. But Lindemann, Hulick, and Ward, who were facing the stiffest sentences, contested the charges and then appealed their convictions. The trials drew the attention of national media like *Vanity Fair, Sports Illustrated, People,* and the *New York Times.* According to a January 1999 article in *The Chronicle of the Horse,* Hulick broke down at her sentencing. "'I'll do anything!' she said. 'I'll help my community. I'll go anywhere! . . . I'm sorry!' she sobbed before collapsing in her chair in tears, leaving the courtroom in shocked silence." Lindemann, Hulick, and Ward were sentenced to jail, and the American Horse Shows Association (now USA Equestrian) banned them for life from recognized shows. The remainder were fined, served suspended sentences, and were also suspended by the AHSA.

Killing horses for money isn't restricted to the horse show world. A 2001 article in *Texas Monthly* reported on the investigation into the death of Alydar, who was, before his death, one of Kentucky's leading sires. He was also heavily leveraged. During the Thoroughbred boom of the eighties, the owner of Calumet Farm, a Kentucky good old boy who had married his way into the most storied breeding farm in the bluegrass, ran up a reported $127 million in debt expanding his empire, buying planes, and acquiring bloodstock. He had packaged free breeding rights to Alydar in with so many deals that the horse was no longer producing enough cash to cover debts. Officially, Alydar died as a result of complications due to a broken leg. According to the *Texas Monthly* article, investigators believed that a chain attached to a truck was used to pull the horse's leg through a bolted stall door until the leg was broken.

The horse show world was disgusted by the brutality and greed of the millionaire horse killers, but not surprised. There had been whispers about such killings for years. They left a pall over the industry. There were so many people investigated and then not indicted that even now, one barn administrator says, people are afraid to lodge complaints about other competitors because in the communal barns that all the competitors share, there is no way to protect your horses at night.

Barney Ward took the AHSA to court to appeal his banishment from horse shows. He had a right, he claimed, to watch his son McLain ride. The court upheld the AHSA decision. Barney's son has had troubles of his own. Although McLain was never indicted, many in the industry believed that he knew what his father was doing. In Aachen, Germany, at one of the world's premier Grand Prix, he was suspended when plastic tacks, which would have painfully pierced his horse's legs if they rapped a pole, were discovered inside his horse's protective leg boots. Ward denied placing the tacks in the horse's boots, but he admitted that he was the person responsible for the horse's care. He was subsequently fined and suspended from competition for eight months by the American Horse Shows Association.

The sourness of these events is still palpable among

competitors. Tommy Serio, a leading hunter trainer, wrote in *Practical Horseman:* "There's a different kind of owner in the show world now. Years ago most owners talked first about what was good for the horse, before talking about where to show next. That has changed." Many of the indicted trainers still work in the business, popular because they produce winning horses and winning riders, even if they're not allowed on the show grounds to watch them compete. In an unsuccessful bid to avoid jail, Marion Hulick appealed her sentencing on the grounds that she couldn't serve time because of her family's needs. She had two disabled children and her husband traveled for work. His work, ironically, was running Horse Watch — the security service that riders use to check on their horses when they are stabled overnight at shows.

Anne's stiffest competition in tonight's Grand Prix is McLain Ward. He's been the leading rider at Devon now for three years in a row. Her team is hoping she wins partly because she's Anne and partly because she isn't McLain. Christy can joke with the ring stewards because they aren't suspicious of Anne. Anne's excesses, when she's accused of them, are the new-agey kind: ultrasound, magnetic, laser, and radio wave therapies; regular massage, acupuncture, and chiropractic; and occasional consultations with an equine psychic. Her barn is full of affectionate, eager-looking horses. "You can tell we don't beat them," she says with a laugh.

After a week of anticipation, Eros knocks down a rail in the Grand Prix. Escapade is spooked by an overhead camera on a crane that swoops down on him like a giant bird of prey when he enters the arena. Anne gets him settled for the first couple of jumps, and then, to his horror, he is faced with a fence whose standards are in the shape of leaping killer whales. Rattled, he tears around the ring and dumps Anne by the in-gate. "He didn't realize he was supposed to jump Shamu," she jokes. McLain Ward wins again, taking leading rider honors for the fourth year in a row.

It's a disappointment, but there are Grand Prix almost every weekend, and the really important shows, Spruce Meadows in Calgary and the selection trials in California, are still ahead.

Escapade doesn't go home, because Anne wants him to compete again, just to get over his scare in the Dixon Oval. Kym's disappointment is outweighed by the news that she's been picked to go with the team to Calgary. "I've never flown with the horses before," she says.

Friday night's jumper class, a Gambler's Choice, doesn't start until 9:50 p.m. Kym still has to be in the barn at six a.m. that morning to feed. She has plenty of time during the day to second-guess her preparation of Escapade for the previous evening's Grand Prix. "It was really exciting that my horse was getting to go in it," she says. "Then I felt bad when he didn't do well. I kept going through my head: What was different? What was different? You just feel like, Is there something that I could have done different that would have helped?"

Hours before the jumper class, bright flashes of heat lightning spark on the horizon. The day has been taken up with driving classes and saddle seat classes — those that show off the fancy gaits of the American saddlebred. On this penultimate day of the 2002 Devon Horse Show and Country Fair, the spectators are ten deep at ringside to watch the Coaching Class Obstacle Course. Teams of four matched horses pulling park coaches, the kind that would have been pulled by Black Beauty through the streets of London, thunder past the barn, harnesses jingling, spooking Escapade in his stall. Even though they're spooking her horse, Anne says that these coaches are her favorite. Seated on top, along with the driver, are four to six passengers in top hats or long skirts. Two liveried grooms stand on the rear running board. The obstacle course is marked by traffic pylons with oranges balanced on top: The driver who knocks down the fewest oranges while passing between the cones wins. It's just getting dark as the coaches rumble into the Dixon Oval under a sign that reads, "Devon Horse Show: Where Champions Meet." As they pass under it, each coach's horn player, in full livery, stands up and blows an introductory tune with a long, slender brass horn. The musicians are competing too. They're judged on their "ability to sound the horn on a moving and stationary coach." The program adds, "Requested are old melodies played by the guards in the 1800s or any of the player's melodies that would provide the most entertainment for the passengers." The winner of this arcane competition is basically the one who gets the loudest applause.

For the spectators crowded alongside the ring, those who don't have box seats, this is what the world of horses looks like: anachronistic, Victorian, stylish, and charming. Populated by people who have the money and leisure to maintain matching horses and antique coaches. People who have the kind of extended family and friend networks that can produce up to six attractive individuals who can carry off long dresses and top hats. The world they don't see is the one of high-tech equipment, the one of workers whose job descriptions are pretty much the same as those of the playacting grooms on the coaches, and one where people have their horses electrocuted in their stalls.

After the carriage competition the Budweiser Clydesdales, those jolly, gentle giants, jingle mightily into the arena. The Budweiser theme song, "Here comes the king, here comes the king, here comes the big number one!" plays loudly as the announcer yells out factoids for the cheering crowd. Each of the eight horses is about eighteen hands high, they each weigh 2,300 pounds, and tonight they are driven not, as you would expect, by a burly Teamster, but by a slender young woman. The men on her team sit quietly in their places on the wagon as she holds ten tons of horsepower to an obedient trot. Her cries of "Gee" and "Haw" to the lead team snap them into position. Their footfalls on the ground carry so much impact that the baby strollers at ringside bounce when they go by.

Just before Anne mounts up, it starts to rain. She looks at the sky and says, "Maybe we should just pack up and go home." She looks tired, as if she's ridden in the rain enough times in her life. As if she's mounted up on enough horses, won enough ribbons, traveled enough, hired and fired enough grooms, fallen off enough, and lost enough. In the warm-up ring, she jumps her fences under a deluge. When she's done, she stands still on Sincere, her young horse, who's calm and relaxed even with the thunder booming and even though a huge tractor is rattling around behind him. Now, Anne's face is radiant as she looks down at him from the saddle. "Look at this," she says, pointing to the loose reins in her hands. "What a good horse."

Gambler's Choice is the kind of jumper class that has all but disappeared from less traditional shows. Each fence has a different point value determined by its difficulty. The object is to race around and jump as many of the big-value fences as possible in the allotted time frame. The rain passes, and Sincere and Anne go first, holding the lead for the first few rides, until everyone else gets ingenious. Margie Goldstein-Engle, a pint-size firecracker of a rider who has worked her way up through the ranks the hard way, by hiring out at shows to ride other people's horses, spins her horse on his haunches, angles her jumps, cuts corners, and races over the finish line twenty points ahead of the second-place horse. The crowd cheers. Anne laughs and then smiles wryly at the announcer. "I think I'll stick to my plan," she says, which is to give Escapade a nice, easy, confidence-producing round. But she's tempted. She practically twitches with self-control as she takes Escapade out for a clean, slow round over the low fences. Then it's over. One more class tomorrow and Market Street can go home.

In the barn, Kym is babbling about how much work she has left. She has to poultice and groom the horses, clean the tack, and pack for tomorrow, when she'll arrive at work at six a.m. She and Anne talk quietly at the end of the barn while the horses stare at them, waiting for the carrots that both women distribute at the end of the day. Kym is supposed to have one day off a week, but she's only had two since she arrived at Market Street over a month ago. While she's been at Devon, another groom has moved out of the apartment above the barn that the Market Street grooms share. That means more work for her when she gets back, but she doesn't mind. "It's Anne's barn," she says. "It's a great place to be. As long as I can have a day off now and then, as long as I can get on my horse and canter and let all my day's stress go out," then she's happy with her job.

By 11:10 p.m. on the penultimate day of the Devon Horse Show and Country Fair, the barns are finally quiet. Trailers have been hauling away horses all day, and the barns are almost empty. In the Dixon Oval, the driver of a single gaited carriage horse works in big circles until the lights of the ring are turned off. The Ferris wheel in the midway is still, though its lights are on, glowing neon tubes of red, blue, green, and yellow. In the last few barns that have horses in them the lights are dim as the grooms put them to bed. In the Team Budweiser tent, the Clydesdales are asleep, resting

up for another day of exciting fans with their power and offering their faces and necks to the fluttery petting of hundreds of sticky little hands. Bright orange and ochre heat
lighting pulses in the night sky, and a handful of security
guards, their shift just beginning, waves goodbye energeti-
cally to the exhausted riders and barn staff heading to their
cars. In two days, the barns will be closed, the white-and-
blue cottages of the country fair shuttered up, empty of
their wares. Bryn Mawr hospital will have another install-
ment in the more than $10 million this show has raised for
them since 1919, and the Devon Horse Show and Country
Fair will be over until everyone comes back next year.

Chapter Nine

GETTING LUCKY

A fter the tension and high drama of Rolex, the summer horse trial season is like the O'Connor Event Team unplugged. At the end of June, they make the long drive from Virginia to Hamilton, Massachusetts, for the Groton House Farm horse trial, with just five horses and two grooms. David has Tex, Tailor, Percy, and one of his young horses, Dante's Tale, who will be completing his first preliminary-level event this weekend. Karen has just one, a horse given to her by a student who left the competitive life to work with Pat Parelli.

Sam is along as well as Donna Smith, a rider from New Zealand who has qualified for her country's show jumping and Three-Day Event teams. She's spending the New Zealand winter working with the

O'Connors. Sam arrives at the barn on Friday morning to find poor Tailor covered with bug bites the size of half-dollars. "I know, I know," she says as she's braiding him. "You need to scratch." He suffers in silence, frowning, his ears halfway back, until she's done. "Go ahead," she says, and he reaches around to nip at his sides and flanks. Tailor is the only one in the aisle with so many bug bites, and Sam surmises that the greenhead flies swooped in, found Tailor, and fed to their limit on him. Brewster is across the aisle with his horse, Derrick. The bugs wouldn't have dared bite Tailor, he says, if he'd been wearing his gold medal.

After Rolex, David's plan for his top three horses, Tex, Tailor, and Tigger, was to compete them aggressively at the summer horse trials to get them fit for the World Games in Spain in September. Tigger's not here this weekend because he colicked back in Virginia and had to have surgery. He's recovering, but he's out of competition for the rest of the year. Tigger, David said, has "never had the kind of luck to make a true career." Waylaid by a tendon injury early in his career, he came back to finish at the Fair Hill CCI three-star, only to miss the flag at Rolex. He still made the short list for the World Games, but now he's colicked. The other bad news is that the U.S. Eventing Team has dropped Karen's horse Grand Slam from the short list, though they've added Regal Scott, so she still has a shot at the team for the Worlds. The O'Connors have lost a groom too. Andi Dees left. Grooming, she decided, wasn't what she wanted to do, according to Sam. Her replacement, Donna Smith, has impeccable riding credentials but no experience as a groom. "I'm not a groom," she reminds everyone every time she does something wrong. At the dressage arena, David notices that Donna has put Tailor's girth on backward. Sam is embarrassed that she didn't catch it before

David. Tailor's huge bug bites, which cast shadows on his back in the bright sun, prompt David to call him the Elephant Man. "I am not an animal!" he cries, mounting up.

The spectators and lower-level competitors at Groton House are thrilled and awed to have horses like Tex and Tailor in their midst. Four-star horses don't always make it to Groton House. The horses who complete Rolex get a holiday after that competition and are not usually fit in time for Groton House at the end of June. David's competitors who completed Rolex are here, but they've left their best horses at home. Every time David, mounted on Tailor, is out of the stabling area, the announcer exhorts the gathering to remember Tailor's accomplishments, to consider how lucky they are to see a horse like this compete.

Tex and Tailor, David says, have a public presence, an identity that is "bigger than me and beyond me." When the fans descend on the big bays, David steps out of the spotlight, allowing his horses to shine. He would like his horses to be ambassadors for the sport. Their health and good nature show that horses are happy in their line of work and can still compete at sixteen and seventeen, late middle age for a Thoroughbred. Improving the sport's image and expanding its popularity are, along with his endorsement of Parelli's training techniques, part of David's vision for creating better relationships between horses and their riders in every discipline and in every backyard where horses languish because they're misunderstood. He's a quiet man who loves animals, but he's also an ambitious man, one who's bursting the narrow confines of the eventing world. He admires Pavarotti, he says, because the tenor "crossed out of his area of expertise and influenced the whole world through music. I would like to do something like that with horses."

Warming up next to David at the dressage arena is a

novice rider on a chunky, wild-maned chestnut who's ambitiously named Sir Galahad. David is glancing at her out of the corner of his eye and smiling. The rider is so focused on her routine that she doesn't seem to notice that she's passing David and Tailor, stirrup to stirrup. Ninety percent of the members of the U.S. Eventing Association ride at the beginner level of the sport. These are the riders David is trying to reach. The ones who squeeze in time for their horses around work hours, the ones who show up faithfully for their once-weekly lessons, and the ones who will never compete at the one-star level, much less at the four-star.

At the end of dressage day, David is in first and second on Tex and Tailor as, Karen says, "he should be." Cross-country day is hot, though the humidity of dressage day has broken. Last year at this competition, after galloping through slick, muggy heat on cross-country day, the horses spent the night in tents while lightning bolts pierced the woods around them. In the morning, the horses in the lower tent were ankle deep in water.

Percy and the young roan Dante are further down in their divisions, but they're not being ridden to win here, as Tex and Tailor are. Sam and Donna take the horses out to graze, weaving them through the picnic tables in the lunch area located at the end of the O'Connors' aisle. Tex and Tailor bounce Sam around between them as they aim for different patches of grass in the parking lot. The novice division is already galloping the cross-country course, and Sam winces as she hears them pounding by on the hard footing. With the Worlds in sight, every competition between now and then is a risk. Hard ground, an awkward step, a stone in the wrong place, could mean the difference between going to Spain and an early holiday.

After the horses graze, Sam and Donna walk the intermediate-level cross-country course that Karen and

David will be running on Louisiana Purchase and Percy. David appears out of nowhere, bumping up against Sam's back and saying hey. Karen and her eleven-year-old niece, J. J. Lende, who comes down from Alaska to spend the summers with them, are at his side. One of their students is with them, and a former student who's just returned from training and competing in England pops up with a cup of coffee in her hand. Eyeing David and Karen, she grins. "I guess this is a good time to walk the cross-country course."

Alaska is an inhospitable place for horses, so little J. J. has to pack in as much time with them as she can while she's with her horsey aunt and uncle. In Virginia, David has been letting J. J. ride Tailor, and at Groton House she's excited and fresh and never far from Karen's side. The group is alone in a cool, deep stand of trees inspecting the sharp drop and loose dirt on the landing side of a fence. At the bottom of the hill, David challenges J. J. to run up it. Calling him "Mr. Diet Coke and Pop-Tarts," she challenges him back, to a race. David calls, On your mark, get set, go, and then lets J. J. race up the hill by herself. She's almost at the top before she realizes that he's not following her. Two of Karen's competitors in the intermediate division pass by, telling her to "stop abusing that child." Okay, okay, David promises. He'll race her this time, but when J. J. gets ahead of him, he grabs her belt, cheating again.

Bouncing up and down under the weight of her back-pack, J. J. claims she won. She's a fast runner, she tells Karen. One day she had to chase Grandpa when he left the farm without her. "That's great, J. J.," Karen says. "He's old and overweight; that must have been tough for you." Karen and David don't have kids; they have horses and students, which is too bad, because Karen's sarcastic wit is a perfect match for a wisecracking eleven-year-old.

Sam and Donna are going to be walking all day, so they spin off from the group halfway through the course and head back to the barn. Sam has an eye for the good common equine Joes, like Sir Galahad, who are faithfully humping their riders around the course. "There are so many cute horses here," she says to Donna. Watching one lift his neck to catch his rider, who's pitched forward on landing, Sam speaks in the horse's voice: "That's okay, c'mon. No, no, don't adjust my stride, you usually do it wrong. I got it. You just hang on. You could get out of the saddle a bit, but if that's too much, okay. I know what to do."

David's first cross-country ride is at 11:16 a.m. on Percy and his last is at 5:30 p.m. on Dante. "Don't be surprised," he tells Sam, "to see me pull up after each jump." Percy, David believes, is such a great jumper that his previous riders have rushed him to the fences, trusting that he'll figure out how to get over them, which has undermined Percy's confidence. When he lands, he bolts away from the fence. At the lower competitive levels, he's a little out of control. When he gets to the upper levels, where the fences are bigger and come in combinations, he'll be dangerous. Stopping him is David's way of teaching Percy to listen to him. Watching David splash through the water jump, Sam laughs, because he's already been passed by the horse who started after him and it looks like the next one might pass him too. After clearing a table jump at the top of the hill, David halts Percy and backs him up. "What's he doing?" the spectators ask one another. "Why did he do that?" At the finish line, before he is even off the horse, one of those spectators wanders over from the patron's tent, his finger holding his place in his book. "I gotta ask," he says. "I'm dying of curiosity." David hands Percy to Sam and she leads him back to the barn as David, the compulsive teacher, explains his methods to a stranger.

Tailor is clean cross-country and fast, and at the finish line David halfheartedly scolds him for pulling too hard on him, for being bad. Even when he's bad, Sam says, he's still better than everyone else. Acquaintances of David's, friends of friends, show up with their four-year-old son. David picks him up and puts him on Tailor's back as Donna is walking him. Tailor spooks at first, then, feeling that tiny weight in his saddle, the grubby fingers twisted in his mane, calms down, as if he understands that, fierce as he is, he's now required to be gentle, to give a tender pony ride to his fragile passenger.

David's solicitousness to children doesn't seem to jibe with his reputation as the consummate competitor. When he's not surrounded by kids at competitions he's quiet and intensely focused. His riding style is unemotional, with an economy of movement that reflects his technical mastery. The hinges of his body — hip, knee, elbow, and ankle — open and close just as much as they need to to help his horses over the jumps. Pictures of him on course rarely reveal the effort it takes to clear the obstacles, because he rides so quietly; they all look small and easy under him.

Success came late for David. He lost his first three ponies. The first two fell victim to equine infectious anemia, and his third broke a leg in his paddock. Because his family didn't have money, he says, "I didn't think my life was going to go this way." As a young rider, he was spotted at Radnor by Jack LeGoff, the former *chef d'equipe* of the U.S. Eventing Team, who invited him to join the developing-riders program at their headquarters in Hamilton, Massachusetts. David had to borrow a horse. He spent three years with the team, he says, riding their "little horses," before he was approached by someone who wanted to buy him an international competitor. Even after that, though, his career progressed slowly, a "one-horse-at-a-time kind of thing." It wasn't until after the Barcelona Olympics, in 1992, when he and Karen didn't make the team because their horses were injured, that they made the decision to "play the game at the multiple-horse level." Through the nineties, he says, his experience started to catch up with his education. Still, even after he was part of the silver medal–winning team at the Atlanta Olympics, in 1996 the Badminton commentator referred to David as a rider who "promised a lot but never actually really produced the goods." Ian Stark, a member of the British Olympic team, confessed that he had doubts about David too. "Having watched him in the beginning," he said in an interview, "I wasn't sure he was a four-star rider." David's eventual success, according to Stark, was a result of his having "worked so religiously at getting it right." He placed third at the 1996 Badminton four-star and subsequently racked up so many wins that no one now dares to accuse him of being an underachiever.

David says he's comfortable with his place in the public eye, but he gives the impression that he's holding part of himself in reserve. Even when he jokes at press conferences, his levity seems to have been prepared, rather than a spontaneous outburst of good cheer. Negotiating his way through the battle between the two governing bodies of American horse sports, USA Equestrian and the United States Equestrian Team, he has been politic and diplomatic, one of the only public figures of the feud who hasn't resorted to accusations and name calling. He is quoted often in the equine press but never in the kind of droll sound bites that his competitors quip to the media. His answers arrive in the form of complete sentences, well thought out and articulate, and he never, ever complains in public.

He's not unlike his best horses, Tex and Tailor. In public, they are gracious and tolerant of all the patting hands reaching toward them. Tex, David says, actually loves to perform and compete. According to Sam, Tex is the horse who would most appreciate having a mirror in his stall. But back in their barn, they're private and reserved.

"We say they're expressive," Sam says. "David wants them to have their own personalities." They act aggressive in their stalls because they're protective of themselves and their private space, and, she adds, they learn to make faces from each other. "Percy does the same thing now," she says. "Pins his ears back at other horses, and you're like, 'Give me a break. You don't even know what that means. You're just trying to fit in with the old boys.'" Deep down, Sam says, all of David's horses are big teddy bears.

Unlike Anne Kursinski, who thinks aloud and second-guesses her decisions constantly as she tries to figure out what's best for her horses, David is closemouthed when something goes wrong, reluctant to answer questions and eager to put the best face on it. Privately, though, when he is confronted with a problem he can't figure out, his confidence can disintegrate. The previous fall, he acquired a horse who had a bolting problem, who was panic-stricken by anything that touched his body behind the saddle or that spooked him from behind. On one occasion, he ran away with David and didn't stop until he skidded into the grain bin in the barn. David called Pat Parelli in to help him. In the barn that morning, he told Sam that he hadn't been able to sleep the night before. "I was terrified," he said, "that he was going to go in there and fix the horse in five minutes and I'm the worst horseman that ever lived. I had nightmares about it. I was ready to quit." Sam was astonished. "I was like, you know better, David. The horse has problems."

David admits that he's been incredibly lucky to have not one, but two horses with Tex's and Tailor's ability, and to have had them at the same time is almost more luck than he can bear. He knew from the beginning that Tailor was a four-star horse, but he didn't know until the Atlanta Olympics that Tex was one. Most of that good fortune he created for himself through discipline, creativity, talent, and professionalism. Some of it, though, really was pure luck. He had the early support of Jack LeGoff, who, according to David's father, said that David was the most talented rider he ever worked with. He got two great horses at the same time before his career was established and everyone rushed to provide him with mounts, and neither of those horses was beset by the injuries that can curtail the careers of so many potential champions, like Tigger. David's generosity with his fans seems to stem not only from his sense of responsibility to the sport and the horses he loves, but from a sense of responsibility to his own good fortune. Sharing his luck instead of hoarding it, a kind of insurance policy. He's dispensed so much of it around the world that it's sure to be there when he needs it again.

In the midst of all the free love that David is dispensing to his fans, tension about his last ride of the day, on young Dante, is rising. Even with all her worries about the hard footing and keeping Tex and Tailor sound, Sam is most concerned about David's ride on Dante. The pushy gray Thoroughbred is having difficulty "getting with the program." His gestures, like chewing on the grooms and rubbing against them, seem affectionate, unlike Tex's and Tailor's pinned ears, but they violate the rule that the horse must respect his handler's bubble of personal space. When he doesn't get what he wants, like Tigger, he pitches fits. Unlike Tigger, Dante has yet to demonstrate his brilliance over fences.

Since he's arrived at Groton House, he's been amusing himself by banging his hoof on the metal frame of his stall, as if he likes the sound of it. Donna jokes that maybe that's why he knocks all the poles down in show jumping, because he likes the way they sound when they thump to the ground. Sam is afraid because cross-country fences don't come down.

David's ride on Dante is the last one of the day for the O'Connor team. The students are lying on the tack trunks and napping on the picnic table. Karen appears, having changed into jeans, and orders them out onto the cross-country course to cheer David on. "Why?" someone asks. "Because he's scared," she says.

The cross-country schooling ring hasn't been watered all day. Great clouds of dust mushroom up under the horses' hooves and drift out over the edge of the ring, settling on the grass and turning it a dusty, grayish green — the color of wild sage. The riders, trainers, and grooms at the ring are sunburned, sweaty, covered with grit, and wiped out by the heat and the long day. The preliminary division that Dante is jumping in is the dividing line between the pros and the lifetime amateurs. For horses like Tex and Tailor, preliminary is the start of their careers; for horses like Sir Galahad, it's the culmination of one.

Galloping out of the start box ahead of David are middle-aged executives, housewives, moms and dads, talented adolescents who are making their first moves up the ranks, and professionals like David on young horses. As David heads to the start box, there's a fall on course. Sam winces when she hears the announcement. The fallen rider is a mom whose professional daughter gave her a retired advanced horse. Recipients of the payback ethos that guides David, these moms, the genetic distributors of horse-crazy genes, find themselves mounted on beautifully trained and athletic, if aged, horses. The horses are an expression of their children's gratitude for the years of grooming, and getting up in the wee hours, and scrimping to keep their kids in horses and lessons, and believing that their kids could do as unlikely a thing as make their living riding horses.

The fallen mom, with dust streaked down one side of her body and bits of greenery stuck in her wiry gray hair, is driven back to the schooling ring in one of the farm vehicles. She's got one leg propped up on the dash, a possible broken ankle, but she wants to check on her horse before she heads to the first aid tent.

David gallops out on Dante, and Sam and Donna race down from the warm-up ring to the center of the course where they can see most of the jumps. At the first tough combination, Sam has her hands to her face. "Dante, focus, focus, please," she begs. He scrambles awkwardly through but is clear. Why, she wants to know, did David have to move this horse up to preliminary this year, with the Worlds in sight? "It's not like this isn't an important year," she says to Donna. "Can't you start that horse next year?"

Karen and her cheering section are stationed around the water. As Dante jumps out of the woods and turns toward it, they chant, "Go, Dante, go! Go, Dante, go!" The rest of the spectators join them. "Go, Dante, go! Go, Dante, go," they call as the skinny, astonished-looking gray splashes through the water. David is laughing as he gallops up the hill for the table jump. A crack of his crop sends Dante over. Sam and Donna run down the hill to the finish line in time to see Dante make an ugly jump along the tree line. "C'mon, Dante. Don't fall at the last fence," Sam pleads as they head for the finish line.

They clear the last fence and David is elated. Dante looks as if he's just been through the worst five minutes of his life. Karen and J. J. have appropriated a farm vehicle and a driver and they zoom up. "Well," Karen says to Donna as Sam leads Dante away. "He says the horse has got a big jump; we just haven't seen it yet."

Back in the stabling area, the team jogs the horses, making sure they're sound, before they put them to bed. David and Tailor lead a parade through the tent as he and Karen, the grooms, and the students take their horses outside. When he's done with his jog, J. J. tugs Tailor's lead shank out of David's hand. "I'm just going to take him over there," she says, trying to turn Tailor away from the hay bale that he's diving toward. She digs in her heels and pulls as he keeps eating. David smiles. "If he'll let you do that, then go ahead."

After everyone has jogged, a woman who's been hovering around the O'Connors' stalls all weekend, and whom Karen has never seen before in her life, asks Karen if she'll watch her horse jog. "Sure." Karen shrugs.

The competitors' party starts before Sam and Donna are done with chores. "Why is it," David asks proudly, "that we're always the last ones done?"

Putting away the last of the grooming tools, Sam closes the trunk and straightens up. Karen is next to her, holding out a beer. "Can you drink yet?" she asks Sam.

Sam sits down heavily on the trunk, next to Brewster. She pulls off her shoes, then peels off the wet socks underneath. When Brewster turns to her, she has the shoe in front of his face. "Smell this," she says, laughing.

There are more autograph seekers prowling the barns. They hover shyly at the edge of the party, clutching posters and programs to their chests. Down the aisle, a young rider has draped her protective vest over a chair. Its blue surface is covered with signatures in white marker: David and Karen, Phillip Dutton, Bruce Davidson, Kim Vinoski, as though she's hoping their signatures will bring her the same luck on cross-country that her heroes have had.

The party is getting silly as competitors dance to the Top 40 music coming out of the CD player. Brewster has brought a stocked cooler, and the O'Connors dip into that instead of the wine bottles and keg next door. They're a little separated from the rest of the crowd, many of whom take it upon themselves to visit them. Sam is avoiding one of the professional riders, who tries to kiss her whenever he gets drunk. He lurches over with his arms out, and she backs up against Tailor's stall. David doesn't have long to relax because the president of an equine catalog company wants to talk to him about another sponsorship. When David first made his move into the top ranks by soliciting owners who could buy horses for him, he described it as taking a chance. Now that he and his wife are a medal-winning juggernaut, everyone is trying to climb aboard. By association, the O'Connors' success could be their success. The ever-attentive Brewster slips up to David's side as soon as his cup is empty and replaces it with another rum and Diet Coke.

Tex and Tailor are in first and second places going into show jumping on Sunday. Dante is twenty-fourth out of twenty-six in his division, and Percy, who racked up eighty-two time faults on cross-country, dropped from second place to third to last in his, ahead of a rider who fell off and another who had two refusals.

Donna is complaining. She woke up at two a.m. in a frenzy of itching. On Saturday, not happy with the location of the walkways on the cross-country course, she bushwhacked through brush and hedges, taking shortcuts back to the barn and dragging Sam behind her. Now she's covered with angry red welts that no one can diagnose.

Dante is the first horse to jump. He's so pushy this

morning that Sam can't get the studs screwed into his shoes or get his boots strapped on. He's shoving Donna, who's trying to hold him, and he's pushing on Sam's back. Sam leaps to her feet, throwing her arms in Dante's face until he circles backward around his stall. He's worse than usual today because he spent the previous afternoon playing push-and-shove with the beefy younger brother of one of the junior competitors. While Sam worked and frowned, the boy pushed on Dante's nose, giggling when Dante pushed back. Sam didn't say anything. From where he sat on the tack trunk, David just smiled. Better to teach the horse to behave than to deny a kid a chance to enjoy one of his horses.

While Dante crashes through the jumps in his warm-up, forcing Sam to fetch and replace them, Donna leans against one of the cross-country fences, tilting her feet forward onto her toes one at a time, trying to get the weight off them even for a few seconds. "Now I know why grooms look the way they do at the end of the day," she says.

For two days, Donna and Sam have been delivering and retrieving horses for Karen and David at the dressage ring and the cross-country start, both of which are a half mile away from the barn. They've had to run their errands on foot, because Groton House has banned minibikes. They've mucked stalls, carried bags of shavings and bales of hay in their arms, and hauled buckets of water, two at a time, from the trough around the corner from the barn. They've hand-walked and hand-grazed the horses. In addition to Donna's creepy rash, they're covered with the kinds of petty, irritating injuries that come from working with big animals in cramped spaces: stepped-on feet, bucked shins, torn cuticles, and bruises. Half the work they do is *under* the horses: strapping on boots, checking legs, screwing in studs, applying poultices, wrapping bandages, reaching for girths, picking feet, and always, always painting on hoof polish. All their gear is stashed in three trunks, but with so many people in and out of them, they can never find what they're looking for. They root through one and then the next and the next. The surfaces of the trunks become littered with coffee cups, soda cans, juice bottles, riding clothes, cell phones, and car keys, and all that stuff needs to be moved each time they open a lid. First thing on Sunday morning, the hinge on one of those lids breaks. When Sam opens the trunk, the lid slips through her fingers and slams down loudly. "Oh," she says, wincing at the noise. "That just makes me so sad."

They've cleaned tack and bathed the horses behind the Porta-Potties in a communal wash area that's slick with mud. The humid weather takes the shine off the brass, and they've polished and repolished it. They've kept track of everyone's start times and are expected to know where David and Karen are whenever someone is looking for them. They've had to find misplaced medical armbands, without which the riders are not allowed on course. Not once since they've arrived has either one of them lost her temper or gotten irritable or said no to a request. Sam even waited patiently at J. J.'s side while she practiced poulticing a horse's leg.

Every groom out here is working just as hard. Halters and lead ropes slung over their shoulders, towels in their pockets, they're sprinting between warm-up ring, barn, and arena. They fold their riders' hunt coats over their arms, gently brushing away the dirt; they gingerly hold on to their helmets by the straps, trying to keep their fingers away from the slimy, slick sweat under the brim. They joke about the smell of their own bodies and apologize for the stubble in their armpits when they raise their hands to bridle a horse. When they ask for help, it's only from one another. They lend out gear that they never get back and give their hay to people who haven't brought enough. Their cell phones are overloaded with calls from their riders' friends, who wouldn't think of disturbing the riders while they're working.

Donna has never groomed before. "I never knew," she says, so tired she's not even watching Dante's warm-up. "I'll never yell at a groom again."

David is stone-faced as he heads into the show jumping ring. Dante canters to his first fence and knocks down a rail. Sam and Donna laugh. He knocks down another and another. "C'mon, Dante," Sam says. "Leave something up." As if he's heard her, he clears the next two fences and then topples another one. David is fighting to control him. At the last combination of three fences, Dante doesn't even jump the first one, just runs through it, trips, and falls to his knees, chucking David up his neck, then he slams on the brakes, pitching David to the ground. They're eliminated. As Sam leads Dante away, the other riders gathered around the ring shake their heads. What was David thinking? they ask one another.

Tex and Tailor are the last two rides of the day. Tailor goes clean and is in second place as David canters into the ring for the final ride on Tex. Standing with him at the side of the ring, watching Tex clear the jumps, Sam tells Tailor that he's going to get beat by his brother. For the award ceremony, David rides back in on his winner, Tex, leading Tailor, in second place, next to him. There's a groom's award on the table, a pair of Blundstone boots that Sam is eyeing, but she's never won a groom's award. "I've got all plain bays," she wails. "I've got nothing to work with!"

The riders have to wait for the intermediate division in the neighboring ring to finish before they get their awards. The patrons, whose tent is adjacent to the ring, invite the riders down to the far end of the tent for a drink. As David sips from an oversize red plastic cup, Tex and Tailor stand quietly, their heads low, each with a hind foot tilted forward and resting on the ground. The other horses spook at the red plastic cups. Their heads high, they imagine predators in the treetops and behind the tent. David sips his cocktail, watching as his peers try not to fall off or spill their drinks as their horses leap and bolt off. Tex and Tailor look embarrassed for the other horses. "C'mon guys," Sam says in their voices, "this is the award ceremony. This is what we do."

When the awards are presented, David calls J. J. in from the side of the arena. He leans down in the saddle to talk to her and then hands her Tailor's reins. As they pin the class in reverse order, the other horses roll their eyes at the crowd and spook at the ribbons the judges are trying to affix to their bridles. When it's his turn, Tailor drops his head behind J. J.'s shoulder; she's half the size of the obstacles he jumps. He plods along behind her, adjusting his stride to her short legs. He raises his head slightly to accommodate the judge who's pinning his ribbon and then drops it behind J. J. again as they plod away. Sam laughs. "What a good horse."

The tents have been emptying out all day long as riders finish their last round and go home. The O'Connors are leaving in the morning. The grooms, David, the students, and Brewster pack the rig with everything except the horses' shipping boots and their breakfasts. The weekend jumble of students and relatives has left behind one more person than they have motel space for. Sam listens silently as they try to figure out where everyone will spend the night. As her seniority has increased, so have her demands, and one of them is that she have her own motel room. Nobody wants to share a bed with Donna because of her creepy rash, and J. J.'s male cousin is mucking up the sleeping arrangements.

"We haven't eaten all day, have we?" Donna asks suddenly.

Sam shakes her head.

"I didn't even notice."

"You get used to it."

It finally occurs to someone that there is an extra bed in Sam's room. When asked, like Tex and Tailor, she accommodates. One of the show officials has cornered Karen and David, and the rest of the team sits on the picnic tables, waiting for their bosses so they can all go to dinner.

There are easily twice as many nudging spectators demanding Karen's and David's attention at the Over the Walls horse trials in Hardwick, Massachusetts, a town just east of the Berkshires. It's the last competition of the season before the unimaginatively titled "mandatory outing" that will determine which riders from the short list and the alternate list are going to Spain. David has Tex and Tailor and Percy with him again, as well as ET, whom Donna will be riding in the intermediate division. Karen has four horses, and Max and Vicky are along to take care of them.

Even though it's a long drive from Virginia, Sam likes the Over the Walls horse trials. It's a new competition, only three years old, organized by a former U.S. team member and current competitor who once supported her horses by modeling. She's outfitted the volunteers here in matching teal-colored T-shirts. There are so many of them traveling around in bands that from a distance they look like floating banners. The O'Connors ride well, but there's bad news on cross-country day. Bruce Davidson and his horse High Scope crash at the third fence on course. High Scope breaks his neck, and Bruce is taken to the hospital with a broken pelvis, a broken shoulder, and a crushed lung. His son Buck withdraws his remaining horses and follows his father to the hospital.

Joe Silva, a director of the MSPCA and the driver of the equine ambulance, admits that it's been a bad year for eventing, though he characterizes Bruce and High Scope's fall as a freak accident, not an eventing one. He agrees with David that the speed and the jumping the sport requires make it dangerous, but he explains that all pet ownership comes with risk. Dog owners take a risk when they let their dogs off the leash in the park. "Every year," he explains, "a dog gets hit by a car or killed by another dog. People let their cats out and they get hit by cars. Does that mean they love their cats any less?" The risks of horse ownership, he believes, are not just inherent among people who compete their horses. Ninety-five percent of the calls that his three equine ambulances respond to are "in-yard, not-in-use emergencies" — colics, split pelvises from a fall, a horse kicking at a fly and breaking the leg of the horse he's standing next to.

Event riders choose the sport because they're enthralled by the challenge, the demands of the three phases, and the courage it takes to run cross-country. The horses they ride, Silva believes, thrive on that challenge as well. "The animals we surround ourselves with are like ourselves," he explains. There are riders who make bad decisions, he concedes, who push on with horses who are clearly not enjoying their work. But in the event riders' defense, he states that all their horses are pets, not, as is the case with polo ponies and racehorses, tools in a broader enterprise. Even with the risk, Silva shares David's belief that competitive horses have fulfilling lives. They're meticulously cared for and they're loved. Their lives are full of the kind of social interaction they crave. It's not the eventing horses who have hard lives, he says, it's all those horses who sit in a field or a stall doing nothing, their owners too busy or too unskilled to create a purposeful life for them. The scrutiny of event horses and their riders, the criticism of the sport, he says, are misplaced. Given the amount of neglect and real abuse out there, "We should be celebrating anybody who takes responsibility for the life of their animals."

Hardwick isn't as "horsey" as Hamilton, which is why, Max thinks, the spectators don't really know they're not supposed to be in the stabling area. It's an unwritten rule, one that is rarely, if ever, enforced at these informal horse trials, but it's one that members of the community of horsemen know. The spectators thronging the aisles, judging by their questions and the fact that they're treating the stabling area like a SeaWorld exhibit, are not members of that community. They pester the grooms with questions: Why are the horses' legs bandaged? Why does that one have an intravenous tube running into his neck? What are the horses' names? How much do they cost? What kinds of horses are they? Most eventers are not as open about their stable-management practices as the O'Connors are, and the majority of spectators seem to have landed here not because they were looking for David and Karen, whom they don't know, but because they've gotten a cold shoulder everywhere else. "I think it's cute," Sam says about the adoring fans. "But when I've got eight horses in the barn and there's twelve kids coming down the aisle . . . You can see ET winding up like, 'C'mere, little girl.'" Tailor, Sam says, really wants interaction, even though he pretends he doesn't. Tex wants to draw people to him so he can turn away and ignore them. As for ET, Sam says with a laugh, "as soon as he sees those little kids enter the barn, he's like, 'Hmmm. Yes, look how cute I am. I'm not interested in you, but I do want to bite you.'"

Karen comes back from the snack stand with a burger. She raises it to her mouth and over the top of the bun she spies a group of adolescent volunteers; in their teal shirts they look like a single blob with pens and posters sticking out of it. "Hold that burger," she says to one of them, exchanging it for a pen. "And don't eat it."

Outside, David has just come back from cross-country on Tailor. "I'm up there in the air," he says, looking skyward, "and I don't know when I'm going to come down, and all I can think is that I'll never, ever sit on a horse like this again." Girls swarm around him and Tailor for photos. David tickles Tailor's belly, trying to get him to drop his head over one lucky girl's shoulder. Vicky, Max, and Sam are answering questions, explaining what the bandages are for, that the IV bags of fluid dripping through catheters in the horses' necks are just a precaution because of the heat. Up and down the aisle, the other grooms who couldn't escape the spectators are doing the same thing. The fans don't know about High Scope. As with Titleist, no announcement is made that a horse died here today. If they notice anything, it's the empty aisle. The closed tack trunks, the gear stashed away. No grooms to ask questions of, just horses closed in their stalls, their aisle strangely still.

After cross-country day, David and Tex are in the lead. The advanced division is jumping late in the afternoon, giving the crew the rare opportunity of taking a lunch break. Sam, Vicky, Donna, and a couple of the students are sitting cross-legged in the aisle, eating huge, drippy sandwiches with Karen. David has decided that the team will drive back that night, arriving home at four a.m. Karen is trying to enlist the grooms to help her talk David out of this plan, which they don't like either because they have to be at work at six a.m. In turn, for the record, they each assert that David's plan sucks. Karen leaves, and Sam is in the process of detailing in how many ways this is a bad idea when David walks in. Everyone else stops talking. Their eyes drift up from Sam's face and stare over her head at David, who's standing behind her. She finishes her sentence and then looks at him over her shoulder. "What studs do you want for show jumping?" she asks. He makes a joke of his answer. "Don't be a smartass," she says. "What studs do you want?"

Later, in defense of his driving plan, David points out that the grooms and students are traveling at least three to a car; he's the only one who has to drive more than three hours, even though Donna has been learning to drive Blue Thunder. "When *she* drives," David says, pointing at her, "I don't sleep."

"I love my boss," Donna says, laughing.

David is the last to ride and he's clear on Tex, winning not only the advanced division, but the national championship taking place at Over the Walls. As he's accepting his award, Karen points out to anyone who passes by that Tex has won nine competitions in a row. She repeats the sentence over and over, as if she can't believe it herself. In the barn, Sam adds that Tex has not lost a competition in three years, except once when David made a mistake. There's little fanfare in the barn. The grooms literally run the horses back from the show ring and start chucking them into the rig. Winning is what they do, what they're expected to do. They would work as hard for any rider as they work for David and Karen. They would take as good care of a losing horse as they do of a winning one. Their good luck is that they're working for great riders at the peak of their careers.

One of the last riders to jump on Sunday was Buck Davidson on the horse who had finished cross-country before his father fell and Buck withdrew the others. Spectators and competitors offered their good wishes for his father, and he thanked them briefly; his father was going to be okay, and he had a show jumping round to do. Standing next to him as he watched other riders complete the course was a friend and fellow competitor who'd been sidelined by a broken foot. "What?" she asked him, as he stared at the jumps.

"He doesn't like liverpools," he said, indicating a blue rectangular inflatable pool holding several inches of water.

"Oh, oh, oh," she said, rummaging in her bag and pulling out a little pot of glitter. "Magic fairy dust," she said.

Buck looked at her impatiently; he was just about to go into the ring.

"For good luck," she said.

"Do it quick." He leaned down in the saddle, one eye still on the course as she brushed glitter over his cheeks and brows and onto his horse's face.

His horse jumped the liverpool and every other jump on course as well. When Buck came out of the ring, his friend waved to him. "It was the fairy dust," she said.

Chapter Ten

CLOSING RANKS

The O'Connor Event Team, after training in England for several weeks, has arrived at the World Equestrian Games in Jerez de la Frontera, Spain, with one horse, David's veteran Tex. "You should have seen how we got to Spain," Sam says. "They take us off these lorries and there's this plane that looks like it's five thousand years old and they pull up this wooden ramp. I'm like, 'C'mon, Tex.' Up this enormous ramp onto the crazy-ass old plane. Tex's head is touching the *ceiling*. It was *unreal*."

Karen O'Connor has made the trip with the team, but her horse, Regal Scott, stepped out of his stall the morning of the mandatory outing back in July with torn cartilage in his shoulder, leaving Karen with no horse for the Worlds. The mandatory outing took its toll on Tailor as well. The day after cross-country, he came up lame. After two days of diagnostic work on the part of "like a million vets," Sam says an abscess was found in his hoof from a puncture wound caused by something, a nail, a rock, that he stepped on as he galloped cross-country. He went to England to train anyway, and though he eventually came sound, David ended up choosing Tex as his partner for the World Equestrian Games.

Anne Kursinski didn't make it to Spain either. At Calgary, just before she headed south to the selection trials in California, she found Eros in his stall one morning with scrapes all over his neck. "It looked like the Boston Strangler had gotten to him," she jokes. He had spent the night fighting through the stall walls with Great Point, who was stabled next to him. "Great Point said, 'I'm moving up to the Grand Prix,' and Eros said, 'Oh, no, you're not,'" Anne says with a laugh. The abrasions were superficial, but in the battle, Eros hurt his back and he wasn't able to complete the selection trials.

Horsemen have been competing in games for at least 2,500 years, so it's appropriate that there is pomp and pageantry in abundance at Jerez. The opening ceremonies begin with speeches by the president of the International Equestrian Federation (FEI), the Infanta Doña Pilar de Borbón; and King Juan Carlos of Spain. Fighter jets scream over the stadium, trailing yellow and red smoke, the colors of the WEG. By a colossal arch constructed of thousands of balloons, the official mascot, himself a balloon, is introduced. Fino is a chubby, smiling white horse with blue wings whose plump jowls make him look as if he's chewing an apple. His name, Fino, not coincidentally, is also the name of the wine of Jerez de la Frontera. In a rather obvious marketing move, the organizers of the games have taught all of the non-Spanish-speaking attendees the one word they need to know to order the local sherry in the city's restaurants and cafés.

The opening ceremonies are a two-hour celebration of the Spanish horse. There are caballeros demonstrating the use of the *garrocha,* a fifteen-foot-long pole used to separate livestock. Members of the Royal Andalusian School of Equestrian Art parade in on their Andalusian stallions and demonstrate the levade, passage, piaffe, and cabriole — all ancient dressage skills that were taught to warhorses so they could be kicking, leaping, and fighting warriors themselves. Charming and coy broodmares, roped together in strings of six by collars around their necks on which bells jingle invitingly, are wheeled and turned by a single rider. Mounted on a stallion, he uses his voice, the body of his horse, and the occasional pop of a whip to keep them in formation. The mares' movements demonstrate how farmers once used strings of horses as threshing machines.

The Jerez Military Stud, driving Break-Pitter carriages, huge wagons used to haul cannons to the front lines, harnessed to six horses, execute drill maneuvers in conjunction with the Andalusian stallions. In the midst of this extravaganza, more than four hundred flamenco dancers clap their way into the center of the arena. Seven of the dancers, wearing dresses that represent the seven different disciplines of the games, are mounted behind caballeros on their stallions. The women sit serenely, their legs over one side of the horse, their ankles crossed, and their hands in their laps as the broad-backed stallions canter across the arena.

The riders here to compete are introduced in a parade, each nation following its flag. Countries like Great Britain, the United States, and Germany, who have fielded teams for all seven of the disciplines, have almost a hundred riders behind their flags. Interspersed with those generously horsed nations are countries like Greece, whose sole competitor, an eventer, makes her lonely walk across the arena in a pale blue suit. Breaching the alphabetical order, the Spaniards come last and loudest. Cheering, they throw their arms in the air and generate a wave among the spectators that undulates around the entire arena, even across the gaps of empty seats.

There are more dancers, surreally outfitted in blue, copper, and white horse heads. Others are carrying Mylar banners with geometric shapes stitched onto them. Three hundred volunteers race into the ring, sit down, watch a dance, and then race out again, the seats of their pants coated with dust.

The competitors and the equestrian press, bemused by the theatricality of the ceremonies, are won over by the exuberance and the beauty of the Spanish horses. Other than that of the single Spanish rider competing in dressage, there are no Andalusian horses in the games. Heavyset and broad-backed, with flowing manes and dark, languid eyes that gaze at their admirers, they embody the mythic beauty of unicorns. Andalusians have paid the price for their rich beauty by being deprived of athleticism. They are powerful horses and breathtaking as they leap in formation, but they're simply not fast enough for most of the disciplines represented here.

For the grand finale, all the horses come back into the arena. Two lines of horses canter diagonally across the arena, crossing paths one at a time at the center as they head to the opposite corner. Around them, the Break-Pitter carriages are circling and crossing diagonals with mounted riders. Individual horses, controlled by long reins held by people on the ground, leap and buck in the air — a move known as the levade. The entire arena is in chaos. Hundreds of horses are cantering across the paths of carriages and other horses. Erupting over the top of their heads, as if they are traveling on a separate plane, are the horses in levade. A crash seems imminent. Many of the spectators have their hands over their eyes. "Oh, my God!" Sam says. "Something awful is about to happen!" Leaping, cantering, disobeying, the horses are expelling enough energy to fuel the city. As the riders leave the arena, some still in formation, some tugging frantically on their horses' reins, one of the horses pulling a carriage jabs his head toward the ground and bucks, launching a passenger into the air and breaking the shaft of the carriage. The crowd gasps, but the passenger leaps nimbly to his feet and waves to his audience with both hands like a gymnast who's just finished a tumbling routine. He jogs off after the disabled vehicle, which is being chased by half a dozen men trying to stop the spooked horses before they stab themselves with the broken shaft.

The disciplines of the games are designed to demonstrate the athleticism of horses and the skill of their riders. The opening ceremonies, on the other hand, demonstrate the other side of horses: their sexy, virile beauty, their power to seduce, their virtuosity as they raise the functions of farm, ranch, and military to an art form, and, in their disobedience and excitability, their expressive personalities.

The competition begins the next day, on Wednesday. While the dressage horses are completing their first round of competition in the main stadium, the Chapin arena, the event horses gather on the far side of the grounds for their first vet inspection. Twelve countries have fielded full teams of at least three and up to four riders. In addition, countries like the United States, Australia, and Great Britain have an additional two riders competing as individuals. India, Greece, and Croatia have only individual riders. Gathered around a stretch of tarmac, the inspectors to one side and a small, knowledgeable crowd in bleacher seats, the team riders keep to themselves. Despite the ethnic diversity of the riders, they are similarly outfitted for this dressy stage of competition. Slacks and skirts are topped by blazers in the dominant color of the riders' national flags. A French rider and member of the military wears a brass-buttoned uniform. The Irish wear spring green blazers, but most riders, like the Americans, are in khaki and dark blue. The American women, Kim Vinoski and Amy Tryon, sport red, white, and blue silk scarves.

Samantha walks Tex in a holding area next to the jog, waiting to hand him off to David. There is even less diversity among the horses. Eventing is a game for Thoroughbreds and their ilk — long, lean, and ribby horses. The Brazilians, who've combed the circle-within-a-diamond pattern of their national flag onto the horses' hindquarters, have brought a team of handy-looking small horses, similar to the polo ponies they breed in abundance. The Germans, whose warmblood breeds dominate show jumping and dressage, have heavier, bigger-boned horses than the rest of the riders. Every horse is neatly braided. Like Tex's, their coats shine in the saturated sunlight of southern Spain. Their hooves are oiled, and their tails are trimmed in the British style, in a straight line just below their hocks.

Tex wasn't David's first choice for these games. He had planned to bring Tailor until the injury after the mandatory outing. Fit, strong, and eager, even at seventeen, Tailor had a terrific summer. David actually had to keep Tailor from running away with him on cross-country. His injury after the mandatory outing panicked the selectors for the U.S. Equestrian Team. "No selector has ever seen this horse take a lame step," Sam says. "This horse is Iron Man; that's what they call him." Tex, on the other hand, struggled over the summer in the Virginia heat, his energy sapped, his coat dull.

Once they got the horses to England for training, Tailor came sound and Tex improved. Choosing between them, Sam says, was the "hardest thing ever." When she and David galloped them, they were stride for stride with each other, eager to race ahead. "They were both brilliant," Sam says. "Every day it was like, 'What do you think?' 'I don't know, what do you think?'" In the end, fearful that the hard footing of Spain would cause Tailor's injury to flare up, David chose Tex.

He takes his turn on the jog, the first of the American team to be inspected. Tex's hooves sound out evenly. His ears flick forward toward the crowd and back toward David. He is passed and handed back to Sam, who takes him to the barn. David watches him walk away. "We'll know in a couple days," he says about choosing Tex over Tailor, "if I made the right decision."

At sixteen, Tex is one of the oldest horses here. Competing in late middle age is a fairly recent development for competition horses, one that is attached to advances in veterinary medicine. Using high-tech diagnostics like ultrasound and magnetic resonance imaging, horsemen are now able to monitor minute changes in horses' ligaments and tendons — the most likely location for injuries. Treatments for joint health that have developed in tandem with similar treatments for humans have allowed horses who might have been sidelined by the arthritic changes of middle age to stay competitive. The O'Connors, like their fellow competitors, make ample and regular use of dietary supplements and injections designed to keep the horses' joints well lubricated and supple. Even with those developments, though, a sixteen- or seventeen-year-old horse who is still competitive is the exception rather than the rule. The youngest horse here is eight years old, very young for this level of competition. It takes so long for horses to develop the skill and confidence they need to compete at this level that even those who have been meticulously trained from babyhood don't usually debut until they're around ten — giving most only about five years as international athletes. Tex and Tailor are a testament not just to veterinary developments, but to the meticulous care they receive on a daily basis — the eye and touch of grooms like Sam.

Thursday is the first of two days of dressage tests for the eighty competitors in the Three-Day Event. While they perform their dressage tests in a side arena, accompanied by slightly distracting classical music, the real dressage horses, those who perform at the highest level of competition, called, like show jumping, the Grand Prix level, have taken over Chapin stadium. Spectators who love dressage are turning out not for the running and jumping event horses who perform dressage tests with the limited enthusiasm of students reciting their catechism, but for the heavy, powerful warmbloods. In the stadium, big-boned horses, most over seventeen hands, propel themselves straight up into the air for the piaffe — trotting in place. They spin themselves slowly in canter pirouettes. Their legs cross underneath them in perfect rhythm as they trot sideways in the half-pass. Their movements are huge and expressive, and their execution has all the theatrical brio of a Broadway dance routine.

But the eventers are no slouches when it comes to dressage, at least not anymore. In the bad old days of eventing, the horses were known for performing their tests resentfully, an attitude they acquired from their riders, who knew that nothing counted until cross-country day. In the age of enlightened eventing, cross-country courses are more technically demanding and less punishing, which means that more riders cross the finish line without major penalties — only time faults. Since mere fractions of penalties separate the top riders on cross-country day, dressage has become more important. The event horses don't have the artistry of the horses who compete solely in dressage, but overall their gaits are more rhythmical and elevated than they used to be and they look happier in their work. One spectator, cutting past the eventing dressage on her way to the Grand Prix, stops and stares. "These horses can do *everything*," she says to her friend, shaking her head.

There are four members to each national eventing team, but only the top three scores count. David, the veteran, is the first to ride for the American team. Of the other three members, John Williams had his last outing as a team member eleven years ago; Amy Tryon, a firefighter from Washington state, has competed on an international team only once, and that was as an individual; and Kim Vinoski has never been a member of the team. It will be David's job to lead this team all week. Even off his horse he's proven very useful. When they missed their connecting flight in Madrid and were left to fend for themselves by their coach, Captain Mark Phillips, it was David who rounded up his panicky fellows and shuffled them off to the train station.

Even though this is Sam's first competition as a team member, David's status extends to her as well. Other grooms look to her to sort out snafus in the stabling area, and the team's administrator has put her in charge of the load plan for all the horses. "Do you think they realize that I've never been to a games before?" she asks David.

At least as far as his dressage test is concerned, David's

choice of Tex over Tailor appears to have been the correct one. His penalty score is a 34.2 out of a possible 100, putting him in first place. Outside the arena, he's swarmed by the other blue-shirted members of the American team. Karen flips open her cell phone, dialing the Stonehall barn manager back home in Virginia, where it's four o'clock in the morning. "Wake up! Wake up! Wake up!" she screams into the phone.

David's teammate John Williams, on the charming and steadfast Carrick, also scores a 34.2, sharing first place with him. They remain tied for first until Phillip Dutton of Australia beats them. No one is celebrating yet, though, because there is still another day of dressage to go, when Amy Tryon and Kim Vinoski will ride.

David's and John's hold on second place is shattered on Thursday, when Bettina Hoy of Germany scores a record-breaking 20.8 penalty points. Although competitors often complain that judges score more kindly on the second day of dressage, no one is complaining about Hoy's score. Her big gray horse, Woodsides Ashby, floated through his test happily, his ears pricked, showing off just how beautiful he was and doing his best to please his rider, whom, even spectators in the most distant stadium seats could see, he obviously loved. The Americans slip from the lead. Amy Tryon is the third team member to compete, on her horse of indeterminate breeding, Poggio II. She scores a mediocre 43.4, a score that would have been excellent just a few years ago, but in the current eventing climate is in the middle of the pack. The team is neither disappointed nor surprised — dressage is not Poggio's strong suit.

The dressage riders are demonstrating a disconcerting range of ability. Along with Bettina Hoy's score of 20.8, there are also scores in the nineties. The disparity may be attributable to bad luck on the day, a lack of emphasis on the horses' dressage training, or, more ominously considering the four-star cross-country test ahead, the possibility that not all of the horses competing here are true four-star horses. The powerhouse teams of Australia, New Zealand, Great Britain, Germany, and the United States comprise riders who have experience at the four-star level. In those countries, the selectors can choose from a full stable of horses and riders who've competed at places like Badminton, Burghley, and Rolex. Countries with fewer resources have qualified their riders for the games, it seems, simply because they were the only riders in the nation who competed in Three-Day Eventing.

In the stabling area, the teams keep to themselves. The Americans are stationed at the end of one row of stalls. While they wait for Kim Vinoski's dressage test, they're ironing out administrative details. The WEG stable managers have rebuffed the grooms' attempts to get into the stabling area early, and the U.S. team has dispatched an administrator to resolve the problem. She returns with the news that the grooms will be allowed in at four a.m. on the morning of cross-country and, more important, that they'll be allowed to stay until 11:30 the night after cross-country. She also reports the news that an international contingent of *chefs d'equipe* have convinced the officials that they need to move a sponsor's Volvo from the middle of the second water jump on the cross-country course. Smiling and adopting a Spanish accent, she says, "We are going to move the car, but we have lost the keys." Throughout the first week of WEG, these administrative difficulties have been frequent, and mainly interpreted as a culture clash between representatives of countries that perceive themselves to be models of bureaucratic efficiency and their Latin counterparts. The credentialing process was stymied by the various nations' interpretations of who exactly was considered essential personnel, and the two-hour-long siestas that many didn't anticipate left riders and press stranded outside the gates in the hot sun. The press liaisons are multilingual, but the stable managers are not, putting the few individuals who speak Spanish and English in high demand. Frustration levels are high as team delegates accustomed to the well-oiled efficiency of the annual four-star events at Badminton, Burghley, and Rolex are stymied by the inexperienced and slow-moving WEG officials.

Sam listens to the news while she sews an American flag patch onto Tex's saddle pad. Not the least of the problems the team has encountered is the condition of the grooms' housing. Sam is lodged in the kind of metal shed most often used to store gardening supplies. She's in there with five other grooms, divvied up between three sets of bunk beds. She's been on the road for six weeks, and all of her gear is piled on the floor at the foot of her bunk. The sheds are hot, their air conditioners noisy and drippy. They're afraid to leave the windows open during the day because people have been stealing things. There are 350 beds for almost as many grooms, but only two showers, neither of which has hot water. There aren't enough toilet facilities, and the ones they have are far away. That is discouraging enough to compel someone to use the shower as a toilet.

Sam goes to lunch with Lilly Bennett, Kim Vinoski's groom. Their jobs and their lives as professional grooms are similar, and they share a comradely affection. In addition, before she came to the O'Connors, Sam was a working student for Kim, so she and Lilly naturally gravitate to each other. The other two riders on the team, John Williams and Amy Tryon, don't run the eventing conglomerates that Kim and the O'Connors do. John Williams's horse Carrick is being groomed by his wife, and Amy Tryon, who supports her eventing as a firefighter, has coerced some friends into coming along as grooms.

What Sam thinks of the other grooms, the riders, or the more than a dozen members of the support staff here with the American team she's keeping to herself. "You see these people all the time," she says. "You have to get along with everybody." There isn't much jocularity or bonhomie in the stabling area. The riders are tense, the grooms are tense, and whatever personal complaints or private ambitions they may have, they've subordinated them to the goals of the team, which is, David says, the best he's ever been on.

The grooms, the riders, and the rest of the team contingent have closed in on themselves and shunted aside their individuality because they have to compete as a team. The difference for David is that he's under someone else's orders, which he doesn't mind, because the team medals, for him, are more satisfying in some ways than the individual ones. But it's not just the American team that has closed ranks; the entire eventing community has. A morning press release on the second day of dressage announced that the International Olympic Committee is threatening to drop eventing from the Olympics.

The obvious reason, the IOC states, is that it's a terribly expensive sport to stage. The cross-country course alone at WEG cost $3 million to build, for just eighty riders. The course designer, Mike Tucker, started working on it two years before the competition. Presented with a relatively flat, arid landscape, he first hired turf specialists, who recommended the installation of Bermuda grass. Once that was installed, it raised the overall height of the course by two meters. Miles of pipe were laid to keep the grass watered, and then the pipe had to be removed before the competition. The terrain itself needed to be altered, to provide more hills to slow the horses down, and then, finally, the fences were constructed. After WEG, the course will have to be dismantled, after which the grass will need to be maintained or it will die. The eventers know their sport is expensive, and one of the demands they make of themselves is to come up with uses for cross-country courses when they're done, as in Barcelona, where it was converted to a golf course after the Olympics.

The other two Olympic equestrian events, dressage and show jumping, are much cheaper, requiring footing only for the arenas and schooling areas. They don't require, as eventing does, a satellite site that has enough room for cross-country, so the organizers don't have to worry about transport for the spectators. Nor do they have to construct the jumps, which in show jumping are portable standards and poles. The cost of eventing has caused even officials from the FEI to shake their fingers at eventers as if they were the profligate stepchildren of the equestrian world.

The eventers are angry. After Barcelona, when their sport was first threatened in this way, they were told that it would stay intact as an Olympic discipline through the 2008 games. They feel betrayed and unfairly chastised, partly because they've been trying to come up with a solution for the excessive expense, but also because they suspect that the IOC is picking on their sport because of its reputation as one that is abusive to horses. Horses like Tex and Tailor are evidence that event horses can live long competitive lives. The mandatory vet inspection that has always been part of eventing passed every single horse that showed up for the World Games. The dressage horses, on whom vet inspections were more recently imposed by the FEI, were not as sound as the event horses. The vaulters, horses who canter on a lunge line in a twenty-meter circle while up to three teenagers in leotards execute gymnastic exercises on their backs, lost six horses to the preliminary inspection. That the FEI could be critical of the eventers and support the vaulters, Sam says, is "so unfair. Those horses are so lame. I don't see how a vaulting horse could be a happy horse. How it could go out and love its job, going in circles and having people tread on its back."

Already a small coterie, the eventers can look forward to becoming an even smaller one if their sport is dropped from the Olympics. Without the international prestige of the Olympic Games, individual nations will be unwilling to support their country's event riders. The cost of transporting a horse to Europe for one of these huge competitions, according to Sally Ike of the United States Equestrian Team, runs about $20,000 per horse, which the USET pays. Added to that are the costs of the people who accompany the horses. Per diems, as high as $500 for the veterinarians, are paid for the support staff. The grooms' housing, such as it is, is provided by the venue, but the riders need their hotels paid for, and everyone needs a meal allowance (fifty dollars a day, according to Ike, whether you're *chef d'equipe* Mark Phillips or a groom like Sam). Stabling at the competition venue is provided, but at an event like the WEG, where the horses have to be moved off the grounds once their discipline has finished to make room for the horses in the next discipline, stabling must be provided until all the horses can fly back to the States together. The riders provide the grooms' salaries, and sponsors pick up some costs — Pennfield Feeds, for instance, has paid to ship over grain and hay so the horses will not have to undergo a drastic change in diet during the stress of international competition. An Olympic medal, no matter how arcane the sport in which it is won, is a universal symbol of excellence and superiority, one that translates directly into international goodwill toward the winning nation. A world championship, except for the fans of a sport, doesn't translate to anything. Individual standard-bearers like Badminton and Burghley for eventers mean even less. Corporate and individual sponsors, government programs, international governing bodies of sport, understand an Olympic medal. Without that goal in sight, eventers worry that funding outside of the dominant countries will dry up — reducing an already small contingent to a very exclusive group, not unlike what happened to polo when that sport was dropped from the Olympic roster.

The riders from other disciplines are silent about the eventers' plight. Eventing supporters warn that dropping the sport from the Olympics is the thin edge of the wedge, the beginning of the elimination of all equestrian sports, but that seems unlikely given the enormous popularity of both dressage and show jumping throughout Europe. The riders in other disciplines have refrained from criticizing their eventing peers about the expense or hazards of their sport, but they have not spoken out on their behalf.

It's eight p.m. by the time Kim Vinoski turns down the centerline for her dressage test. The sun is low in the sky, casting shadows across the arena. Swallows swoop overhead, and the stands are now full of spectators eager to watch the last individuals ride for their teams. Kim's horse, Winsome Adante, is rattled by the atmosphere in the arena. Even though he scores two 9s (out of a possible 10) for his extended canter, he turns in a 43.4, the same score as Poggio II, which for him is disappointing. Kim is flushed and teary eyed as her fellow team members rush to her side outside the arena. Mark Phillips throws an arm over her narrow shoulders, dwarfing her with his bulk and military bearing. The journalists are waiting for their interviews, and Kim turns her back to them, blinking away tears and composing her game face before she takes their questions.

Lilly and Dan return to the stabling area. In the barn, she tells Sam that she feels like crying. Sam tugs on the horse's ears. "Dan," she says, "you were bad." Lilly leads him away for his bath. Away from the team, she rubs his face. "You're so bad," she tells him, "you really are." Kim's disappointing score has dropped the Americans behind Great Britain. The top four teams, Great Britain, the United States, Germany, and Australia, are now separated by less than three points.

Over the two days of dressage, the riders have been bussing out to Garrapilos, a satellite site almost an hour away where the cross-country phase will be staged. They need to walk the four-mile-long course several times before they jump their horses over it. The problem that Mike Tucker had to surmount in designing this cross-country course has already appeared in the dressage tests — the range of ability demonstrated by the riders and their horses. He needed to build a course that would be challenging to the elite eventers while not being too punishing for the riders whose trip to the Worlds is their first four-star. What Tucker has done is to build fences in combinations with turns in between them that require the horses to be extremely obedient so the riders can quickly adjust their stride or change direction as the jumps demand. Ideally, the horse and rider combinations who are not equal to the challenge will accumulate penalty points by running out at fences rather than crashing into them. The turns required by the fences will also slow the horses down so they are not approaching the fences at top speed. Tucker's goal was to have every team in the competition complete the course. "If I could do that," he says, "I'd be walking on air."

The riders are not so sure. They don't like all the turns on the course, some of which are literally 180 degrees. The direct routes through at least two of the combinations the riders don't think are possible, and even Tucker admits that he doesn't think anyone will take the direct route through the second water complex. "Why build it, then?" Karen snaps when she hears this. "Just to prove what we can't do?" The turns and indirect lines interrupt the flow of the course, discouraging the horses from jumping forward positively and boldly, the kind of jumping that Lucinda Green, former British team member and WEG commentator, says deposits credit in the horses' "bank accounts of good experience."

The first really questionable obstacle on course is the eleventh jump — the first water, an obstacle whose ingenuity approaches the bizarre. Tucker has built an enormous and steep bank that the horses gallop up on their approach. When they reach the top of the ramp, the entire confusing and complicated combination opens out below them. For the horse and rider, he says, "it's quite an eyeful." From the top of that ramp, just as they are required to jump over a small log, the horses see a steep downward pitch, about forty-five degrees and about twenty-five yards long. At the bottom, they jump into water whose depth is unknown to the horse and then have only one or two strides, depending on how fast they've come down the ramp, before they jump up onto a small island and bounce over a little stone house. Once over the little house, they jump over some stacked timber and then descend several feet, landing in water. According to Sam, the American riders don't think this direct route is doable. They're worried that the footing on the ramp is going to give out and the horses are going to slide down it uncontrollably and then not be able to sort themselves out in time to jump up onto the island. The optional route for this obstacle takes horse and rider through a tunnel under the ramp and then *around* the island, slogging through fairly deep water and jumping several fences — a route that Tucker believes will add fifteen or twenty seconds to the rider's time in a competition in which the top riders will be separated by only a few seconds.

These time-consuming alternate routes, according to David, are not really a legitimate option. Riders trying to catch the time will be forced to gallop through the deteriorating footing. "Even if you rode it perfectly," David says, "there's less than a fifty-fifty chance that you'd go clear."

The second controversial fence, number twenty-four, called La Barca Village, comes almost two thirds of the way through the course — after the horses are tired from having run almost eleven miles. It's a complex of scattered miniature houses arranged to resemble a village. There are multiple routes through this complex, but again, the longer ones are very long. Tucker refers to it as more of a show jumping test than an eventing one, meaning that the horses have to be extremely adjustable and capable of powering over a huge fence with only a couple of strides to set themselves up for it. The direct route, he hopes, will have riders jumping into the village over an imposing timber fence. ("Did you see that fence?" David says, eyes wide. "It's huge!") Four strides later, following what Tucker calls a "zed line," they'll jump the first house, turn on the landing side, gallop four more strides, and jump the second house. They'll turn again on landing after the second house and, in three strides, jump the third.

What's at stake over this cross-country course is not just the success of the teams or the individuals riding it, but the reputation of the sport. WEG is a televised event, one that is open to the world, and the riders are rightly concerned that yet another public outing of crashes and falls on cross-country is going to do damage to the sport they've worked so hard to improve. Publicly, the riders are very circumspect about their fears. Phillip Dutton, at the press conference after dressage, says simply, "It's very different than any course we've jumped for a while."

Sam and the grooms arrive at four a.m. on cross-country day and are trucked up to Garrapilos, where they discover that there is no electricity in the barns. The WEG organizers triumphantly announce that they've sold thirty thousand tickets for cross-country day. The skies are overcast, which is a relief because it protects the horses from the hot southern sun. Before anyone can get to cross-country, though, they have to complete the roads and tracks phases, where the footing, unlike cross-country, has not been doctored.

The hopes that the course will ride better than it looks are dashed when the first rider on course gets a refusal at the brush complex. That will be the last time all day that anyone tries the direct route there. The second rider, from Canada, stumbles and falls at the water; his horse limps away and they retire on course. The fifth rider is eliminated, and the seventh, Herbert Blocker of Germany, comes off the roads and track phases with a horse too spent to go on and withdraws, reducing the third-placed German team to three riders, which means they have no drop score for the final tally. Rider nine from France falls and retires; rider ten from Spain is eliminated. In the press tent, the equine journalists hang their heads, dismayed at the early carnage.

David is the twelfth rider on course. Until he got to the start box, Sam says, he didn't know which route he was going to take through the first water. "I was terrified," she says. "I didn't know what he was going to do and I wasn't about to ask him." Karen has been scouting the fence all morning and reports back to the team that the direct route is possible, that the footing is holding up. Watching on the monitor in the vet box, Sam says, "I saw him go the direct route. I was like, 'Oh, my God! I can't look.' I was scared to death."

There's an uncomfortable moment when David loses a rein coming off the island. Having gotten no instructions to turn, Tex gallops gamely directly toward the line of photographers behind the rope, completely prepared to jump over them if asked. The photographers dive out of the way just as David gathers up his reins and steers Tex toward the next obstacle. Describing it later, David laughs. "He thought we were going to see some people."

Though he's clear through the water, Tex is obviously struggling on course. He's slipping on the turns, scrambling to keep his feet under him, and he's knocking into even the straightforward fences. It's an ugly ride on a horse that David described in an NPR interview as a "semi-geek," a master technician who "would know exactly how fast he's going and where his feet are going to go." It isn't until later that an explanation is offered. David and Mark Phillips confess that they used the wrong studs in Tex's shoes. Trying to protect his feet from the hard footing, they chose the small studs over the bullet-size ones that give the horse greater traction but can bruise his feet on hard footing. But Tex, the horse who tries harder when the going is difficult, soldiers on. He lands crookedly and rights himself. His front legs knock into the fences, but he scrambles to get them under him before he lands. He's running his heart out because David is asking him to. At La Barca Village, after slipping and approaching the last fence at an awkward angle, he powers straight up into the air to get over that last little house. "Look at that jump!" commentator Lucinda Green gasps. "Conjured out of nothing."

David comes across the finish line with no jumping penalties, but he has thirty time faults — a penalty higher than the twenty faults of a refusal. Tex has never been the fastest horse. As Sam says, he "doesn't have an accelerator" like Tailor does. Thirty time faults is huge, and though he has no other penalties, the team's medal is now at risk. Going out there and making mistakes, David says, was his job as the lead rider for the team. He has returned with valuable information.

David delivers Tex to Sam, and she jogs him in between the buckets of ice water, holding on to his head while half a dozen people strip off his gear, slit open his leg wraps, and fling ice water on him with oversize sponges. She walks him in a circle and then returns him to the ice water. "I was worried about him," she admits later. "He pulled up really stung because the footing was horrible." Tex's whole body looks pinched, as if every step hurts. Sam walks him back to the ice water station for another dousing, circling and returning to it again and again to get the horse cooled out. Despite his discomfort, Tex has his head up, lifted above the hands that are trying to soothe him. He looks down his long nose at Sam. "You spend so much time with these animals," Sam says. "You get to know them a million different ways and they know you. Tex looked at me on Saturday like, 'Help me. Put me on the ice.'"

Once he's cooled and his heart rate has returned to normal, she walks him back to the barn, looking over her shoulder, clocking his ouchy pace.

John Williams is the next rider out, on Carrick. "A great partnership, these two," Lucinda Green says. "They think alike." Carrick is deceptively fast, his speed cloaked by his long stride. He has a few sticky spots at some of the fences but gallops over the finish line with just 2.8 time penalties. "I got him in a couple tough situations," Williams says. "It wasn't the prettiest round I've ever done." Nevertheless, he rode precisely through La Barca Village, showing the rest of the riders, according to David, how to do it.

Falls, eliminations, and withdrawals continue to rack up over the day. Amy Tryon heads out on Poggio II, a horse she describes as one who "doesn't like to be fiddled around with." He's irritated with all the pulling and turning and adjusting of his stride; he wants to run and jump. Stylistically, Poggio is a horse who dives at his fences, yanking Amy out of the saddle, and at the Euro combination, an E-shaped obstacle requiring three jumps with off-striding in between, she comes off. Under the second part of the obstacle is a small ditch with a rail, and she lands on her back over the middle of the rail. Poggio drops his head and dances his way around her and then takes off, going for "quite a little wander," as one of the commentators says. For a few frightening moments, Amy doesn't move. Then she rolls over and pushes herself stiffly and painfully to her feet. Ready to get back on, she has to wait until someone catches her horse, whose "little wander" costs her four minutes' worth of time penalties. In the press tent, watching her remount, a journalist sucks her breath through her teeth. "Brave girl," she says.

After her ride, sweaty, dirty, and obviously in pain, Amy limps into her press conference. "Every fence," she says, "required you to jump and turn. The horses got discouraged or argumentative. There wasn't one combination where you could keep being straight." Throughout the day, other riders will echo this criticism. "I can see what he was after," Amy says of Tucker's course design. "I'm not sure it was the right thing."

Amy's fall and the subsequent time faults make her the drop score on the U.S. team. For them to stay in contention for a medal, twenty-eight-year-old Kim Vinoski has to go clear and fast. Kim is a petite, steely-eyed blonde, and her position on this team has been a long time coming. At Rolex, *Chronicle of the Horse* handicapper Jimmy Wofford referred to her as the best rider who didn't have a team coat, which wasn't quite true. She'd been given one for the 1999 Pan Am Games and then had to withdraw at the last minute because her horse was injured. It's been sitting in her closet since.

The footing at the first water, as predicted, has not held up. Horses going the direct route have been stumbling in what appears to be a hole under the water. The judge at this fence isn't sure it's the footing; she suspects that the afternoon's shifting light has made it difficult for the horses to see the jumps on the island. Kim picks up the extra seconds taking the long route at the water but shaves so much time off the rest of her ride that she completes the course with only 2.4 time penalties, the fastest time all day. In the media tent, the journalists watch speechless as this young woman, on her first team outing, makes a course that has felled some of the mightiest riders in the sport look easy.

Other than David and Captain Mark Phillips, the American riders look whipped at their press conference. Amy Tryon isn't there; she's at the hospital getting her back X-rayed. (The results will reveal no broken bones, but after she returns to her duties as a firefighter, a second set of X-rays will reveal that the spines of two of her vertebrae have been broken off.) The team is in the lead, and in the individual standings, John Williams is in first place. The journalists fling questions at the team, but none that lead to criticism of the course, which might be because Michael Tucker is at the press conference with them. "We've seen some brilliant riding today," he says. And he's quick to point out that no horses have been hurt.

Out of the eighty riders who started cross-country, only fifty completed. The Americans and the British are the only teams who got all of their members through the course. Four teams lost one member, another four lost two members, and the Spanish and the Germans lost three.

In the stabling area, the horses look like the losing team at the Superbowl. Tex is much better than he was in the vet box. He was footsore, Sam said, but "we've dealt with that a million times. You just ice him and ice him and ice him." The horse they're really worried about is Carrick, who grabbed one of his front heels with a hind hoof on course.

The lorries pull up to take all the horses back to Jerez. Their grooms lead them out of their stalls, away from the hoses and ice buckets. They're walking stiffly. Some of them have knees and hocks swaddled in bandages. No one is celebrating yet. At the American press conference, journalists pester the team with questions about the strategy for tomorrow's show jumping. Mark Phillips leans forward and interrupts them. Before show jumping, he reminds them, there is another test to get through: the Sunday-morning vet inspection.

Out of fifty horses who completed the cross-country, forty-eight show up for the third vet inspection. One was withdrawn for being too tired. The other, Bettina Hoy's brilliant gray, Woodsides Ashby, who received the best dressage score, racked up penalties on cross-country. The German team is already out of contention for a team medal, so Hoy withdrew from competition so she could spend the day at the hospital with her husband, Andrew, who fell on course the day before while riding for the Australian team. The oblique angle of the early-morning sunlight dapples the ground where the horses will jog. Spectators and riders watch nervously as the horses are trotted out for the ground jury. The horses look somewhat battered by their run over the hard ground of cross-country. Only one is actually lame, but almost all of them look stiff, the bounce and energy of their first vet inspection gone.

For the show jumping round, the riders compete in reverse order of their standings — the lowest-placed rider going first and the highest-placed, John Williams, going last. Despite the pain she's in, Amy Tryon wants to complete her show jumping round. Expressing a theme repeated by the Americans throughout the event, she says, "I wanted to finish for the team." She spends the morning pierced with acupuncture needles and then drops only one rail in show jumping. "She's tough as nails," Sam says, shaking her head.

The eventers are keeping the jump crew busy on course. Poles are flying, as horse after horse knocks them down. By the time David arrives on Tex, there have been very few clear rounds. The big-hearted technician, the horse who loves to perform and get a chance to go back into the ring for his victory gallop, pulls off a clear round for David. Unless there is a total disaster with either Kim Vinoski's or John Williams's rounds, the United States has the gold medal in hand.

Winsome Adante, again rattled by the atmosphere in the arena, drops three rails, which keeps the team in the medals but drops Kim out of a shot for an individual one. The last three riders on course are Jean Teulere of France, Phillip Dutton of Australia, and John Williams of the United States. Despite the previous day's exertions, Teulere's horse, Espoir de la Mare, looks sharp and excited, jumping easily. Espoir de la Mare is relatively inexperienced, though, and a moment's distraction causes him to drop a rail, but Teulere is still assured of at least a bronze medal. Phillip Dutton drops three rails and gets two time penalties, knocking himself out of the medals.

John Williams enters the arena more than eight points in the lead; he can knock down two fences and still have the gold medal. His boyish face is clouded with nervousness. At the in-gate, he goes over the course mentally one more time, using his finger to point his way from fence to fence. Carrick, who was exuberantly disobedient in his jog, looks stiff as he canters around. At the first fence, he drops a rail and then another at the second. For the individual gold, John needs to jump cleanly from here forward. Carrick drops another rail, and John loses the gold but is still in contention for the bronze. Normally, Carrick is a good show jumper, careful and obedient, but the hard footing of the day before is evident as he jumps a bit flat, leaving little room between his hooves and the fence rails. He's clean through the grid of blue poles that makes up the triple combination, but at the very last fence, he drops another rail. John ends up in fourth place, less than one point behind the bronze medal winner, Piia Pantsu of Finland.

With three of their horses in the top ten, the Americans take the gold medal, their first team gold at a world championship since 1974, but no individual medals. After cross-country, David confessed to Sam that he thought Tailor might have handled the footing better. But Tex is the better show jumper, and his round is what the Americans have to thank for their gold medal. David, Sam says, was thrilled with his horse: Tex's job was to "get the worst dressage score because he was the first out. He was here to set the pace and make a mistake in cross-country so no one else would, because David can get him around with the wrong studs. And he show jumped clean. He totally did his job."

Outside the arena, the American riders collapse into

one another's arms. Karen is screaming into her cell phone again, and David is looking for an American flag that they can carry on their victory gallop. The grooms throw white sweat sheets on the horses, and the riders scramble back on for the medal ceremony. On the podium, they accept their awards from the flamenco dancers and then stand at attention while the national anthem is played and the American flag raised. In the middle of the arena, the grooms, in their matching polo shirts, stand quietly, holding the reins of their horses. Before the victory gallop, the grooms are presented with their souvenirs, small silver-plated plaques, given "in acknowledgement of their hard work towards the success of these horses."

The Americans, followed by the French and the British, gallop around the ring, and then the games, for which these riders have been preparing for years, are over. Sam leads Tex away, stopping outside the ring to rub his face. "Texie," she says, "you want to go back to the barn?" He lowers his mighty medal-winning head, needy and exhausted, and leans into her. As the grooms file out, someone from the stands shouts out to them, "Hey, grooms! Good job, ladies!"

There's a celebration, of course, in the joint U.S. / British hospitality tent. A drunken one, by all accounts. Jimmy Wofford, writing about it for the American press, reported that his favorite moment was when Karen asked top British rider William Fox-Pitt to autograph her butt. For the first time all week, Sam catches up with David's father, who attends almost every one of his son's competitions, quietly stationing himself on course in his O'Connor Event Team baseball hat. At WEG, he wasn't able to get a stable pass, and Sam missed his regular and stalwart presence in the barn. At the party, she says, "He gave me a huge hug. He was like, 'Your boy was amazing,'" and then he choked up and started crying.

This was Tex's last competition. The less generous members of the eventing community, pointing to his thirty time faults on cross-country, grumble that it is high time he be retired. "Please tell me," one of the dressage team's grooms says to Sam, "that David's going to retire him." Sam is angry: "She doesn't know my horse."

At the final press conference for the American riders, David officially goes on record saying that there were too many falls on the cross-country course. In Tucker's defense, those falls weren't entirely the fault of the course design. Some of the riders out there simply were not prepared for a four-star course. Saddened by what she saw, Sam shakes her head as she recalls a big gray who arrived in the vet box exhausted from the roads and track phases. "That horse was done when he came into the vet box," Sam says. "Go home. Take your horse home. He doesn't want to play anymore."

What angers her about the groom's comment is that Tex doesn't belong in the category of horses who were being forced to compete. "They love it," she says of David's horses. "For horsemen like David and Karen," she explains, "if the horse doesn't want to do it, they're not going to do it. They're going to have another career." It wasn't just Sam's eye that was making judgment calls throughout cross-country day. In the press box, the international journalists, sitting side by side, called fouls on the riders whose horses were struggling too much and on the judges who were not exercising their prerogative to step up and tell the riders they were eliminated. One journalist from New Zealand kept a personal inventory of who was and wasn't patting their horses at the finish line. "Look at that," she said with disgust as a rider pumped his fist into the air and then leaped off his horse into the arms of his teammates. "Not even a pat for the horse." The implication was that these riders didn't deserve to participate in this sport; their participation in it sullied its name. Only the best horsemen deserve to be eventers. As Jean Teulere, the individual gold medal winner from France, and a former show jumper, says, "Eventing, of all the horse sports, should stay in the games because it requires the best riding and training and horsemanship."

The American riders leave early Monday morning to catch their flight back to the States. Amy Tryon is due back at her firehouse in three days, and the others all have young horses competing at different horse trials next weekend. David's years in the sport, like Karen's, he said on NPR, mean that "the highs are not as high and the lows are not as low." At this point in their career, no single competition is going to make or break them. "You try to keep everything in the middle ground," he said. "Tomorrow is another day. There's always another competition."

The horses leave Jerez on Monday too, emptying out their stalls for the driving and show jumping horses, but they aren't being flown back to the States until after the second week of the games, when all the American horses are done. In keeping with her practice of not filling up her head with information she doesn't need, Sam knows only the name of the resort the grooms are going to in the meantime, not its location.

After six weeks on the road culminating in a metal box and no hot water, the grooms are transported to an exclusive resort, Montemedeo, about an hour south of Jerez. Rather than five other people, they share their rooms with one other person in a tile-roofed hacienda where cool, fragrant, thick-walled hallways lead to rooms of opulent luxury. There are leather sofas to recline on and artworks to admire and peacocks who shake out their magic tail feathers for the grooms to find. At the end of their day, the grooms sit in the courtyard, frosty cocktails in one hand and Spanish cigarettes in the other. Except for the staff members who pad around silently delivering drinks, the grooms have the courtyard to themselves. A fountain splashes soothingly, and the grooms are giggling about the U.S. Equestrian Team's decision to house them here. "We think they made a mistake," they say.

Sam has been looking forward to some afternoons on the beach, a chance to sneak in a little vacation between the six weeks in Europe and the roster of fall competitions she faces when she returns to the States. It's been a grueling year for her. "There were some rough spots," she says. "Some really rough spots." She can't remember her last day off, but in Spain, now that the competition is done, she has only one horse, who needs very little care. There's no riding to do and no tack to clean. But the resort staff will not let the horses use the paddocks, which were the reason this location was chosen for the horses in the first place — because it had ample paddock space. The grooms can see them as they stand in a field hand-grazing their horses during the afternoons they had intended to spend at the beach. And the driving competitors have left behind their extra horses for the grooms to take care of. "Crazy driving horses," Sam calls them as she describes how they've been dragging Lilly and her around at the end of their lead shanks.

The grooms leave the courtyard for dinner, picking up the Canadian grooms along the way. Even though their horses are lodged next to the American ones, their team made the thrifty decision to house the grooms in what can only be called a roadhouse. The small convoy makes its way up a steep, winding road to the village of Vejer de la Fron-tera. One of the Moorish pueblos blancos (white towns) of Andalusia, its central square is a crowded nest of houses, restaurants, and an iron-fenced plaza where children, under the watchful eye of their grannies, play soccer. There is wine and sangria at dinner, along with Moroccan food whose subtleties may well be lost on this chip-eating, Diet Coke–guzzling crowd.

This was Sam's last trip with the O'Connor Event Team. She'll groom for David through the fall season, and then she's leaving. This news has not come as a surprise to David; Sam warned him about it almost a year ago. "I want to still love horses and still love working with horses when I leave here," she says.

She gave David a year because she wanted to do the games and because she couldn't bear leaving her horses be-hind in the hands of someone she didn't know, someone she hadn't trained. Vanessa can feel a tendon now, Sam says. She's completely competent. "She does things the way I do things and she knows these horses better than anyone else."

It's going to be hard for David to lose her, to have any-one besides Sam taking care of his horses. She predicts that he'll treat Vanessa the same way he treated her when she first took over from his previous head groom Colleen. "He'll go around behind you and it's very offensive, but then you realize, of course, he doesn't know me yet. You just have to earn his trust. He has to trust you with these ponies."

Sam won't be going far, though. David is loath to let her go altogether. "Get comfortable in your little house," he tells her. Ms. Mars and her barn manager are trying to put something together for Sam training the young horses — finally a true riding job. "We'll see," Sam says. She hopes in her new position to be more of a student than she has been as a groom. "They're the best of the best," she says of Karen and David. "And I love this sport."

The past year hasn't offered a specific highlight. "Everyone has a bad season," she says, referring to the disastrous outings at Rolex and Foxhall; and the travel, the months on the road away from her fiancé, has been hard. Her joy this year has been the same as the joy of every year, and that's keeping company with her horses. "They're so perfect," she says of Tex and Tailor. "They're so amazing, so professional. In every event they go to, they win."

Tex and Tailor are also done. Tailor will compete at Fair Hill in the fall and then retire. Tex will never do a CCI again. Retirement, Sam thinks, will be easier on Tailor. "You can put anybody on him and he's fine," she says. Like so many of the great event horses before him, he'll retire to the hunt field. For Tex, Sam says, retirement is going to be harder. "We're going to have to give him the illusion that he's still competing. He gets upset when the truck leaves and he's not on it."

The restaurant is emptying out. The other grooms have gone home, leaving Sam behind to get back on her own. She's exhausted, and thinking about the horses who were fatally injured during the year brings her very close to tears, imagining how easily their fate could have visited her horses. "You wouldn't see me again," she says. "I would be in a hole somewhere." As she prepares to move on, to leave behind her beloved horses, she's been talking to David's former head groom Colleen, who trained Sam to be a groom and is now preparing her to be an ex-groom. "She said it was much easier to walk away than she thought it would be. When she sees the horses now, she says, she sees them as my horses, not her horses anymore." Sam isn't sure she's going to feel the same way, that she'll ever look at her horses as anything but hers. "I'll have to see." She shrugs.

The wine is gone and so is the coffee. The ashtray is full and the waitresses are lined up in the doorway, shifting their weight from one tired foot to the other. All this talk about her horses, the grooms who loved them before her, and those who will love them after her has Sam thinking that they've been very lucky horses indeed, though they're not always as gracious about it as they could be. "No," Sam says with a laugh, "they know. We're here for them, period. And that's fine."

ACKNOWLEDGMENTS

There are so many people who contributed to this book that, rightfully, it must be called a team effort. First and foremost, thanks to Maria Koundoura and Pam Painter, my teachers at Emerson College, who convinced me that people write books all the time and there was no reason I shouldn't be one of them.

Thank you to my agent, Lisa Bankoff, who had faith in an unproven writer and to my first editor, Deborah Baker, who labored patiently over the manuscript and marshaled this project to its conclusion, and to my second editor, Reagan Arthur, who adopted this project and treated it as one of her own.

Thanks to those practitioners of the ancient art of hospitality without whom I never would have been able to complete my research: John Barjuca, Doug

Spontak, Jill and Paul Valliere, Pat Craddock, Nina McKee and Josh Wender, Steve Johnson, and Tom Olofson.

For her technical expertise and for helping me to lose money on the 2002 Kentucky Derby, I'd like to thank Glenye Cain of the *Daily Racing Form*.

Thanks to Dr. Sandra Olsen for setting me straight about the prehistoric horse.

To the gentlemen at Schuhmann's Click Clinic in Lexington, Kentucky, without whose advice every one of my photographs would have been fuzzy and dark.

Tim Bennett shared his knowledge and expertise about the gentleman farming culture of Lexington.

For allowing me free and unfettered access to their barns, thanks to David and Karen O'Connor, Anne Kursinski and Carol Hoffman, and Jill McCully and Bill Sellers at Lane's End.

And finally, thanks to the grooms of the O'Connor Event Team, Market Street, Inc., and Lane's End, who tolerated my intrusion into their work and lives and whose dedication to their horses continues to serve as a daily inspiration.

BIBLIOGRAPHY

Budiansky, Stephen. *The Nature of Horses: Exploring Equine Evolution, Intelligence, and Behavior.* New York: Free Press, 1997.

Clutton-Brock, Juliet. *Horse Power.* London: Natural History Museum Publications, 1992.

Conley, Kevin. *Stud: Adventures in Breeding.* New York: Bloomsbury, 2002.

Dent, Anthony. *The Horse Through Fifty Years of Civilization.* London: Phaidon Press, 1974.

Englade, Ken. *Hot Blood: The Millionairess, the Money, and the Horse Murders.* New York: St. Martins Paperbacks, 1996.

Hediger, Heini K. P. "The Clever Hans Phenomenon from an Animal Psychologist's Point of View." *The Clever Hans Phenomenon: Communication with*

Horses, Whales, Apes and People. Ed. Thomas A. Sebeok and Robert Rosenthal. New York: Annals of the New York Academy of Sciences, 1981. 1-25.

Herodotus. *The Histories.* London: Penguin Group, 1972.

Houpt, Katherine. *Domestic Animal Behavior for Veterinarians and Animal Scientists.* Ames, Iowa: Iowa State University Press, 1991.

Klinkenborg, Verlyn. *The Rural Life.* New York: Little, Brown and Company, 2003.

McGuane, Thomas. *Some Horses: Essays.* New York: The Lyons Press, 1991.

Mitchell, Elizabeth. *Three Strides Before the Wire: The Dark and Beautiful World of Horse Racing.* New York: Hyperion, 2002.

Nack, William. *Secretariat: The Making of a Champion.* Cambridge, MA: Da Capo Press, 2002.

O'Connor, Sally. *Practical Eventing.* Official Publication of the United States Combined Training Association, Inc. Richmond, VA: Press of Whittet and Shepperson, 1980.

Olsen, Sandra, ed. *Horses Through Time.* Lanham, MD: Roberts Rinehart, 2003.

Scanlon, Lawrence. *Wild About Horses.* New York: Harper Collins, 1998.

Schafer, Michael. *The Language of the Horse: Habits and Forms of Expression.* London: Kaye and Ward, 1975.

Schwartz, Jane. *Ruffian: Burning from the Start.* New York: Ballantine Books, 1991.

Sewell, Anna. *Black Beauty.* Racine, Wisconsin: Whitman Publishing Company, 1951.

Squires, Jim. *Horse of Different Color: A Tale of Breeding Geniuses, Dominant Females, and the Fastest Derby Winner Since Secretariat.* New York: Public Affairs, 2002.

Thomas, Keith. *Man and the Natural World: Changing Attitudes in England, 1500–1800.* Oxford: Oxford University Press, 1983.

Toby, Milton C. *Ruffian.* Thoroughbred Legends No. 13. Lexington, Kentucky: Eclipse Press, 2001.

Waring, George H. *Horse Behavior: The Behavioral Traits and Adaptations of Domestic and Wild Horses, Including Ponies.* Park Ridge, New Jersey: Noyes Publications, 1983.

Xenophon. *The Art of Horsemanship.* London: J. A. Allen and Company, 1962.

The following magazine articles were consulted for research:

Anthony, David, Dimitri Y. Telegin, and Dorcas Brown. "The Origin of Horseback Riding," *Scientific American,* December 1991.

Budiansky, Stephen. "Too Fast to Get Faster," *U.S. News and World Report,* April 28, 1997.

The Chronicle of the Horse. "In the Country" News Summary, December 24, 1999.

————. "Lindemann Gets Maximum Sentence as Hulick Confesses in Court," January 26, 1996.

Cunningham, Patrick. "The Genetics of Thoroughbred Horses," *Scientific American,* May 1991.

Gaines, John R. "Crisis or Opportunity," Bloodhorse.com, June 12, 2001.

Gladwell, Malcolm. "Listening to Khakis: What America's Most Popular Pants Tell Us About the Way Guys Think," *The New Yorker,* July 28, 1997.

Journal of the American Veterinary Medical Association. "AVMA Animal Welfare Forum," April 15, 2000.

Levine, Marsha. "Eating Horses: The Evolutionary Signif-
icance of Hippophagy," *Antiquity,* March 1998.

Levine, Marsha, Yuri Rassamakin, and Aleksandr Tatarint-
seva. "Late Prehistoric Exploitation of the Eurasian
Steppe," *Antiquity,* September 2001.

Nack, William. "Nobody Knows Their Names: Working
Anonymously and Often Living in Squalor, Grooms
Are the Unsung Heroes of Thoroughbred Racing,"
Sports Illustrated, June 10, 1991.

———. "Pure Heart," *Sports Illustrated,* October 24, 1994.
(reprint)

Vila, Carles. "Widespread Origins of Domestic Horse
Lineages," *Science,* January 19, 2001.

The following magazines were also helpful: *Equus, Practical
Horseman,* and *The Chronicle of the Horse.*

About the Author

Susan Nusser received an M.F.A. from Emerson College. She was a recipient of Emerson's Cecil and Helen Rose Ethics in Communications Scholarship and was also a finalist in 2002 for Nimrod's Katherine Anne Porter Prize for fiction. She has worked as a groom and barn manager for international competitors in the Three-Day Event. Previous to her writing and teaching career, Susan worked in AIDS research, as a private investigator, and in television and video production. She lives in Vermont's Northeast Kingdom with her husband, the artist Michael Brunelle.